南京城墙与罗马城墙比较
Comparative Study on the City Walls of Nanjing and Rome

陈 薇　〔意〕路易吉·戈佐拉
Chen Wei　〔Italy〕 Luigi Gazzola

东南大学出版社
SOUTHEAST UNIVERSITY PRESS

EDIL STAMPA
editrice dell'ANCE

序一

路易吉·戈佐拉

Preface I

Luigi Gazzola

一个地区的文化特色只有通过不断更新才能有效地延续并且永葆生机。本书的出版便是源于这个共同的信念。

近些年来,中国与意大利两国在文化与专业领域方面的交流日益增强。在建筑与城市研究领域,特别是遗产的保护、修复和政府举措方面的合作有显著进展。两国数千年的文化,塑造了两国人民不同的性格,也成为双方寻求合作的根源。概括来说,首先,意大利针对文化遗产的保护措施,不论是理论还是实践,都得到了中国学者的高度关注。其次,中国对于文化遗产的保护措施,不再仅仅停留于对历史建筑物的关注,而开始考察建筑物与其所处环境背景之间的关系。此外,合作交流,也开启了历史脉络的保护——关注意大利文化,这对已有详尽成果与成熟实践经验的罗马时期文化研究,同样具有十分重要的意义。

南京东南大学和罗马萨皮恩扎大学(Sapienza Università di Roma)在各自国家的历史文化研究中均有重要建树。双方试图利用各自的研究成果展开合作交流,但是不可避免地遇到了选择研究对象的问题。研究对象必须是双方所共有的,既可以满足在理论与实践上进行对比分析,又可以使研究成果在实际工作过程中得到运用,而不只存在于"学术"讨论中。

南京东南大学建筑学院与罗马萨皮恩扎大学建筑系(Dipartimento di Architettura e Progetto Sapienza Università di Roma)回顾历史发现:研究与比较两座城市的城墙可以立刻成为最为合适的合作项目选题,原因有以下三点:

1. 罗马与南京城墙均为了限定城市范围而建造,当时,两座城市均是帝国的都城;两者基本完整地保留了原貌,建造范围内地形多变,平原、山川、河流交替出现;城墙沿途都经过陡峭的山坡、曲折的河岸,穿越了高度城市化的区域和公共绿地;并且两者在建造技术方面有诸多可比性。

This publication is born of the common conviction that cultural identities can continue to grow in quality and remain vital only through continuous updates that are part of an incessant and reciprocal confrontation.

During recent years, cultural and professional exchanges between China and Italy have intensified. In the field of architectural and urban studies there has been a particular growth in those related to the conservation, restoration and valorisation of heritage. The roots of this reciprocal interest are also to be found in the millenary culture that characterizes both populations, but above all in the attention that Chinese intellectuals focus on everything produced by Italian culture in relation to both theory and practice in cultural heritage safeguarding. What is more, China's culture of safeguarding no longer considers exclusively the historical monument, but also examines its relationship with the context in which it is located. In addition there is also an opening towards the conservation of historical fabrics, a field in which Italian culture, and that of Rome in particular, has elaborated studies and matured practical experiences of specific importance.

However, when the Southeast University of Nanjing and the Sapienza University of Rome (Sapienza Università di Roma), important university structures from both countries with differing millenary cultures, intended to compare their work and collaborate, their inevitably arose the problem of identifying a common object of research for a comparison of theory and practice, a theme of research that would allow for a parallel in the real world, and not only in an academic setting.

The School of Architecture at the Southeast University of Nanjing and the Department of Architecture at the Sapienza University of Rome (Dipartimento di Architettura e Progetto Sapienza Università di Roma) were assisted by history: the study and comparison between the city walls of the two cities immediately appeared the most suitable topic for a coordinated research project. This was the case for three reasons:

– The walls of Rome and Nanjing were constructed to defend two cities that, at the time, were capitals of enormous empires; both are almost wholly conserved and run across a variegated terrain, comprised of alternations between plains, hills and rivers; they climb steep slopes, run along watercourses and cross highly urbanized areas, public parks; what is more, they are constructed using techniques that offer various analogies.

– Both have been or are the object of interventions and/or projects of restoration, consolidation, urban requalification and the application of new restrictions, etc., by different public entitles.

2. 罗马与南京的城墙曾经或当今正是所在城市维护与修复的对象，经历了被不同朝代的执政者重建以用于重新限定城市范围。

3. 两所大学里的学者均参与过或正在进行与古城墙相关的规划设计工作，这个幸运的巧合使得对城墙的合作研究成为可能。

以上原因表明了此次研究项目的可操作性，也为避免研究沦为纯理论探讨提供了基础性条件。

由此，双方决定从五个方面（历史演进、城墙与所处环境背景的关系、城墙的修复、城市规划与城墙、城墙与都市计划）对城墙进行研究，为已完成的（或即将完成的）项目中出现的问题和亟待解决的问题提供文化和技术上的综合性视角。联合研究以两地同步的方式展开，学者们在已达成的共识下从五个角度出发，分别研究南京明城墙和罗马奥勒良（Aurelian）城墙，并进行比较分析。

这项联合研究是两校长期深入合作的成果之一：东南大学与萨皮恩扎大学之间的学术交流已持续了多年。两校合作始于2004年6月德阿申齐奥（D'Ascenzio）校长率团访问南京。同年11月，南京召开了第三届东亚建筑文化国际学术会议，会上正式确定了两校联合研究的计划。在会议过程中，双方共同描绘了项目研究的方式，确立了联合研究计划的发展方向，同时互派教授、博士生，共享资源信息。城墙在当代扮演了特殊而重要的角色，修复工程方面的合作将进一步深入，并且两校都在各自城市的城墙发展和历史研究中作出过杰出的贡献。这些事实促成了合作研究的深入发展。2008年，两校正式签署了文化合作协议文件，将两座城市的城墙定为首个研究对象，补充了项目研究的具体细节，规定了合作形式、研究时间表，并任命陈薇教授和路易吉·戈佐拉教授作为双方合作牵头人。

2008年11月，第四届国际城市化论坛在南京举行。论坛中，两校的学者举办了南京与罗马城墙比较研究研讨会，将合作的初期和中期成果进行了展示。这本书收录了联合研究的最新成果，研究成果包含了在文化、技术与操作层面上的类比与差异。新增了两国学者如何利用研究成果丰富本国文化的实践对比。

中国正处在急速发展、寻求新的国际地位的时期，在这一过

– It was possible to exploit the fortunate coincidence that many professors from both faculties are, were, or were about to be commissioned to design varying interventions involving the historical walls in these two cities.

The above data projects this research into a field of operability, a fundamental condition for avoiding the purely theoretical nature of the results developed by the studies.

As a result, five interrelated fields of research were selected (historical evolution, the relationship between the walls and their context, the restoration of the walls, planning and city walls, city walls and urban projects), with the intent of providing a comprehensive vision of the cultural and technical problems related to completed interventions (or to be completed), and problems yet to be resolved. A joint research was thus developed by moving along parallel lines of analysis, treating each of the five themes from common points of view and comparing the results of the Chinese research involving the walls of Nanjing with those of the Italian scholars examining the Aurelian Walls in Rome.

This coordinated study is one of the first results of a collaboration matured over time: the academic exchanges between the Southeast University and the Sapienza University of Rome have been underway for many years. They began in occasion of the visit by a qualified delegation of professors from Rome, under the guidance of its Rector Mr D'Ascenzio, to Nanjing in June 2004. A common line of research was identified in November of the same year, during the " 3rd International Conference on East Asian Architectural Culture", held in Nanjing. This occasion was also used to delineate a number of approaches and to define the modalities for the development of a coordinated research project and an exchange between professors, doctorate students and scientific information. In particular, it was established that relations in the field of restoration would continue to grow, both due to the contemporary nature and importance of this subject, as well as because both universities have made the greatest contributions to the development (and history) of this field in their respective countries. This approach was rendered more concrete in occasion of the official signing of a Cultural Agreement between the two universities, in 2008, when the urban walls of the two cities were selected as the first theme of joint research. This occasion was also used to define the modalities and timing of the study and nominate its coordinators, professors Chen Wei and Luigi Gazzola.

An initial and interim conclusion to the coordinated research was provided in November 2008 with the Seminar "International Forum on the Comparative Study for the City Walls of Rome and Nanjing", in occasion of the 4th World Urban Forum, held in Nanjing, when scholars from the two universities presented the results of their research . The most recent conclusion, instead, is presented in this publication, which reveals cultural, technical and operative analogies and differences, in addition to explaining how the comparison between the work of scholars from the two countries offered responses that enriched both cultures.

程中必然会与其他重要文化产生碰撞。中国与意大利距离遥远，语言系统建立在不同的（如果说不是相反）逻辑上。然而，我们能否在两个国家间建立一种意义深远而不同以往的紧密合作关系呢？也许是有这种可能的。

中国在上个世纪初已经开始了文化交流方面的工作，此项工作在毛时代结束后的1980年代得到延续。中国在文化遗产保护方面的开端可以追溯到20世纪初，这也正是中国文化观念和技术发生剧烈变革的时期。1919年，朱启钤先生创立了中国营造学社，创办刊物《中国营造学社汇刊》。学社成员大多拥有国外教育背景，他们试图将所学到的方法运用于中国的古迹修复、古建筑的历史研究和测绘工作中。但不幸的是，在接下来的时间里，中国动荡的时局阻碍了学者的研究活动，物质与非物质的文化遗产遭到大量破坏，中国传统文化体系也遭到严重威胁。

时至今日，两国高层次的文化交流合作仍需要一个相当漫长的时间。因此两校间的学术人才交换也是一个长期的项目。持续的合作才能确保研究向更深层次发展，中意两国还将逐渐扩大研究范围，使得研究不但取得理论上的成果，而且可以运用到操作实践中。

China currently finds itself in an era of boundless change and the pursuit of a new global position, in many cases confronting other important cultures. However, is it possible that two countries, in this case China and Italy, can develop a significant intellectual affinity without any tradition of past exchanges, given both their geographic distance and the fact that their languages are based on different (if not opposing) logics? It is possible.
The Chinese people began working in this direction at the beginning of the past century, with a return after 1980, following the period of Maoist rule. In the field of cultural heritage conservation, the bases and beginnings of a radical theoretical and practical change can be dated back to the early 20th century, when Zhu Qiqian, in 1919, organised the Society for Research in Chinese Architecture, publishing the *Bulletin of the Society for the Research in Chinese Architecture*. His students and followers, many of whom were educated abroad, sought to impose some methodologies within Chinese research into practices of restoration, historical studies and surveying. Unfortunately, the historical events of the following decades impeded any significant practical follow up to these theories, while the destructive force of material and immaterial objects proved all too powerful, threatening the formation of a modern Chinese cultural identity. However, the confrontation between two important cultures at an elevated intellectual level requires a lengthy period of time, and thus the exchange between the two faculties is a long-term programme. Successive collaborations are ensuring ever more in-depth investigations, involving other research bodies (both in Italy and China), extending it into progressively vaster fields and producing research that is not only theoretical, but also operative and practical.

序二

陈薇

长时间以来，我们比较敏感和注重研究东西方文化的差异。往往在这种寻觅中，发现各自的独特魅力，并力图进行心理上的认可和行为上的发扬。在文化冲突、社会变迁、探寻途径的过程中，这种比较研究的现象和心态尤为突出。但是从文明发展的角度而言，人类在认识事物的本质、理解自然的规律、探求技术的进步、提高认知的心性、追求社会的美好上，其实是相通和一致的。也就是说，文化的果实各滋各味，但在孕育和浇灌形成果实的过程中，其内驱力是基本相同的。从这样的视角来考察中西方文化，既可以观赏到它们的千姿百态，也可以领略到它们拥有的境界。

对南京城墙和罗马城墙的比较研究，乃试图揭开这两个世界著名历史城市的城墙存有差异的形成过程，而不是从结果图解和剖析它们的不同。本书的篇章结构和内容试图展示这样的思考。如筑墙史与城市史相关联，如城门启闭、开墙打洞与城市道路发展相关联，如城壕功能与城市变化相关联，如修缮保护技术与城墙遗址相应的材料和风土相关联，如保护规划与都市发展相关联等，尽管在具体的两座城市的城墙遗址上表现的形态不一，但从方法论上看，不同文化体系下的建设成就、发展思考、技术运用等，是有着共同追求的，乃对先人智慧的尊重，对文化遗产的珍重，对城市生活的关注，对城市文脉的理解。

另一方面，我们还从两个不同历史城市的城墙史、发展变化和保护经验中，体会到城墙作为一种载体所透射出的文化差异和技术手段的异趣，这是十分有价值的，也是在不断加强的文化和学术交流中，值得比较推敲、相互学习、共同探讨、形成见识的。

从个人的角度，偏爱这两个历史城市的城墙、发现彼此的相关、又流连差异的追寻，源于16年前在欧洲的建筑考察。1998年，我独自登上意大利罗马台伯河侧的雅尼库伦山（Gianicolo），鸟瞰罗马城墙，其曲折变化、其顺山依水、其沧桑巨变，一时梦回南京，宛若在紫金山看到"龙脖子"（城墙蜿蜒曲折的形象俗称）、在九华山视及"台城"（六朝宫墙的北段），游子之心怦然而动。但只是瞬间，意大利语、德语不绝于耳，幡然梦醒，此乃西方文

Preface II

Chen Wei

We have long been sensitive to the cultural differences between the East and the West, and paid addictive attention to study them. The scrutiny of cultural differences, however, would sometimes bring out unexpected charms embedded in each other's unique culture, heralding a psychological recognition and encouraging a behavioral acceptance. In a world teemed with cultural conflicts, social changes, and explorations, it is understandable that people would automatically use comparison to satisfy their curiosity. From the perspective of human civilization, people, no matter what country they are originated from, are quite consistent in understanding the nature of things, reading the law of nature, exploring technological advancement, improving their perceptions, and in pursuing a positive social development. In other words, different cultures, though differed in the flavor of their fruits, are essentially stemmed from the same internal driving force that shapes up the breeding, developing, and fruiting process of human society. In this context, one would be overwhelmed by the unexpected charms gushed out from Eastern and Western cultures, and thus led to feel what they are meant for him or her.

The comparative study of the ancient walls in Nanjing and Rome is designed to understand the differences in the process of shaping up the two world famous historical walls, rather than to anatomize and illustrate the differences in results. This book's structure and content are therefore aligned to show the intention. One would, from a methodological point of view, see the same pursuit for achievements, development, and technological advancement under a different cultural system, when examining the historical ties between the wall and the urban development, between the opening/closing of a city gate and running through the wall to facilitate the traffic flow of urban roads, between moat functionalities and changed urban life, between wall repairing and protecting techniques and traditional materials applied to build the walls, and between protection planning and urban development. The comparison helps people respect their ancestors' wisdom, cherish the cultural heritages they left behind, look at today's urban life in an enlightened context, and understand the city's culture from a new perspective.

On the other hand, one can enjoy the different charms of cultures and techniques embedded in the walls, from reading the history of two different historical walls and their development, change, and protection, which makes the study worthy. Thanks to the increasingly enhanced cultural and academic exchanges, people are given opportunities to scrutinize the walls, discussing and sharing the anecdotes behind the walls, and deepening their knowledge of the walls.

My personal curiosity to know the ancient walls in the two historical cities, and to see the relevance as well as the difference between the two was originated from an architecture tour I made in Europe 16 years ago. In 1998, I climbed up to the top of Gianicolo on the left bank of the Tiber River in Rome, taking a bird's eye view of Roman Wall and its twists and

明之地，非金陵故乡。这样的兴趣和记忆一直萦绕于心。

2007年，我和我的工作团队受南京市政府委托，承担全国重点文物保护单位南京城墙的总体保护规划工作，开始全面认识南京城墙——历史的和现在的、保护的和发展的、本体的和环境的等等，2008年我们完成了这项艰巨而重要的工作。恰逢机缘，通过东南大学和罗马萨皮恩扎大学的学术交流平台，也因为阅读过意大利学者路易吉·戈佐拉（Luigi Gazzola）教授的《凤凰之家——中国建筑文化的城市与住宅》（*La casa della Fenice: la città e la casa nella cultura architettonica cinese*），得以了解西方学者视野下的城市，以及以路易吉·戈佐拉教授为领衔及其同事长期在罗马城墙研究方面的学术积累和操作经验。于是经过磋商，在南京东南大学召开"南京城墙和罗马城墙比较研究"国际研讨会，本著作乃这个会议后双方深入研究的成果。

从两校学术交流和东西方文化交流的角度而言，这本著作只是开端，但已领略况味：艰辛和乐趣。

感谢罗马大学路易吉·戈佐拉教授对于著作目录的编排建议，感谢他带领的团队对罗马城墙研究和实践的贡献并予以分享，感谢他多次为出版事宜亲赴南京共商切磋，感谢他联系的意方多米齐亚·曼多莱西（Domizia Mandolesi）女士为出版出谋划策，感谢罗马大学建筑学院前副院长乔治·迪·乔治（Giorgio Di Giorgio）亲临南京参加研讨。作为南京城墙保护规划的负责人，感谢南京市文物局、规划局、建设局及东南大学城市与建筑遗产保护教育部重点实验室主任董卫教授在此过程中的组织、指导、建议和帮助，感谢南京城墙管理处杨孝华先生和文物局姜继荣先生在盛夏酷暑导引我们开展调研，感谢南京各界专家和国家文物局专家的建设性意见。作为尝试用双语出版的著作，尤其是进行中文和意大利文之间的转换，实际上我们开展了中、英、意三国语言的沟通和交流，这是一件十分费力和需要严谨态度操作的事情，感谢所有学者和研究者、译者、出版社和友人及留学生杨慧的无私贡献以及共同的认真负责。即便如此，还是存有不少错误，出版之际，难免忐忑。

《诗经·小雅·鹤鸣》曰："它山之石，可以为错；它山之石，可以攻玉"。如果说进行南京城墙和罗马城墙比较研究有什么体会的话，或许可以改为："它山之石，可以润玉"，"它山之石，可以固玉"，横批："玉石一体"。在繁琐的后期校核和制作过程中，想到这些，不禁喜上眉梢。

turns along the mountains and waters, and envisioning the vicissitudes, which stirred in me a nostalgia for a range of similarities of things in Nanjing, including the zigzagging "Dragon Neck" Wall on the Purple Mountains, the landscape view of Jiuhua Mountain, and the northern section of the city walls built in the Six Dynasties. Then, I was awakened by the Italian, German, and other undistinguished languages murmuring around me to the reality that I was on the land of Western civilization, rather than in Nanjing, an ancient Chinese city. The curiosity and memory stemmed from that trip has been lingering in my mind for a long time.

In 2007, my team and I were assigned by the Nanjing Municipal Government to make a master plan for wall protection, which prompted the team to have an in-depth look at the past and present pictures of the city wall, its protection and development, and its survival and environment. In 2008, the painstaking planning work was completed. My personal curiosity led me to acquaint myself with the ancient walls under Western scholars' eye, either through academic exchanges between Southeast University and Sapienza University of Rome, or through reading the *Phoenix City* (*La casa della Fenice: la città e la casa nella cultura architettonica cinese*) by Prof. Luigi Gazzola, a Roman scholar. An international symposium was then held at Southeast University to discuss the ancient walls in Nanjing and Rome. This book reflects the results derived from the joint study conducted after the meeting.

The book is a beginning, in the context of academic and Eastern and Western culture exchanges between the two schools, though we have already tasted joys as well as difficulties doing that.

I would like to express my gratitude to Prof. Luigi Gazzola for his suggestions concerning the arrangement of contents, and for sharing with us the findings derived from the studies conducted by him and his team. Prof. Luigi Gazzola also showed untiring support to the publication of the book by personally visiting Nanjing several times, and by inviting Ms. Domizia Mandolesi to be part of the publication planning. I would also like to thank Giorgio Di Giorgio, former vice-president of University of Rome School of Architecture, for his personal attending the meeting held in Nanjing. Additionally, I want to acknowledge the following for their guidance, suggestions, comments, and assistance: Nanjing Cultural Heritage Bureau, Planning Bureau, and Construction Bureau, Prof. Dong Wei, dean of key Laboratory of Urban and Architectural Heritage Conservation (Southeast University), Ministry of Education, China, Mr. Yang Xiaohua of Nanjing City Wall Management Division, Mr. Jiang Jirong at Cultural Heritage Bureau, and specialists from involved disciplines and from State Administration of Cultural Heritages. The book, published in both Chinese and Italian languages, went through a process of communication and exchange made in three languages, including Chinese, English, and Italian. Here, I am especially grateful to all the scholars, researchers, translators, publishers and friends and overseas student Yang Hui who are part of the process for their hard working and devoted contributions. Even so, I would ask for forgiveness if a mistake is found here or there.

It says in an ancient Chinese book discussing poems and songs that stones from the hills that produce no jade can be borrowed to polish or carve jade. When studying the ancient walls in Nanjing and Rome, we perceive that stones from the hills that produce no jade can be applied to nourish and strengthen jade, making jade and stone into one. These are the feelings cropped up in the tedious process of publishing the book, though to my delight as enlightenment.

凡例 / General Notices

1. 本书为中英文双语，图片共用，图版采用原图及文字。

2. 外文人名、地名、书名一般均于首次出现时加注原文；中文人名、地名、书名一般均以汉语拼音在英文中出现，个别书名和地名，辅以意译，便于读者理解。

3. 个别意大利人名和地名在相关字典未检索到的则直接引用。

4. 各节图片分别顺序编号，注释和参考文献附于各节之后。

5. 书中所用图表、照片，未注明出处的，均系作者绘制和拍摄，相应版权分别归本合作研究的中、意双方负责人所有。

1. This book is in bilingual of Chinese-English but shared same photos. The original languages and drawings are used in the plates.

2. The original texts of people's names and place names are given when first from foreign language to Chinese. Chinese Pinyin codes are used when from Chinese to English for names of Chinese, place and book. English explanation for some important Chinese book titles and place names are provided, in addition to Pinyin.

3. Some Italian names and place names are cited directly if they cannot be found in dictionaries.

4. The figures in each chapter are numbered separately. The notes and bibliography are listed after each chapter.

5. Except for the ones with citation notes, all the drawings, pictures and tables in this book are produced by the authors, and all rights are reserved. respectively by the cooperation research principals of Chinese and Italian.

目录
Contents

序一
序二
凡例

第一章　历史演变　　　　　　　　　　　　　　　　　1
　第一节　南京城墙建置史　　　　　　　　　　　　　2
　第二节　南京明城墙的功能演变　　　　　　　　　20
　第三节　罗马城墙、城门及道路的发展和演变　　　30

第二章　城墙、景观与城市肌理　　　　　　　　　　47
　第一节　南京明城墙环境　　　　　　　　　　　　48
　第二节　"围"与"穿"——南京明城墙的城门与道路　71
　第三节　奥勒良城墙和城市肌理的关系　　　　　　84

第三章　城墙修复　　　　　　　　　　　　　　　109
　第一节　南京城墙的保护与修缮　　　　　　　　110
　第二节　19世纪至今奥勒良城墙的修复过程　　　121
　第三节　奥勒良城墙修建和维修　　　　　　　　131

第四章　城墙规划　　　　　　　　　　　　　　　147
　第一节　明城墙保护总体规划　　　　　　　　　148
　第二节　城墙系统与罗马的新城市总体规划　　　168

第五章　城墙与都市项目　　　　　　　　　　　　175
　第一节　南京明城墙风光带规划与实施　　　　　176
　第二节　新罗马城总体规划与战略规划区　　　　188

结语　　　　　　　　　　　　　　　　　　　　　196
作者及简介　　　　　　　　　　　　　　　　　　201

Preface I
Preface II
General Notices

1　Historical Evolution　　　　　　　　　　　　　　1
　1.1　A History of Constructing the Nanjing City Wall　　2
　1.2　The Evolution of the Nanjing Ming City Wall's Function　20
　1.3　The History and Evolution of the Rome City Walls, Gates and Roads　30

2　City Walls, Landscape and Urban Fabric　　　　　47
　2.1　The Environment of the Nanjing Ming City Wall　48
　2.2　"Enclosure" and "Traverse" – Gates and Roads under the Nanjing Ming City Wall　71
　2.3　The Relation between the Aurelian Walls and the Urban Fabric　84

3　Restoration of City Walls　　　　　　　　　　　109
　3.1　The Protection and Maintenance of the Nanjing City Wall　110
　3.2　The Restoration of the Aurelian Walls from 19th Century until Today　121
　3.3　The Construction and Restoration of the Aurelian Walls　131

4　Planning for City Walls　　　　　　　　　　　　147
　4.1　The Conservation Master Plan for the Nanjing Ming City Wall　148
　4.2　The Walls System and the New General Urban Plan in Rome　168

5　City Walls and Urban Projects　　　　　　　　　175
　5.1　The Landscape Planning and Implementation of the Nanjing Ming City Wall　176
　5.2　The New Master Plan for Rome and its Strategic Planning Zones　188

Conclusions　　　　　　　　　　　　　　　　　　196
Authors and Introductions　　　　　　　　　　　201

第一章 历史演变

1 Historical Evolution

第一节 南京城墙建置史
1.1 A History of Constructing the Nanjing City Wall

诸葛净 Zhuge Jing
张剑葳 Zhang Jianwei

南京城墙的建设可追溯至公元 3 世纪的前半叶，自那以后的近 2 000 年里，南京城墙被不断地建设、毁弃、整修与重建。现存的南京城墙，包括城墙和郭墙，基本为 14 世纪后半叶明代所新建或在前代基础上改扩建而成。南京明城墙实测总长为 35.267 km，目前保存较完好的有 25.091 km，遗迹（地面有 4～5 m 以下高度）、遗址（地面无城墙）共 10.176 km；郭墙总长 60 km，目前走势尚存的有 42 km（图 1）。其规模在中国古代城市的现存城墙中首屈一指。

The Nanjing City Wall was initially built in the first half of the 3rd century. The wall has experienced expansion, demolition, repairing, rebuilding, and restoration over the past 2,000 years. The surviving walls, including the city walls and defensive walls, were mainly rebuilt or expanded in the second half of the 14th century, based on the wall foundations built in the preceding dynasties. The city walls built in the Ming Dynasty measured 35.267km long. The sections, deemed reasonably well preserved, ran 25.091km long, with the remains walls (under 4～5m in height) and the sites (without walls) at 10.176km in length. The defensive walls have a total length of 60 km, though only 42km of them showing the course (Fig.1). The Nanjing City Wall has topped other ancient Chinese city walls survived the times in terms of scale.

图例
- 河流湖泊
- 明代外郭（有遗迹）
- 明代外郭（无遗迹）
- 明代内城墙（有遗存）
- 明代内城墙（无遗存）
- 明代皇城遗址
- 明代宫城遗址

图 1 南京明城墙范围、规模和保留现状
Fig.1 The spread and scale of the Ming City Wall of Nanjing

1. 南京古代城墙建设

1) 明代以前（1366年以前）[1]

建于周元王三年（公元前473年）的越城是南京城市区域内有明确记载的最早古城，周显王三十六年（公元前333年）楚在此筑金陵邑，则是南京地区第一个行政治所[2]。但明以前南京城墙的大规模修建主要集中在两个建都时期：三国两晋南北朝（220—588年）及南唐五代（892—960年）。

中国古代历史上的汉代和唐代之间，经历了300年左右的大分裂，即三国两晋南北朝，在此期间中国被三个或更多的地方政权割据。今天的南京先是成为三国时吴国的都城，之后成为南朝各王国的首都。这些地方割据政权都面临来自北方的威胁，对这些王朝来说，长江是天然屏障，江边的丘陵山岗则提供了良好的据守高地。

212年吴国国王孙权改秣陵为建业[3]，并改筑金陵邑城为石头城以储存粮食与武器。至229年，孙权定都建业，在石头城以东的腹地新建了一座城池。东晋六朝皆因之[4]，但317年城名改为建康。

石头城清凉山一带，长江绕其西侧而过，是石头城的天然护城河，成为都城建业西面最重要的军事堡垒。今天在清凉山还能看到一些石头城遗迹，斑驳迷离，雄踞城西，由于其砖石表层剥落，原深红色山石和脱落的白色表层，形成一些图面，被称为"鬼脸城"。尽管这段遗迹表面砖石已非六朝原物，但墙体走向与山崖紧密结合的关系仍非常清晰，展现出当年"因山以为城，因江以为池"的险要地势（图2）。

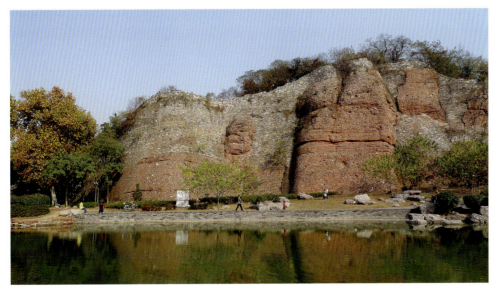

图2　石头城
Fig.2　The Stone City

1 – Historical Evolution

1. Constructing of the Nanjing City Wall

1) Before the Ming Dynasty (before 1366) [1]

The Yue City, appeared in 473 BC, is the earliest city on the territories of the Nanjing City having a written record. In 333 BC, the Chu State founded there a city named Jinling. It was the first administrative district in the Nanjing area[2]. However, before the Ming Dynasty, major activities to build and expand city walls were mainly made during two periods: the period of the Three Kingdoms, the Two Jins, and the North and South Dynasties (220–588), and the period run by the Five South Tang Dynasties (892–960).

In the Chinese history, a major split occurred between the Han Dynasty and the Tang Dynasty, which lasted for some 300 years. Historically, the period is referred to as the period of the Three Kingdoms, the Two Jins, and the North and South Dynasties, where ancient China was split into three or more local domains. Today's Nanjing was then the capital of the Wu State (one of the Three Kingdoms), though served as the capital of other kingdoms in the South Dynasties as well. Local warlords had to deal with the threats stemmed from the north. To them, the Yangtze River made a natural barrier to fence off the possible attacks from the north. The hills and mountains sitting along the River became a desirable fortification.

In 212AD, Sun Quan, the King of the Wu State, changed Moling into Jianye in name[3], and renamed the Jinling City a "Stone City" to keep food and arms. In 229AD, Sun Quan founded his capital in Jianye, and built walls and moats in the east part of the Stone City. The East Jin and the Six Dynasties followed suit[4], though the city was renamed Jiankang in 317AD.

The Stone City sat in an area called Mount Qingliang . Passing by the Stone City in the west, the Yangtze River was apparently a natural moat, and the most important military fortification in the west of the capital city Jianye. In today's Mount Qingliang, one is still able to see some traces left by the Stone City in the west. The weathered original bricks showed some weird patterns, as the color faded from crimson to whitish. Folks termed the mutated wall patterns as "ghost face". The wall went in a well-defined course heading for the nearby mountains, indicating the tough terrains it had worked with to be a city defended by mountains as the walls and rivers as the moat, even though the surface bricks on the relics were no longer the one laid in the Six Dynasties(Fig.2).

公元589年，建康城被隋的统治者平毁。隋在这个地区设置了蒋州，治所安置在石头城中。

这一阶段的城池建设基本揭示了南京所在地区地理环境特点对城市建设的制约，即适合城市建设发展的区域主要在北至覆舟山、南至秦淮河、西至清凉山、东至燕雀湖的范围内；该区域周边的山岗，尤其是沿江的丘陵，提供了扼守水、陆通道，据险防御的地势。因此城市建设也形成以建康城为中心，周边堡垒相环护卫的态势（图3、图4）。

In 589 AD, Jiankang was flattened by the ruler of the Sui Dynasty. Authorities set up an administrative district called Jiangzhou there, and homed its headquarters in the Stone City.

The development of city walls and moats in the period suggests the limits imposed by the geographic environment on the development of a city, confining the major development of the city to an area stretching to Mount Fuzhou in the north, the Qinhuai River in the south, Mount Qingliang in the west, and Yanque Lake in the east. The surrounding hills, especially the one sitting along the rivers, made a fortification to both land and water ways, desirable for defense. As a result, the urban area was developed with Jiankang as the center, protected by an array of strongholds in the vicinity(Fig.3, Fig.4).

图3 玄武湖南侧的明城墙（上）
Fig.3 The Ming City Wall on the south of the Xuanwu Lake (up)

图4 南朝都城建康图（引自《金陵古今图考》）（下）
Fig.4 The map of the capital city Jiankang of the South Dynasties (from: *Jinling Gujin Tu Kao*) (down)

唐朝末年，中国再次分裂。南京所在地区先为杨吴所占据，接着直到宋代都在南唐的统治之下。公元914年，杨吴改筑为金陵府城。932年，徐知诰主持改筑，在原有基础上拓广甚多，奠定此后数百年城池规模。937年，南唐以金陵为都城。金陵城同样以西侧长江及南侧秦淮河为天然屏障（图5）。

宋沿用了这一城池，城周二十五里四十四步，有八门[5]。而因宋金对峙之特殊形势，长江南岸的宋建康府城是前线的军事要地，采取了增立女墙，加厚墙身，建硬楼瓮城，浚城壕，立羊马墙等一系列措施，使围绕城墙建造的一套防御体系得以加固与完备[6]。

元代该城作为集庆路治，城墙仍保持南唐初建时的规模走向，直至1366年朱元璋大规模扩建才使城墙规模、形制发生巨大变化。

2）明之建设（1366—1911年）

元末朱元璋起兵抗元，至1366年，朱元璋虽未称帝，但已在钟山（今紫金山）之南新建宫殿，并初次拓展元之集庆路旧城，将新宫纳入城中[7]。

公元1368年，朱元璋以元集庆路（已改名为应天府）为明帝国的都城，其后虽有

China split again at the end of the Tang Dynasty. The area where Nanjing stands today was occupied by the Yang Wu State, and then placed under the rule of the South Tang Dynasty till the Song Dynasty. In 914 AD, Jinling was rebuilt into a capital city in Yang Wu period. In 932 AD, Xu Zhihao presided over the city expansion. The massive expansion efforts created a solid foundation for the expansion of walls and moats in the following hundred years. In 937 AD, the South Tang authorities made Jinling its capital. In the same manner, Jinling enjoyed the role played by the Yangtze River in the west and the Qinhuai River in the south as a natural barrier (Fig.5).

The city wall and moat stretching over 13km and associated 8 gates [5] also survived the Song Dynasty. The confrontation between the Song and the Jin made the Jiankang City built in the Song Dynasty on the southern border of the Yangtze River a military fortification. The city wall was enhanced and fortified with a range of practices, including erecting the parapet wall, thickening the wall, building the bastions, and deepening the moat [6].

In the Yuan Dynasty, the city was made a prefecture named Jiqing, though the city wall retained its original course and scale as it was built in the early South Tang Dynasty. In 1366, Emperor Zhu Yuanzhang ordered a massive expansion of the wall, which led to a huge change of the walls in both scale and structure.

2) City walls in the Ming Dynasty (1366—1911)

Zhu Yuanzhang launched a rebellion uprising at the end of the Yuan Dynasty. In 1366, Zhu built a new palace in the south of Mount Zhong (today's Purple Mountain), though not yet made himself an emperor [7].

In 1368, Zhu made the Jiqing prefecture that was established in the Yuan Dynasty (already renamed as Yingtianfu) the capital of his Empire. The city struggled to keep its capital status in a range of changes. Zhu expanded the city in a well-planned manner. The city was made up of four inner parts: the palace, the imperial city, the capital city, and external defensive enclosure. The so-called Nanjing Ming City Wall is technically the walls built to defend the capital city at the time. In 1373, the wall of the capital city underwent another round of expansion [8], with raised height and width. The expansion was basically completed in 1386. The city wall was rebuilt on the foundation built in the times of the Stone City in the west, and on the wall remains left by the South Tang Dynasty in the southwest part of the city [9]. The rest of the city walls went further eastwards and northwestwards, encompassing the highlands along the rivers from Mount Shizi to Mount Qingliang.

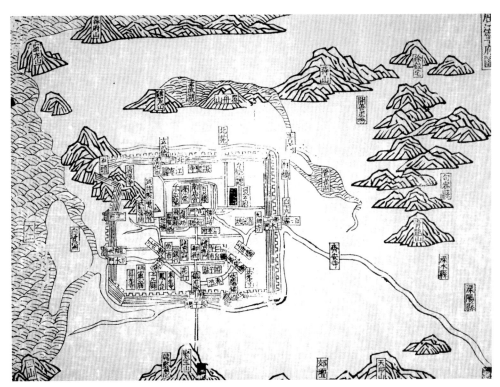

图5　南唐江宁府图（引自《金陵古今图考》）
Fig.5　The map of the Jiangning (Jinling) city in the South Tang Dynasty (from: *Jinling Gujin Tu Kao*)

反复，但最终确立应天府都城地位，并逐次营建，形成宫城、皇城、京城与外郭四重城的规模。通常所说的南京明城墙指的就是京城城墙。1373年京城城墙再次改扩建[8]，将第一次拓建城墙加宽加高，至1386年基本完成。新的城墙西侧一部分以石头城的遗存为基础，西南段的走向以南唐城墙为基础[9]，其他部分除向东扩展，亦向西北扩展，将狮子山至清凉山一线的沿江高地纳入城中。

最后建造完成的南京城墙总长实测为35.267 km，高度在12～26 m之间，城顶最宽处达19.8 m，包围了城市三个不同的功能分区：①从东水关经聚宝门到石头山为市区；②石头山逶迤而北而东而南到太平门一带，依山傍湖，据险而设，为军事区；③从朝阳门到通济门围护皇宫[10]。共设城门13座。

到1390年，最外一重郭城也初具规模。外郭西侧以长江为防，自幕府山迤东而南而西，联络岗阜，将南京地区外围的丘陵山岗包绕入城，全长约60 km（图6）。外郭墙体以土墙为主[11]。

The city wall, when completed, reached a length of 35.267km, with a height between 12m and 26m. The widest part of the wall top measured 19.8m. It embraced three functional zones: ① the city proper running from the East Water Pass to Mount Shitou via Jubao Gate; ② a military zone covering the northern, east, and southern part of the city from Mount Shitou to Taiping Gate, against the mountains and lakes; and ③ the imperial palace stretching from Chaoyang Gate to Tongji Gate[10]. The wall had 13 gates.

In 1390, the outmost part of the defensive wall was completed of construction. The outer defensive wall sat against the Yangtze River in the west, snaking along Mount Mufu to meet other mountains, making outside hills part of the city. The defensive wall accounted 60km in length(Fig.6). The outer defensive wall was built mainly with earth[11].

When expanding the city walls, Zhu Yuanzhang employed a strategy to build the walls on the sur-

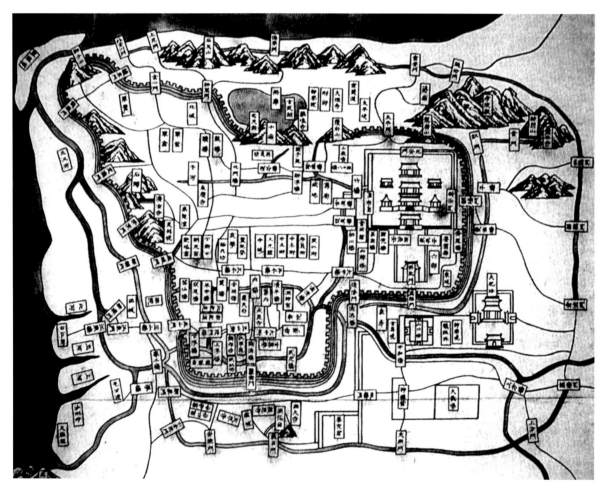

图6 （明南京）街市桥梁图
（引自：《洪武京城图志》）
Fig.6 The streets and bridges map of Ming Nanjing City (from: *Hongwu Jingcheng Tu Zhi*)

viving foundations, rather than dismantling the old walls completely(Fig.7).Meanwhile, he spared no resources to build the new walls, when necessary. According to *Jingding Jiankang Zhi* (The Gazetteer of Jiankang in the Jingding Reign Period), there was a Fugui Castle (The Crawling Turtle Castle) outside of the southeast corner of the Jinling City Wall. The castle was first built in the South Tang Dynasty, and was expanded in the South Song Dynasty. In addition to its fortification functions, it was employed by folks to enjoy a bird's-eye view. The name of the castle was still mentioned in the historic texts even when Zhu attacked the Jiqing prefecture established in the Yuan Dynasty [12]. Archaeologists in Nanjing discovered in May 2001 the remains of an ancient structure when repairing the southeast corner of the Ming City Wall. The remains were identified to be the foundation of a large structure, it was believed that the structure was built in the times of the Yang Wu State, or in the South Tang Dynasty, probably the remains of the Fugui Castle built in the South Tang Dynasty, an auxiliary structure attached to the city wall(Fig.8).

The huge labor force needs for building the city walls had to be addressed in a combined manner, including the labor services provided by servicemen,

图7 明城墙与南唐至元代的城墙
Fig.7 The Ming City Wall and the South Tang to Yuan City Walls

图8 南唐伏龟楼基址
Fig.8 The remain of the Fugui Castle's foundation

在具体的建造中，朱元璋并未将原有城墙彻底拆除，而是尽可能在原有基础上利用改筑（图7），但需要新建之处也不吝人力与物力。

据《景定建康志》等文献记载，南唐金陵城东南隅偏南外侧有伏龟楼。此楼始建于南唐，南宋时增筑，除主要用于军事瞭望守备外，还兼有登高观赏之功能。直至朱元璋攻打元集庆路时，伏龟楼的名称仍出现在文献中[12]。2001年5月，南京文物部门的工作者在维修明代南京城墙东南转角一段时发现了一处古代建筑遗迹。从其形制及构筑特征判断，是一处大型建筑的台基，很可能就是作为旧城附属建筑的南唐伏龟楼基址（图8）。

城墙建造所需的大量人夫以军役、丁役和罪役等几种方式解决。军役是征发部队人员参加城池营建。丁役则是征派民夫，城墙营建期间主要以"均工夫"的方式征派。城墙建造所需之建材则依靠各地方官员督办，从全国各府州县征派调运至京。如城砖即由各地组织烧造，然后运入京城，为此也形成一套专门的组织制度。相应的，为便于检查和管理，南京城墙砖上都模印着府县提调官、司吏、地方总甲[13]、甲首、小甲、窑匠等与砖的烧造和运输各个环节相关的人员姓名，以及造砖年月。从砖上所印地点来看，烧造南京城墙用砖的，除少数南京附近卫所外，绝大多数来自长江及其上游湘江、赣江等支流流经的江苏、安徽、江西、湖北、湖南的州县，已知有28府，160多个县和卫所[14]（图9）。

公元1421年，明帝国迁都北京，南京成为中国东南地区的经济中心。虽然有明清换代之事件，但建于明朝的南京城墙一直沿用到1911年。1645年，满洲入侵者在明朝宫殿的旧基上建立起满洲驻防城，但此举并未改变南京城墙的走势。

2. 南京明城墙系统建置特点

1）城池

自六朝以来，南京城市顺应山水地形而形成的不规则形状就与中原地区方正的都城形成鲜明对比。明代城墙尤以包络岗阜为主，使得城墙走势更为曲折逶迤。通过对

registered craftsmen, and jailed criminals. The labor service provided under the regime of "averaged labor service call" constituted a major labor force employed to build the wall, though servicemen were occasionally called to be part of the construction efforts. The materials needed to build the city walls were shipped to the capital city from different parts of the country upon the imperial demand. For example, bricks would be made by designated local kilns, before shipping to the capital city. This was, obviously, done under a special organizing and dispatching system. To supervise and manage the inflow of building materials, the bricks employed to build the city walls were printed with the names of local officials and folks who made the bricks [13], and the date when the bricks were made. According to the addresses printed on the bricks, most bricks employed to build the city walls came from the counties in the vicinity of the Yangtze River, and the one on the tributaries of upper reaches, including the Xiang River and the Gan River, covering 28 prefectures and more than 160 counties and army units in Jiangsu, Anhui, Jiangxi, Hubei, and Hunan [14], though the armies stationed in the vicinity of Nanjing also contributed some bricks (Fig.9).

In 1421, the Ming Dynasty moved its capital to Beijing. As a result, Nanjing became an economic center in the southeast part of the country. The Nanjing Ming City Wall survived the shifts of dynasties in the following years until 1911. In 1645, the invaders from Manchuria built a defensive wall on the foundation of old palace walls, which, fortunately, did not change the course of the Nanjing City Wall.

2. Highlights of the Nanjing Ming City Wall

1) Walls and moats

In the Six Dynasties, Nanjing, as a city, was built in an irregular shape to go with the contours of the mountains and rivers in the locality, which was quite a deviation from the square shaped city layout prevailed over the middle part of the country at the time. In the Ming Dynasty, the city walls started to encompass the hills and mountains,

图9　南京明城墙砖上的铭文
Fig.9　The inscriptions on the bricks of the Nanjing Ming City Wall

现存城墙所在地形的分析可以看到，明城墙的大部分段落选线顺着岗阜，但并非走山脊，而是尽量将制高点包络入城内，如狮子山、九华山、富贵山都是此种情况[15]。也因此在南京城墙建造中，包山墙是非常显著的特点，即城墙外壁从下到上都用砖石包砌，内侧为土丘或山体，基本没有内壁墙或人工护土坡（图10）。

making the walls more zigzagged in riding. Analysis of the walls shows that in the Ming Dynasty, most part of the city walls were built along the hills and mountains to encompass as many highlands as possible, rather than simply traversing the mountains. For example, Mount Shizi, Mount Jiuhua, and Mount Fugui were the highlands in the locality[15]. The wall built to encompass the mountains was, therefore, a major highlight of the way to build the city wall. Folks built the entire external walls using bricks and rocks with the hills or mountains being the internal part. No internal walls made of bricks or raised earth hills were found on the site (Fig.10).

图10　玄武门段城墙（上）
　　　狮子山段城墙（下）
Fig.10　The city wall near the Xuanwu Gate (up)
　　　　The city wall encompass the Mount Shizi (down)

城墙墙顶外侧有密集的雉堞作为战时掩体，根据《明史》记载，南京明城墙上雉堞共有13 616个[16]。内侧则筑高约1 m的矮墙。据文献记载，城墙上还建有窝铺200余个，为守城者值更与放置守城器械的临时住所。

城墙外侧的护城河是城墙系统的重要组成部分。六朝与南唐时建城即尽量利用长江天险作为城西的天然护城河，同时又以人工开挖整理结合自然水系勾连形成城市护城河。明南京城仍继承了这一传统，利用长江、外秦淮河、金川河与大小湖泊沟通贯连成宽阔的护城河。

南京明城墙另一重要特点是没有中国城墙上通常会有的防御设施——马面。学者认为南京城墙的平面极不规则，各段城墙之间容易组织侧防，已起到了马面的作用，因此南京城墙没有设置马面。

2）城门

对于被高大城墙环绕的中国城市，城墙上开启的门洞对于保证城市内外人与物的流通，并进而保持城市的活力起着至关重要的作用，但同时也成为战争中防御的薄弱环节，因而在城墙系统中，城门也是防御的重点。不仅城门本身有特别的形式与布局，城门上还往往建有高大的城楼。战争时城楼是军队指挥官的指挥场所，平时作为中国城市中较为少见的高大建筑，视野高远，城楼有时也成为城市的一道风景。

南京古代城墙的城门以明代最具代表性。

与明南京城布局之三区相对应，十三座城门中石城门、三山门、聚宝门至通济门围绕着市廛区；自通济门向东，正阳门、朝阳门至太平门围绕着皇城区域；从太平门向北，经神策门、金川门、钟阜门、仪凤门、定淮门、清凉门包绕着军事区（图11）。

城门形制一览[17]：

明南京城的每座城门至少有一个门道，由砖、石或半砖半石砌成拱门。

（1）三山门

三山门位于西侧城墙，是在南唐及宋、元金陵城城门基础上改建的三个门之一，原名为龙光门，又叫水西门、下水门（图12）。洪武十九年（1386年）重新建造，改称三山门。城门形制为三道内瓮城，一门道，共四道拱券门。

（2）聚宝门（中华门）

聚宝门位于城墙南侧中路，原为南唐都城以及宋、元金陵城的南门，1386年在原有基础上改建而成，城门形制为三道内瓮城（图13），一门道，共四道拱券门。东西宽124 m，南北长129 m，占地面积14 572 m²。

Ancient folks also built dense crenels around the top of the city walls. According to *Ming Shi* (The History of Ming Dynasty), there were 13,616 crenels on the Nanjing Ming City Wall[16]. The inner wall was a structure with a reduced height up to 1m. According to ancient literatures, folks also built more than two hundred shelters (bedding areas) on the wall tops for night watchman or for the soldiers guarding the arms. The moat built along the external part of the walls made an important part of the city walls. In the Six Dynasties and the South Tang Dynasty, the Yangtze River, a natural barrier, was borrowed to be the moat for the west part of the city walls. Meanwhile, some artificial ditches were dug out to connect to the natural water systems, forming up a moat protecting the city. In the Ming Dynasty, the city walls were built following suit. A range of natural rivers and lakes, large or small, including the Yangzye River, External Qinhuai River and the Jinchuan River, were borrowed to be part of the massive moat.

Another important feature possessed by the Nanjing City Wall built in the Ming Dynasty is the walls were not built with a Mamian, a projecting part of a rampart at a given distance, or bastion, commonly applied in ancient Chinese city walls for defense purpose. Some scholars believe that, the irregular layout of the Nanjing City Wall and the fact that it is easy to organize a lateral defense within the sections of the walls, has offset the role of Mamian, which explained the absence of Mamian in the Nanjing City Wall.

2) Gates

Ancient Chinese cities enclosed by massive walls had to address the flow of people and goods in and out of the city. In this context, gates in the city walls were meant to be accessible, playing an important role in sustaining the vitality of a city. Unfortunately, city gates also constituted a weak link in the context of defense, and were therefore a focus of defense. In ancient times, city gates were built to meet the defense needs in both form and layout, usually having an impressive gate tower sitting above it. In wartime, a gate tower served as the headquarters where military commanders issued their instructions and orders. In peacetime, a gate tower made a landscape for its unusual height and bird's-eye view.

The city gates built in the Ming Dynasty tell the typical story of a city gate possessed by the Nanjing City Wall. In the Ming Dynasty, city gates were built to match the 3-zone layout of the city. Of the 13 gates, Shicheng, Sanshan, Jubao, and Tongji were accessible to the downtown area. In the east of the Tongji Gate, erected a number of other gates, including Zhengyang, Chaoyang, and Taiping,

第一章 历史演变 1 – Historical Evolution

stretching to the imperial enclosure. In the north of the Taiping Gate, sat a string of gates heading for the military enclosure, including Shence, Jinchuan, Zhongfu, Yifeng, Dinghuai, and Qingliang(Fig.11). Gates and their basic facts[17]:

Each gate built in the Ming Dynasty had at least one gateway made of bricks or rocks, or the combination of the two.

(1) Sanshan Gate

Sitting in the west section of the walls, Sanshan Gate was one of the three gates rebuilt on the gate foundations of Jinling City built in the South Tang Dynasty and the Yuan Dynasty(Fig.12). Before known as Sanshan, it was also called Longguang Gate, or Shuixi Gate, or Xiashui Gate in the past. In 1386, it was rebuilt and renamed as Sanshan Gate. The gate was built to be an internal fortress with three enclosures, one gateway, and four arches.

(2) Jubao Gate (Zhonghua Gate)

The gate stood in the middle of the southern loop of the walls. It was named South Gate in the South Tang Dynasty, the Song Dynasty, and the Yuan Dynasty. The gate was designed to be an internal fortress with three enclosures (Fig.13), one gateway, and four arches. Occupying an area of 14,572m^2, the gate measured 124m wide from

图11 城门汇总图（上）
Fig.11 The map of the city gates (up)

图12 三山门瓮城（下）（引自：《南京明城墙》）
Fig.12 The Sanshan Gate with an internal fortress (down) (from: *Nanjing Ming Chengqiang*)

每门有上下启动的千斤闸和向两面分开的双扇门。城中设有27个藏兵洞，可屯士兵约3 000人及军用物资[18]。

（3）通济门

位于南京城东南转角处，南北向。明初建，1386年重筑。城门形制为内瓮城三道，均为弧形（图14）。主城门门道与瓮城门道在一直线上。主城门上建闸楼和城楼。

the east to the west, and 129m long from the south to the north. Each gate was equipped with a lifting mechanism for opening and closing. The gates could also be opened sideways. There were 27 vaults in the gate complex that could hold 3,000 military personnel and military equipment [18].

(3) Tongji Gate

Tongji Gate was physically located in the southeast corner of the walls. First built in the Ming Dynasty, the gate was rebuilt in 1386. The gate was built as an internal fortress with three enclosures, all in arch shape(Fig.14).The gateway of the main gate sat on a line leading to the gate of the fortress. Above the main gate erected a gate tower and a gate operation room.

(4) Zhengyang Gate

Built in the early Ming Dynasty, the gate sat facing the central axis of the Imperial Palace. The gate had an internal fortress with one enclosure.

(5) Chaoyang Gate

The gate stood in the east part of the city. No fortress was attached in the early Ming Dynasty when the gate was initially built. In the Qing Dynasty, it became a defensive gate in the east part of the city, guarded by the invaders from Manchuria. In 1865, a fortress was added, by north, outside of Chaoyang Gate [19].

(6) Taiping Gate

The gate was built in the early Ming Dynasty without fortress.

(7) Shence Gate

Sitting on the top of a small hill in the northeast corner of the walls, the gate was built in the early Ming Dynasty, and closed in the early Qing Dynasty. It was reopened under Emperor Shunzhi, and renamed Desheng. The gate changed its name to Heping in 1928, and has been kept intact since then. The gate was the only city gate having an external fortress.

(8) Jinchuan Gate

Built in the early Ming Dynasty, and blocked in the late Ming Dynasty.

(9) Zhongfu Gate

The gate was first built in the early Ming Dynasty, and was named East Gate under the rule of Emperor Hongwu. It was renamed Zhongfu Gate in 1378. The

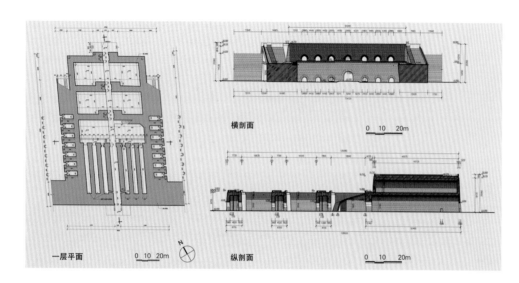

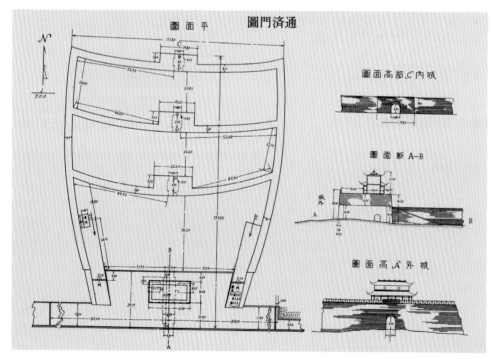

图13 聚宝门测绘图（上）
Fig.13 Drawings of Jubao Gate (up)

图14 通济门测绘图（下）（引自《中国城墙：支那城郭的概要所载地图选》）
Fig.14 Drawings of Tongji Gate (down) (from "Chinese Walled Cities: a collection of maps from Shina Jokaku no Gaiyo")

（4）正阳门

正对明朝宫殿中轴线的门。建于明初。

（5）朝阳门

位于城东，明初建时无瓮城。清代成为满洲驻防城的东门，同治四年（1865年）于朝阳门外城门偏北斜设瓮城[19]。

（6）太平门

建于明初，无瓮城。

（7）神策门

位于城墙的东北角，在一座小山丘的顶上。建于明初，清初关闭，顺治年间又重开，改名得胜门。1928年改称和平门。保存完好。这是唯一一座有外瓮城的城门。瓮城开有两门。

（8）金川门

建于明初，明末堵塞，宣统元年（1909年）重开。

（9）钟阜门

明初建，洪武初年称东门，洪武十一年（1378年）改称为钟阜门。明成化(1465—1487年)前关闭。

（10）仪凤门

又称兴中门，明初建，明成化(1465—1487年)前堵塞，清顺治十六年（1659年）重开。

（11）定淮门

明初建，原名马鞍门。清道光二十三年（1843年）堵塞。

（12）清凉门

明初建，洪武十二年（1379年）改清凉门为清江门。清初堵塞。

（13）石城门

原南唐都城及宋元金陵城之西大门，明初在原址改建。保存较完整，两道城门尚存，但瓮城北墙不存，城门上部楼橹无存。设一道内瓮城。

3）从军事防御角度看瓮城布局

南京城门最有特点的是瓮城布局。

通常说来，瓮城由城门外侧一道或多道城墙组成围合空间，可以增加防御纵深。但在南京，城墙南侧的七座城门却是内瓮城，也就是说由一道或多道城墙组成的围合位于主城墙的内侧。南京城墙最南面的三座门：三山门、聚宝门、通济门皆有三道内瓮城、门券四层。石城门为一道内瓮城，门券二重。正阳门有月城（瓮城）一座。其

gate was closed before the period of 1465–1487.

(10) Yifeng Gate
Also named Xingzhong, the gate was built in the early Ming Dynasty. It was blocked before the period of 1465–1487, and was reopened in 1659.

(11) Dinghuai Gate
Originally called Ma'an(literally means "saddle"), the gate was built in the early Ming Dynasty, and blocked in 1843.

(12) Qingliang Gate
The gate was built in the early Ming Dynasty. It was renamed in 1379 from Qingliang to Qingjiang. It was blocked in the early Qing Dynasty.

(13) Shicheng Gate
It was a main gate guarding the west part of the city in a range of dynasties, including South Tang, Song, and Yuan. It was rebuilt in the early Ming Dynasty. The gate has been relatively well kept with two lines of gates, though the fortress had lost its walls in the north, and the gate tower lost its watch post. The gate was built with an internal fortress.

3) Defensive functions of the fortresses
The layout of the fortresses built in the Ming Dynasty reflects the uniqueness of the city gates.
In ancient China, a fortress was, more often than not, a structure with one or more enclosures built outside the city gates to enhance the depth of the defensive walls. Strangely, the seven gates in the southern part of the Nanjing City Wall were built with internal fortresses only. That means the same structures in Nanjing sat within rather than outside of major city walls. Three gates sitting in the far south of major city walls, including Sanshan, Jubao, and Tongji, were built with an internal fortress having three enclosures and four arches. Shicheng Gate had an internal fortress with one enclosure and a gate with two arches. Zhengyang Gate possessed a fortress. The remaining 7 gates were designed with one gate. Only Shence Gate in the northern part of the city was built with an external fortress. The remaining 5 gates were built without fortresses.
In the context of defense, the city gates in Nanjing were built to match the major military strongholds outside the walls, including the Moling Pass in the southeast, and Mount Yuhua outside Jubao Gate. They were the fortifications that one had to overcome when invading the city from the south. Outside of Taiping Gate stood Mount Zhong. Invaders had to usurp the highland outside of the gate, if attacking the city from the north. As a matter of fact, an uprising army, called the Taiping Army, built a number of fortifications there, including the Tian Castle and the Di Castle. The loyal army in the Qing Dynasty attacked the rebellion army by occupying the said two castles first, before besieging and forcing into the city from

余七门皆为城墙上设门一道。南京城墙只有城北的神策门一座城门是外瓮城，而其余的五座城门则没有瓮城。

从军事防御的角度看，南京城外围的重要军事据点有东南面之秣陵关，聚宝门外之雨花山，此为从南面陆路进入南京所必须攻克的关隘；太平门外为钟山，从北面陆路进入南京也需首先取得太平门外之制高点，后来太平军即就此地势筑了天堡、地堡城，清兵亦先攻占天堡、地堡城方能完成对南京的合围并最终从太平门攻入；城外北面陆上的军事据点为红山（洪山）与北固山。从长江进攻南京，有两种可能，一种在水军强大的情况下，可顺外秦淮河直达城下，直逼石城门与三山门，朱元璋与陈友谅大战时，特意用计将其水军引至龙湾，即是怕陈友谅之水军可沿外秦淮河直达城下，虽然此时尚未建设南京城，但道理同一；另一种如郑成功之战法，在城北登陆占据城北陆上之据点攻城。

故而《南都察院志》中石城门、三山门、聚宝门称为"冲繁"，通济门、正阳门、太平门、金川门、仪凤门称为"冲要"。冲者，本意为交通要道。

显然朱元璋建造南京城墙时，城墙设施的防卫重点在城之西与南。三山门、聚宝门、通济门及东西水关最为森严，三山、聚宝（图15）与通济也都采用了三道内瓮城；其次为石城门（图16），再次为南之正阳门、北之神策门。从地形上分析，南京城的西与南地势较为平坦，且这几座城门外是宽阔的外秦淮河，因而城墙作为防御工事的作用较为突出。这一区域内又是南京城的繁华闹市，特别是聚宝门外有雨花台要塞，

Taiping Gate. Outside the city walls, stood two military fortifications, Red Mountain and Mount Beigu, in the north. When attacking Nanjing from the Yangtze River, one may have two options: sending the navy directly to Shicheng Gate and Sanshan Gate via the Exterior Qinhuai River. For example, Emperor Zhu Yuanzhang had a war with Chen Youliang. Emperor Zhu Yuanzhang deliberately lured the navy of his enemy to the Long Gulf, fearing the possible direct attacks to the city gates from the water way. The tactics worked all the same, even though Nanjing was not yet built into a city at the time. Another proven tactics is the one employed by Zheng Chenggong: taking up the fortifications in the north, before breaking into the city. In *Nan Du Cha Yuan Zhi* (Gazetteer of the South Capital City Supervision), some city gates, including Shicheng, Sanshan, and Jubao, were referred to as "busy junctures", while some others, including Tongji, Zhengyang, Taiping, Jinchuan, and Yifeng "fortification junctures".

When building the city walls, Emperor Zhu Yuanzhang paid more attention to the fortifications in the western and southern part of the city. As a result, three major gates, including Sanshan, Jubao (Fig.15), Tongji, and two major water passes in the east and west, were the heaviest fortifications built at the time. The three gates were all built with an internal fortress in three enclosures. Shicheng Gate (Fig.16) was next in the importance of fortification, followed by Zhengyang Gate in the south, and then Shence Gate in the north. Topographically, Nanjing is relatively flat in both west

图15 聚宝门（中华门）
Fig.15 Jubao Gate (Zhonghua Gate)

图16 石城门
Fig.16 Shicheng Gate

通济门靠近皇城,其本身所处位置也非常重要。而南京城西北包绕岗阜,可充分利用地形凭险制高,西北城区本身也是军事区,屯驻有十几个卫的军队守卫京师。

至于为何石城、三山、聚宝、通济诸门使用了内瓮城而不是传统的外瓮城,研究者有不同的观点。一种观点认为城外紧靠秦淮河,没有足够的空间建造瓮城,因而将瓮城建于城内侧[20];另一种观点认为此做法是对南宋初年陈规在《守城机要》中提出的内瓮城构想的创造性发展[21]。

4)外郭城门

外郭初建时辟城门16座:东为姚坊门、仙鹤门、麒麟门、沧波门、高桥门;南为上坊门、夹岗门、凤台门、大安德门、小安德门、大驯象门、小驯象门;西为江东门;北为上元门、佛宁门、观音门。明晚期又在西面和北面分别增辟栅栏门和外金川门,共为18座城门。

5)水关、涵闸、涵洞

明南京城内外主要水系沟通之处,又建进水水关、涵闸、涵洞8座;出水水关、涵闸、涵洞16座[22]。三山门、通济门旁的西水关与东水关为秦淮河出城与入城的通道,都颇具规模。

东水关又称通济门水关闸、上水关,俗称东关头,为内秦淮河入城处(图17)。位于通济门南侧,设有大小33券洞,分三层,每层11券洞,闸身及券洞均为条石砌筑,只有最上面一层的拱洞周围及顶部以城砖覆盖,内侧砖墙高约5 m。上层22个券洞面向城外一侧封堵;最下一层进水,每个涵洞设三道门:前后两道为防止敌人潜水进城的栅栏门,中间一道为控制水位的闸门,可用绞关闭合。11个进水涵洞中有9个装有固定铁栅,涵洞拱高3 m,洞长30 m。11个涵洞的中间一洞稍大,以通舟楫,以活动式铁栅替代固定铁栅[23]。

西水关为内秦淮河出城处,位于三山门南侧,结构与东水关相同。

最有代表性的闸是玄武湖南流的溢水闸:武庙闸,本名通心水坝,是玄武湖主要泄水入城通道,也是城内珍珠河的主要源头。玄武湖水通过地下管线入珍珠河至南唐金陵城北的杨吴城壕。所用管道150多节,其中铜管107节(径95 cm,长104 cm,厚1.5 cm),铁管43节(径约98 cm,长约81 cm,管壁约2 cm),各节用企口套接,水管经过城墙处上跨以砖券两重[24]。

城内原有两个进水水闸,可单独或同时启动。为减缓湖水的流速,闸口水道建成"之"字弯曲形。闸设矩形条石砌筑的深井,宽3.1 m,长7 m。在深井下方安装两套双合铜水闸,每套闸为方形(重约5.5 t),边长1.30 m,厚0.25 m,呈上下阴阳状。两处闸口都安装了绞刀,刀随水流的作用运转,用以切碎随湖水而来的湖草,防

and south. Additionally, outside of the aforesaid gates sat a massive Exterior Qinhuai River. In this context, the city wall was a desirable means for defense. Furthermore, the said part of the city was a downtown area. There was, in particular, a Yuhuatai fortification outside of Jubao Gate. Tongji Gate was in the vicinity of the imperial palace. All these made the gates strategically important. The northwest part of Nanjing, a military section holding tens of thousands of military personnel, had encompassed the mountains and hills that could be borrowed to make strategic heights. Researchers had differed views on why some major gates, including Shicheng, Sanshan, Jubao, and Tongji, were designed with an internal fortress, rather than the traditional external fortress. Some researchers believed that there was no sufficient space to build a fortress, as the city was closely bordered with the Qinhuai River. Evidently, one had to build an internal fortress instead [20]. Some others held that the practice was a creative realization of the concept of internal fortress proposed by Chen Gui in *Shou Cheng Ji Yao* (The Secrets of Guarding a City), published in the early Southern Song Dynasty [21].

4) Gates of the outer wall

The outer wall initially opened with 16 gates: Yaofang, Xianhe, Qilin, Cangbo, and Gaoqiao in the east; Shangfang, Jiagang, Fengtai, Daande, Xiaoande, Daxunxiang, and Xiaoxunxiang in the south; Jiangdong in the west; and Shangyuan, Foning, and Guanyin in the north. In the late Ming Dynasty, a Zhalan Gate was opened in the west, and a Waijinchuan Gate in the north, making the numbers of gates 18 in total.

5) Water pass, gate valves and culverts

On the junctions which connect the internal and external part of the city water system, there were 8 water passes, gate valves, and culverts for the inflow, and 16 water passes, gate valves, and culverts for drainage [22]. The West Water Pass and East Water Pass sitting near Sanshan Gate and Tongji Gate were the massive tunnels for inflows and outflows of the Qinhuai River.

The East Water Pass, or Tongji Water Pass, was a juncture through which the water of the Interior Qinhuai River flow into the city (Fig.17). It sat on the southern side of Tongji Gate, equipped with 33 arch tunnels, large or small, in three levels, with 11 tunnels on each level. The pass and tunnels were built with rectangular stone slabs. The tunnels on the top level and their covers were built with bricks. The inner brick wall stood 5m in height. 22 tunnels on the upper level were sealed off on end facing the outside of the city. The bottom level tunnels were built to allow river water to flow into the city. Each tunnel was built with three lines of gates: the front and rear gates

图 17　东水关
Fig.17　The East Water Pass

止闸口被堵塞。下合装在条石砌成的方框内，内凹有直径 1.10 m 的阴穴，穴内穿 5 孔，中孔直径 0.28 m，四边四孔直径为 0.21 m；上合呈反"凸"字形与下合相合，即为合闸断流。上合正中有一直径 0.09 m 绳孔的铜钮，以铁索连接地面上的绞关启动。在下合闸的下方，为石质泄水拱洞，向城墙方向延伸约 5 m 处，与铸铁涵管相连；在临近城墙处再与铜管相接[25]。

were designed to fence off the possible penetration of enemy, with the middle gate for regulating water levels and blocking the inflow of water using a winch. Of the 11 inflow tunnels, 9 were equipped with permanent iron fences. Tunnels measured 3m high, and 30m long. Of the 11 tunnels, the one sitting in the middle was a bit wider for boat passing, equipped with a flexible iron fence, rather than a fixed one[24].
The West Water Pass sat at an outlet of the Interior Qinhuai River to the south of Sanshan Gate, built with a structure similar to that of the East Water Pass.
The most representative gate valve was the Yishui Pass that regulated the southern flow of Xuanwu Lake. It was not only a major channel through which Xuanwu Lake discharged, but was also a major water source for the Pearl River in the city. Xuanwu Lake traveled through an underground pipeline to the Pearl River, where it was further diverted to the Yang Wu Moat in the north of the Jinling City built in the South Tang Dynasty. The pipeline was made up of more than 150 pipes, with 107 copper pipes each measuring 104cm long, 1.5cm thick, and 95cm across, and 43 iron pipes with a size of 81cm×2cm×98cm. Pipes were connected with one another using special joints. When passing through the city walls, the water pipes were protected by a double layered brick arch[24].
The city initially had two inflow gate valves that could either be operated independently or together. The water way was deliberately built in a zigzagged manner stretching to the gates in an effort to slow down the speed of water flow. The gate valves had a deep well made of bricks, 7m long and 3.1m wide. At the bottom of the deep well installed two sets of double copper valves in square shape, measuring 1.3m long and 0.25m thick, and weighing 5.5 tons, in a Yin-Yang pattern. The two gate valves were equipped with a rotating cutter. The cutter would rotate along with the movement of water, smashing and preventing the build-up of lake weeds. The lower case sat in a square frame made of stone slabs, and the internal concave was built with a socket 1.1m across. The socket had 5 holes, with the middle one measuring 0.28m across, and the rest 0.21m. When the upper case met with the lower case in reverse concave, the water flow would be cut off. There was a copper button in the middle of the upper case. The copper button had a chain hole measured 0.09m across, allowing an iron chain to run through to be connected to the winch on the ground, starting the rotating cutter. Under the lower valve case, sat a stone water discharge tunnel with a 5m long extension outlet heading for the city walls. The outlet was connected to cast iron pipes, before going further to copper pipes near the city walls[25].

注释

1. 由于南京城市一直在旧有基础上层叠发展，难以作考古勘探，明以前城墙建造情况的实物及考古证据均较缺乏，相关资料主要来自文献记录，包括地方志、正史及笔记，不同学者所作的城市复原也多有差异。
2. 杨国庆，王志高．南京城墙志．南京：凤凰出版社，2008：3
3. 南京城市名称历代都有变动，大抵隋以前："本楚金陵邑，秦改为秣陵，吴改为建业，晋愍帝讳业，改为建康，元帝即位，称建康宫，五代仍之不改。"《建康实录》卷一。
4. "东南利便书曰，孙权虽据石头以扼江险，然其都邑则在建业，历代所谓都城也。东晋及齐梁因之，虽时有改筑，而其经画皆吴之旧。"（宋）马光祖修，周应合纂．宋元方志丛刊：第二册：景定建康志．北京：中华书局，1990：1623
5. （元）张铉纂修．宋元方志丛刊：第六册：至正金陵新志．北京：中华书局，1990：5296
6. "建康府城周二十五里四十四步，上阔二丈五尺，下阔三丈五尺，高二丈五尺，内卧羊城阔四丈一尺。夹淮带江以尽地利。城西隅据石头冈阜之脊，其南接长干山势，又有伏龟楼在城上东南隅，自开宝克复升州，城郭皆因其旧。绍兴初略加修固，乾道五年留守史正志因城坏复加修筑，增立女墙。景定元年大使马光祖以开濠之土培厚城身，创硬楼四所一百七十八间，又于栅寨门创瓮城及硬楼七间，闪门六扇，皆裹以铁。圈门一座，址以石，武台二座，铁水窗二扇。绕城浚濠四千七百六十五丈有奇，以深丈五阔三十尺为率，城之外濠之里皆筑羊马墙，其长如濠之数。"（宋）马光祖修，周应合纂．宋元方志丛刊：第二册：景定建康志．北京：中华书局，1990：1629
7. "八月庚戌朔，拓建康城。初建康旧城西北控大江，东进白下门外，距钟山既阔远，而旧内在城中，因元南台为宫稍庳隘。上乃命刘基等卜地定，作新宫于钟山之阳，在旧城东白下门之外二里许，故增筑新城，东北尽钟山之趾，延亘周回五十余里，规制雄壮，尽具山川之胜焉。"《明实录·太祖实录》卷二十：295
8. "洪武六年六月辛未，诏留守卫都指挥使司修筑京师城周一万七千三十四丈二尺，为步二万一千四百六十八有奇，为里五十有九，内城周二千五百七十一丈九尺，为步五千一百四十三，为里十四。"《明实录·太祖实录》卷八十三：1481
9. 但这一说法仅依据文献记载，尚未得到考古学证据的支持。
10. 潘谷西．中国古代建筑史：第四卷．北京：中国建筑工业出版社，2001：23
11. 蒋赞初认为南京外郭城门及重要地段以砖包砌部分墙体。转引自杨国庆，王志高．南京城墙志．南京：凤凰出版社，2008：230
12. 《明实录·太祖实录》卷四："丙申（1356）三月庚寅，上进兵集庆……福寿闭城拒守……将士以云梯登城……福寿犹督兵巷战，兵溃，坐伏龟楼前指挥……"
13. "明初工夫役中的总甲设置主要指洪武年间修筑南京和凤阳城墙的人夫组织。组织形式为'总甲—甲首—小甲'，存在年代大致为洪武初年至洪武十四年。'总甲—甲首—小甲'组织中，总甲身属均工夫，根据明初均工夫佥选的原则，应由田多者充任。其编制原则可能在明代卫所基层建制基础上有所变通。"王裕明．明代总甲设置考述．中国史研究，

Notes

1. Today's Nanjing City is the result of a continuous building and expansion process. In this context, it is difficult to undertake a meaningful archaeological survey. The evidences and relics showing the regime with which the city walls were built before the Ming Dynasty are scarce. Researchers have to understand the development of the city walls built before the Ming Dynasty mainly through ancient texts, including local gazetteers, historical accounts, and notes. As a result, researchers who consulted different texts would see somewhat a different picture of the old city walls.
2. Yang G Q, Wang Z G. *Nanjing Chengqiang Zhi* (Annals of Nanjing City Wall). Nanjing: Phoenix Press, 2008:3
3. The Nanjing City was named differently in different dynasties, basically following a line as such: Jinling in Benchu, Moling in the Qing Dynasty, Jianye under the Wu State, Jiankang under Emperor Min of Jin, and Jiankang Palace in the Yuan Dynasty. The name of Jiankang Palace lasted for five dynasties. *Jiankang Shilu* (Records of Jiankang City), Vol. 1.
4. "In an ancient book describing the defense facilities in the southeast, it was stated that Sun Quan inhabited in Stone City as the place was a strategic fortification bordering the Yangtze River. However, he built his "city" in Jianye, or "capital" so termed in the following dynasties. The city had kept its basic layout in the following dynasties, though with some occasional changes." Ma G Z, Zhou Y H (Song Dynasty). *Song–Yuan Fangzhi Congkan* (Local annals collection in the Song and Yuan Dynasties): Vol. 2: *Jingding Jiankang Zhi* (The Gazetteer of Jiankang in the Jingding Reign Period). Beijing: Zhonghua Book Company, 1990: 1623
5. Zhang X (Yuan Dynasty). *Song–Yuan Fangzhi Congkan* (Local annals collection in the Song and Yuan Dynasties): Vol. 6: *Zhizheng Jinling Xinzhi* (The New Gazetteer of Jinling City during Zhizheng Reign Period). Beijing: Zhonghua Book Company,1990: 5296
6. " The Jiankang City had a city wall and moat measured more than 13 kilometers long, 25 feet wide for the upper part, and 35 feet wide for the lower part, with a height at 25 feet. An inner fortress 41 feet wide sat inside… taking advantage of the strategic position bordering the river. The city was built against the rocky hills in the west, connecting to the mountains in the south. A Fugui Castle sat in the southeast corner of the walls. The city wall was further repaired and fortified in the following dynasties. In 1169 AD, the city wall was fortified with additional parapet walls. In 1260 AD, authorities adopted a range of practices to further fortify the walls, including thickening the walls, deepening the moat, and building 178 hard houses. Near Shanzhai Gate, ramparts and 7 more hard houses were built with 6 iron armored doors. Folks also built an arch gate, two military procession reviewing platforms, and two iron water windows. The moat surrounding the city reached 47,650 feet long, 50 feet deep and 30 fee wide. Outside the moat built with a parapet wall as long as the moat itself. " Ma G Z, Zhou Y H (Song Dynasty). *Song–Yuan Fangzhi Congkan* (Local annals collection in the Song and Yuan Dynasties): Vol. 2: *Jingding Jiankang Zhi* (The Gazetteer of Jiankang in the Jingding Reign Period). Beijing: Zhonghua Book Company, 1990:1629
7. "In August 552 BC. authorities started to expand the Kang City. The city was first built, taking advantage of the strategic fortification of a large river in the northwest. In the east, stood a vast opening stretching to Mount Zhong. The old palace sat in the town. According to the divination, a new palace shall be built to take in the positive energy from Mount Zhong. As a result, the city had to expand 1 kilometer further from Dongbaixia Gate. The city went further for more than 25 kilometers till Mount Zhong in the northeast. The

2006（1）

14. 郭湖生．中华古都．增订再版．台北：台湾空间出版社，2003：99
15. 郭湖生认为，明南京城墙这一选线也和沿江高地靠近船运可达的河道有关．郭湖生．中华古都．增订再版．台北：台湾空间出版社，2003：99
16. 参见《明史》，但《南都察院志》所记各段城墙雉堞相加的总数与此数不符．
17. 今天所能见到的有关城门形制的详细信息主要来自《南都察院志》以及历史照片．
18. 《南都察院志》："本门冲繁。东至通济门界。西至三山门界。长九百五十三丈五尺。垛口一千二百零二座。城下门券四层。"
19. 《南都察院志》："本门僻静。南至正阳门界。北至太平门界。长七百五十四丈五尺。垛口一千零五座。城下水关一座。"
20. 杨国庆，王志高．南京城墙志．南京：凤凰出版社，2008：155
21. 南京市文化局（市文物局），中国民主同盟南京市委员会，杨新华主编．南京明城墙．南京：南京大学出版社，2006：62
22. 杨国庆，王志高．南京城墙志．南京：凤凰出版社，2008：218
23. 杨国庆，王志高．南京城墙志．南京：凤凰出版社，2008：218-219
24. 郭湖生．中华古都．增订再版．台北：台湾空间出版社，2003：102
25. 杨国庆，王志高．南京城墙志．南京：凤凰出版社，2008：220

massive expansion encompassed the magnificence of the mountains. "*Ming Shilu: Taizu Shilu* (Authentic Records of the Ming Emperors: Emperors Taizu), Vol. 20: 295

8. "In 1373, the city wall underwent another round of expansion for another 7 kilometers. The inner city wall reached 7 kilometers in length." *Ming Shilu:Taizu Shilu* (Authentic Records of the Ming Emperors: Emperor Taizu), Vol. 83, 1481
9. The account is made available only in written records, without the support of archaeological evidences.
10. Pan G X. *Zhongguo Gudai Jianzhushi* (History of Architectures in Ancient China): Vol. 4. Beijing: China Architecture and Building Press, 2001：23
11. Z.C. Jiang believed that the external defensive wall and major part of the Nanjing City Wall were partially built with bricks. Yang G Q, Wang Z G. *Nanjing Chengqiang zhi* (Annals of Nanjing City Wall). Nanjing: Phoenix Press, 2008:230
12. *Ming Shilu: Taizu Shilu* (Authentic Records of the Ming Emperors: Emperor Taizu), Vol.4: "In March 1356, invaders attacked Jiqing. Fushou closed the city gate for defense. Invaders climbed the city wall using ladders. Fushou ordered soldiers to fight against the invaders in the streets, in vain. He sat in the Fugui Castle, commanding the troops…"
13. "In the early Ming Dynasty, the averaged labor force call system was mainly designed to organize the man power needed for building the city walls in Nanjing and Fengyang during the years of Emperor Hongwu. The system, running from 1368 to 1381, had an organizational structure consisting of group leader, subgroup chief, and subgroup. Group leader shall be the one who possessed most land resources, though the designation could be somewhat varied in details." Wang Y M. Community Regime in the Ming Dynasty. Study of Chinese History, 2006 (1)
14. Guo H S. *Zhanghua Gudu* (Chinese Ancient Capitals). second ed. Taibei: Taiwan Space Press, 2003: 99
15. Guo H S. believed that the site selected to build the Nanjing City Wall was associated with the fact that the heights along the river were the accessible water way that can be reached by boats. Guo H S. *Zhanghua Gudu* (Chinese Ancient Capitals). second ed. Taibei: Taiwan Space Press, 2003: 99
16. See *Ming Shi* (History of the Ming Dynasty). However, the number of crenellations on each section of the walls told in *Nan Du Cha Yuan Zhi* (Gazetteer of the South Capital City Supervision) is differed from the number recorded in *Ming shi*.
17. Detailed information people read today about the building of the city walls comes mainly from *Nan Du Cha Yuan Zhi* (Gazetteer of the South Capital City Supervision) and some historical photos.
18. *Nan Du Cha Yuan Zhi* (Gazetteer of the South Capital City Supervision): "The gate was a crowded juncture stretching to the border of Tongji Gate in the east, and to the border of Sanshan Gate in the west, having a length of 9,530 feet. This part of the city wall had 1,202 crenels. The gate was designed with 4 arches."
19. *Nan Du Cha Yuan Zhi* (Gazetteer of the South Capital City Supervision): "The gate was a secluded place, up to the border of Zhengyang Gate in the south, and to the border of Taiping Gate in the north, with a length of 7,545 feet. There were 1,005 crenels on the gate, with a water pass on the ground."
20. Yang G Q, Wang Z G. *Nanjing Chengqiang Zhi* (Annals of Nanjing City Wall). Nanjing: Phoenix Press, 2008:155
21. Nanjing Municipal Culture Bureau, etc,ed. *Nanjing Ming Chengqiang* (Nanjing Ming City Wall). Nanjing: Nanjing University Press, 2006:62
22. Yang G Q, Wang Z G. *Nanjing Chengqiang Zhi* (Annals of Nanjing City Wall). Nanjing: Phoenix Press, 2008:218
23. Yang G Q, Wang Z G. *Nanjing Chengqiang Zhi* (Annals of Nanjing City Wall). Nanjing: Phoenix Press, 2008:218-219
24. Guo H S. *Zhanghua Gudu* (Chinese Ancient Capitals). second ed. Taibei: Taiwan Space Press, 2003: 102
25. Yang G Q, Wang Z G. *Nanjing Chengqiang zhi* (Annals of Nanjing City Wall). Nanjing: Phoenix Press, 2008: 220

参考书目

1. （唐）许嵩撰，张忱石点校．建康实录．北京：中华书局，1986
2. （宋）马光祖修，周应合纂．宋元方志丛刊：第二册：景定建康志．北京：中华书局，1990
3. （元）张铉纂修．宋元方志丛刊：第六册：至正金陵新志．北京：中华书局，1990
4. （明）程嗣功修，王义化纂，程拱宸增修．万历应天府志
5. （清）陈开虞纂修．康熙江宁府志
6. （清）莫祥芝，甘绍盘修，汪士铎，等纂．同治上江两县志．清光绪二年（1876年）重印本
7. （民国）陈乃勋，杜福坤纂．新京备乘．铅印本．南京：北京清秘阁南京分店，1932
8. （民国）叶楚伧，柳诒徵修，王焕镳纂．首都志．铅印本．南京：南京正中书局，1935
9. （宋）张敦颐撰，王进珊校点．六朝事迹类编．南京：南京出版社，1989
10. （明）顾起元撰．客座赘语．北京：中华书局，1987
11. （清）陈文述撰．秣陵集．石印本．上海：扫叶山房，1927
12. （明）陈沂撰．金陵古今图考．南京：南京出版社，2006
13. （明）王俊华纂修．洪武京城图志：北京图书馆古籍珍本丛刊：24．北京：书目文献出版社，1990
14. 杨国庆，王志高．南京城墙志．南京：凤凰出版社，2008
15. 郭湖生．中华古都．增订再版．台北：台湾空间出版社，2003
16. 王克昌，等．明南京城墙砖文图释．扬州：广陵书社，1999

Reference

1. Xu S, Zhang C S (Tang Dynasty). *Jiankang Shilu* (Records of Jiankang City). Beijing: Zhonghua Book Company, 1986
2. Ma G Z, Zhou Y H (Song Dynasty). *Song–Yuan Fangzhi Congkan* (Local annals collection in the Song and Yuan Dynasties): Vol. 2: *Jingding Jiankang Zhi* (The Gazetteer of Jiankang in the Jingding Reign Period). Beijing: Zhonghua Book Company, 1990
3. Zhang X (Yuan Dynasty). *Song–Yuan Fangzhi Congkan* (Local annals collection in the Song and Yuan Dynasties): Vol. 6: *Zhizheng Jinling Xinzhi* (The New Gazetteer of Jinling City during Zhizheng Reign Period). Beijing: Zhonghua Book Company,1990
4. Cheng S G, Wang Y H (Ming Dynasty). Supplemented by Cheng G C. *Wanli Yingtianfu Zhi* (Yingtian Local Annals)
5. Chen K Y (Qing Dynasty). *Kangxi Jiangningfu Zhi* (Annals of Jiangning in the Reign period of Kangxi)
6. Mo X Z, Gan S P, Wang S D, et al (Qing Dynasty). *Tongzhi Shangjiang Liangxian Zhi* (Annals of Two Counties: Tongzhi and Shangjiang), 1876, reprints
7. Chen N X, Du F K (Republic of China). *Xin Jing Bei Cheng* (Historical Accounts of A New Capital City). Nanjing: Beijing Qingmige Printing Shop Nanjing Branch, 1932
8. Ye C C, Liu Y Z, Wang H B(Republic of China). *Shoudu Zhi* (Annals of Republic of China Capital). Nanjing: Nanjing Zhongzheng Book Company, 1935
9. Zhang D Y, Wang J S(Song Dynasty). *Liuchao Shiji Leibian* (Historical Accounts of Six Dynasties). Nanjing: Nanjing Press, 1989
10. Gu Q Y (Ming Dynasty). *Ke Zuo Zhui Yu* (Folks' Historical Accounts of Jinling City). Beijing: Zhonghua Book Company, 1987
11. Chen W S (Qing Dynasty). *Moling Ji* (Moling Collection). Shanghai: Saoyeshan House,1927
12. Chen Y (Ming Dynasty). *Jinling Gujin Tu Kao* (A Review of Jinling Maps). Nanjing: Nanjing Press, 2006
13. Wang J H (Ming Dynasty). *Hongwu Jingcheng Tu Zhi* (Capital City Atlas under Hongwu): Collections of Precious Ancient Books in the Beijing Library: 24. Beijing: Bibliography and Document Publishing House, 1990
14. Yang G Q, Wang Z G. *Nanjing Chengqiang Zhi* (Annals of Nanjing City Wall). Nanjing: Phoenix Press, 2008
15. Guo H S. *Zhonghua Gudu* (Chinese Ancient Capitals). second ed. Taibei: Taiwan Space Press, 2003
16. Wang K C, et al. *Ming Nanjing Chengqiang Zhuanwen Tushi* (Interpretation of Brick Inscriptions in the Nanjing Ming City Wall). Yangzhou: Guangling Publishing House, 1999

第二节　南京明城墙的功能演变
1.2　The Evolution of the Nanjing Ming City Wall's Function

是霏　Shi Fei
杨俊　Yang Jun

1. 古代城墙营建之初的功能（1366—1911年）

1）防卫御敌

"筑城以卫君，造郭以守民"[1]，在中国古代，城墙的营建主要为御敌，因而防御成为城墙在战争时期最原始也最基本的功能。从1366年朱元璋始修应天府城算起，大明帝国用了21年的时间才基本完成南京都城城墙的建设，而这一建设的目的就是为国家都城营建一套完备的防御体系。明代南京四重城垣，尤其京城与外郭临江带山，结合山水地形构筑了坚固的城防系统（图1）。今天我们仍可从明代聚宝门（今中华门）的27个藏兵洞等遗存（图2、图3），清晰地看到古代南京明城墙最基本的功能——防卫御敌。

1 Function at the initial stage (1366-1911)

1) Defense

In ancient China, city walls were mainly built for defense, or specifically: " city walls were built to defend the Lord, and defensive walls were erected to protect people"[1] . In this context, city walls were designed to accomplish a fundamental function of defending a city in wartime. Starting from 1366 when the first emperor of the Ming Dynasty Zhu Yuanzhang (the Hongwu Emperor) decided to build a wall to defend the Yingtianfu City, it took 21 years for the ruler to finish the long wall circling the major contours of the present-day Nanjing. Apparently, the wall was built to defend the capital of the country. In the Ming Dynasty, Nanjing was fenced with four enclosures of walls, a fortified city defense system built to take advantage of the strength of both rivers and mountains in the locality (Fig.1). The 27 soldiers hiding vaults (Fig.2,Fig.3) found in the Ming Jubao Gate complex (or Zhonghua Gate today) were the loud evidences showing the defense function of the walls built in the Ming Dynasty.

图1　山水城防
Fig.1　The city defense system with rivers and mountains

图 2　聚宝门（中华门）城门
Fig.2　Jubao (Zhonghua) Gate

图 3　聚宝门（中华门）藏兵洞
Fig.3　Vaults for hiding soldiers at Jubao (Zhonghua) Gate

2）经济保障

古代中国城墙，有时也是城市和农村的分界，使城市成为一个地区物资交换的中心，推动当地社会经济的发展。明南京当时，"万艘云趋，千禀积粮，贡深浮舫，既富且强"[2]。城墙的围合除了保障城市的经济贸易，南京城墙范围的划定特别特殊，圈地很大，合计 41.07 km²，城内不少土地留作农作，以保障战争年代有足够的经济保障[3]（图4）。

2) Economic security

In ancient China, city walls were sometimes employed to be a line to tell the urban area from the rural one, making the urban area a center where commodities were exchanged, flourishing with economic activities. In the Ming Dynasty, Nanjing was a busy and crowded place with "thousands of ships shuttling back and forth like clouds, and abundant grains stored in the barns. Folks sent their tributes to the Palace in boats, and the country was rich and powerful"[2]. In addition to the function of protecting the city's economic development, the walls also enclosed a large area of land, or 41.07km² to be specific[3]. The city had possessed an impressive amount of arable land, which produced the needed food for wartime (Fig. 4).

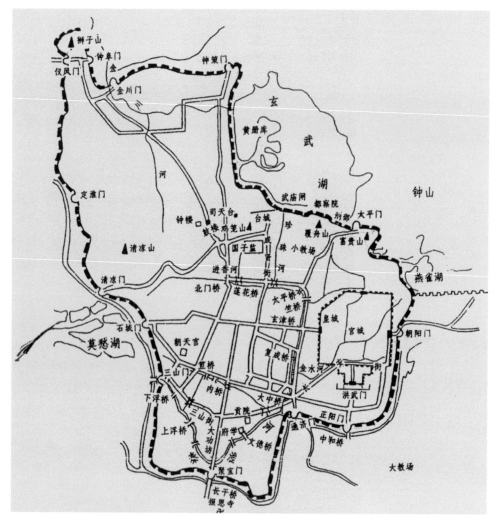

图4 明代南京京城示意图（引自《南京明城墙》第6页）
Fig.4 Capital city in Ming Dynasty (from: *Nanjing Ming Chengqiang*: 6)

3）文化风俗

城墙围起了一方土地，为百姓提供安居乐业的环境，同时也逐渐形成城市生活内容，并成为承载民众美好祝愿和寄托的场所。如南京城正月十六有"爬城头"、"走百病"、"踏太平"的风俗，古代南京的劳动人民在和平时期通过登城墙来表达他们祈盼平安康健的愿望，充分体现了城墙在民众文化生活中的利用，并形成独特的风俗。

3) Culture and custom

The enclosed area created a peaceful environment where people enjoyed their daily life. Meanwhile, it started to build up the contents of an urban life, and became a place where people expressed their good wishes. Some local custom was developed associated with the walls. For example, January 16 (Lunar month) is a day you "climb up the head of the city walls", or "you walk hundred diseases away", or "you walk for peace" on the city walls. In peacetime, folks would like to express their wishes for peace and being healthy by climbing up the walls, suggesting that people made the wall part of their cultural life, though in a unique way.

2. 近现代原始功能退化后的利用（1911—1980年）

1）破墙穿越

近代民国时期，对南京城墙的利用产生了变化。1929年《首都计划》的颁布第一次否定了古城墙的防御功能，"但其界内中部，筑有城垣，近代战具日精，城垣已失防御之作用"[4]，古城墙的价值与新国都的城市发展呈现出矛盾。这种矛盾反映出保存和革新的彷徨，而由于新的经济力量尚未能在社会的变革中取得压倒性的作用，所以《首都计划》并未真正实现。但南京中山大道的开辟，自西而东贯穿南京，一改

2. Utilization after the lost original functions (1911–1980)

1) Traverse through the walls

In the Republican times, the city walls were utilized in a different manner. In 1929, a Capital Plan was published, which declared for the first time that the city walls were no longer a necessity for defense, as "the city walls built in the inner part of the city was no longer a defense barrier in modern wartime"[4]. Apparently, the value of old city

古代城市轴线自北而南的传统格局，昭示出当时快捷为上进行道路设置的速度原则，因此破墙开洞也就成为必然。1927—1936 年，南京城墙内城新开了 8 座城门（图 5），有中山门、中华东门、中华西门、汉中门、新民门、中央门、武定门、雨花门，用以解决城市道路穿越的问题，我们至今仍可以看到这些大部分民国时期建造的城门，依然承担着道路穿越的作用（图 6）。不管这破墙穿越的利用是否存在不足或弊端，我们都应当看到在当时发展条件下产生的这种利用方式实属必然。

walls failed to find its expression in the development of a new capital city. The conflicts made people wander between conservation and innovation. As a matter of fact, the Capital Plan was not materialized as it had been planned, as the emerging economic force was not strong enough to be a dominant force in the reform. However, a new trunk road named Zhongshan Avenue was anyway paved up to run through Nanjing from the west to the east, which changed the traditional north–to–south course a road would take in ancient times. The development suggested that people started to talk about speed when opening a new road. From that perspective, traversing the walls had to be a natural result. During the period of 1927–1936, Nanjing opened 8 new city gates (Fig.5), including Zhongshan, Zhonghua East, Zhonghua West, Hanzhong, Xinmin, Zhongyang, Wuding, and Yuhua, in an effort to improve the traffic in the urban areas. As a passage traversing the walls, most of the aforesaid gates survived the times till today (Fig. 6). Evidently, traverse was a natural choice under the then condition, even though it had been a controversial issue attracted debates for a long time.

图 5　1927—1936 年新开城门（据《南京明城墙》、《古城一瞬间》、《南京民国建筑》整理）
Fig.5　Newly opened gates during the period of 1927–1936 (Sorted accordling to *Nangjing Ming Chengqiang*, *Gucheng Yishunjian, Nanjing Minguo Jianzhu*)

图 6　中山门现状
Fig.6　Today's Zhongshan Gate

汉中门
Hanzhong Gate

中央门
Zhongyang Gate

中华东门
Zhonghua East Gate

中华西门
Zhonghua West Gate

雨花门
Yuhua Gate

武定门路口
Wuding Intersection

中山门
Zhongshan Gate

2) 拆城建房与防空疏散

1949年新中国成立后，古城墙的防御功能，在军事体系和思想体系上均不复存在。1950年代，受经济建设因素的影响，以及城墙保存状况不佳呈多处出现坍塌现象，南京市政府从1954年起开始有计划地拆除城墙。大量的城砖被用于新的房屋建设。而在1950—1970年代冷战时期，城墙又被用作防空隐蔽和疏散。比如1951—1952

2) Dismantling and building bomb shelters

After the founding of the People's Republic of China in 1949, the old city wall was no long a viable choice for defense, either militarily or ideologically. In the 1950s, the old walls started to see collapse or cave-in in numerous places, due to the economic development and poor maintenance of the walls at the time. To deal with the decayed walls, municipal authorities decided to dismantle the city wall in 1954. The bricks recovered from the dismantlement were reused to build new Houses. During the period of 1950s–1970s, some wall sections were turned into bomb shelters for an assumed war. For example, Jiefang Gate was opened during the period of 1951–1952 for evacuating people, and many other bomb shelters were built in the walls in the mid 1960s–1970s (Fig. 7, Fig. 8). In the mid 1970s, the citizens who had been asked to "evacuate" to the rural areas returned to the city, and some of them built their dwellings along the foot of the walls, making the walls a backing of their houses. Objectively speaking, the reutilization of the old bricks dismantled from the walls, or building bomb shelters in the walls, or building houses near the city walls, makes another part of historical information embedded in the

图7　1950年代新开解放门（引自《古城一瞬间》第81页）
Fig.7　Jiefang Gate opened in 1950s (from: *Gucheng Yishunjian*:81)

图8　城墙上防空洞通风口
Fig.8　Bomb shelters' ventilation on the wall

年为疏散方便而开的解放门以及1960—1970年代中期将城墙多处挖空用作防空洞等（图7、图8）。1970年代中期，"下放"（城市居民疏散到农村居住）返城的居民大量在城墙根倚城建房，将城墙利用作为住房的围护结构或者"半壁江山"。可见，无论是拆城墙用旧砖，还是开挖设置防空洞，抑或倚城建房，尽管对古城墙保护产生负面作用，但都是当时人们对城墙加以利用的态度和表现，是历史信息在古城墙上的另一种积累。从特定的角度来说，南京城墙在中国计划经济体制下随着社会的变迁和需求，于城市建设中得到另一种利用。

3. 当代南京明城墙遗产的利用（1980至今）

1）城门

现有城门20座，其中仅用作交通功能的有9座（玄武湖人行隧道、富贵山小门、武定门、伏龟楼北小门、中华东门、中华西门、热电厂南小门、集庆门、华严岗门）；用作公园入口的有8座（玄武门、后半山园小区小门、汉西门、清凉门、解放门、中山门、中华门、神策门），其中后4处设有城墙登城口；另有2座——仪凤门和挹江门上的城楼，作为博物馆起展示作用，以及新民门用作街巷入口的牌坊标志（图9）。

2）城墙

利用城墙组织起城市公园等相关景点，同时，利用相对连续的城墙段进行登城观赏，人们可以行走于城墙之上体验历史的沧桑和变化（图10）。玄武湖公园、前湖、琵琶湖风景区、月牙湖公园、东水关遗址公园、清凉山公园、小桃园、绣球公园、狮子山风景区等，都已成为南京重要而成熟的景区或景点（图11）。

3）护城河

曾经作为城防体系中重要环节的护城河，今天依然是南京城墙系统中极为重要的元素。现状护城河为自然水体与人工水体相结合，保留了较完整的水系（图12）。南京护城河在城市景观建设中的优势非常明显，目前利用护城河展示南京、联系城墙周边诸景点、营建城市优良环境、创造优美景观，作用多元。像玄武湖公园、前湖、琵琶湖风景区、月牙湖公园、东水关遗址公园、小桃园、绣球公园、狮子山风景区都已成为市民和旅客观赏滨水景观的好去处（图13）；清澈的水体与沧桑雄劲的城墙交相辉映、相得益彰；而护城河较好的连续性也得到利用，形成独具特色的水上游览路线，引人入胜，成为南京的独特美景。

4）郭墙

南京外郭现存的郭墙部分现被用作车行道。郭墙用于由土筑而成，俗称"土城头"，而长期的车行压实，从客观上增强了"土城头"的强度，加上两侧植树扎根，削弱了泥土

old walls, showing people's attitude towards the utilization of the old walls, even though the events cast a negative impact on the protection of the old walls. From an angle defined by history, the city wall of Nanjing was utilized in line with the changed needs under a planned economy system.

3. Utilization in the last 30 years (1980–today)

1) City gates

There are currently 20 city gates in Nanjing. 9 of them are the passages through the walls, including Xuanwuhu pedestrian tunnel, Fuguishan Xiaomen, Wuding, Fuguilou Xiaomen North, Zhonghua East, Zhonghua West, Thermal Plant South, Jiqing, and Huayangang. 8 others have been employed to be the gates to the parks, including Xuanwu, Houbanshanyuan, Hanxi, Qingliang, Jiefang, Zhongshan, Zhonghua, and Shence. The remaining four gates have an entrance to the walls. Additionally, the castles on Yifeng Gate and Yijiang Gate have been borrowed to be a museum, and Xinmin Gate became a gateway leading to the streets and lanes (Fig. 9).

2) City walls

Some sections of the city walls were turned into part of the public parks. Meanwhile, some successive walls were made into a scenic spot for climbing and visiting, allowing people to walk on the walls, and to physically feel the change of history and the city (Fig. 10). Many public parks having an old wall section have become popular scenic spots, including Xuanwuhu Park, Qian Lake, Pipa Lake, Yueya Lake, Dongshuiguan Park, Qingliangmen Park, Xiaotaoyuan Park, Xiuqiu yuan Park, and Mount Shizi (Fig. 11).

3) Moats

Moat, a major link in the ancient defense system, remains a major component in today's city walls. The moats currently circling around the city are the combination of natural and man-made water bodies (Fig. 12). Moats are apparently making the city more picturesque. In Nanjing, moats have been borrowed to link the scenic spots in the vicinity of the walls, to beautify the environment, and to create a beautiful landscape. An array of public parks that are associated with the moats, including Xuanwuhu Park, Qian Lake, Pipa Lake, Yueya Lake, Dongshuiguan Park, Xiaotaoyuan Park, Xiuqiu Park, and Mount Shizi, are the water scenes most frequently visited in the city (Fig. 13). The limpid water body mirrors the magnificence of weathered walls, reminding people of their close connection with one another in the past and today. The

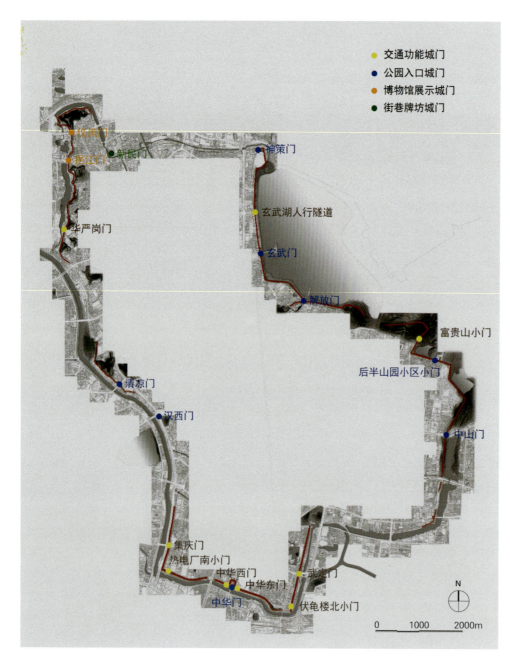

图9 当代城门功能图
Fig.9 Utilization of city gates today

utilization has secured the successive line of moats, making them unique water scenes and routes attracting tourists.

4) Defensive walls

In Nanjing, the defensive walls on the outskirts of the city walls have been partially employed to be roads. The old defensive walls were also called "earth walls" for the materials they were built with. The persistent pressing by vehicles has unintentionally reinforced the "earth walls". Trees have also been planted along the sides of the "earth walls", which objectively eased the erosions of winds and rains (Fig. 14). However, one has to admit that the utilization is passive in nature, and is apparently not a well planned protection.

4.Yesterday's fortification, today's entertainment

In ancient China, most cities were built based on the standards stated in a book named *Kao Gong Ji*. The book laid out strict rules on size, regime, latitude/longitude, and pattern a city should be shaped into. However, the Nanjing City built in the Ming Dynasty was an exception. It was built borrowing the contours of natural terrains, and using the rivers and mountains as a natural defense barrier.

被风雨剥蚀破坏的程度（图14）。但也不得不承认，这样的利用是被动的、不尽如人意的。

4. 南京城墙借古山水之险，营今山水之乐

中国古代都城的建设多遵循《考工记》的礼制要求："匠人营国，方九里，旁三门。国中九经九纬，经涂九轨，左祖右社，面朝后市，市朝一夫。"但明初的南京城，采取自由的形制，因地制宜，利用自然山水作为天然的屏障，城墙的高度随地形而异，

第一章 历史演变　1 – Historical Evolution

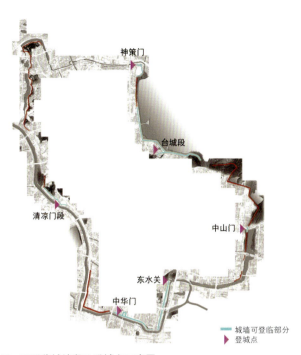

图 10　可登临城墙段及登城点示意图
Fig.10　Sections and sites where people can access the walls

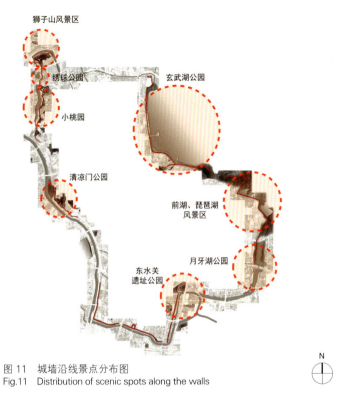

图 11　城墙沿线景点分布图
Fig.11　Distribution of scenic spots along the walls

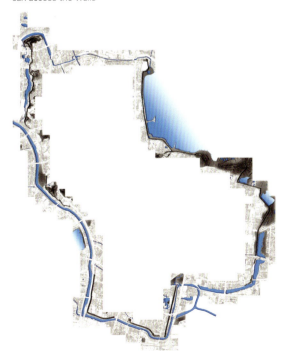

图 12　护城河水系图
Fig.12　Moat water system

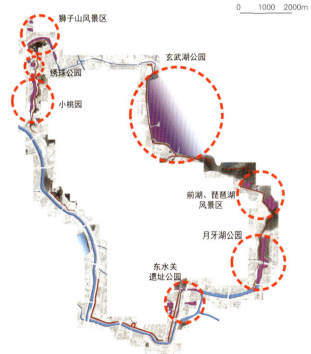

图 13　护城河滨水景点分布图
Fig.13　Distribution of scenic spots along the moats

图 14 郭墙用作道路现状
Fig.14 Defensive walls used as roads

视各段所处的地势，而采取不同的结构和材料。京城南墙利用南唐金陵城墙加筑而成，又因近秦淮河水，故加固和建置时，用石块垒砌；而西墙则充分利用孙吴石头城旧址，加以拓宽和增高；又由西而北利用清凉山、马鞍山、四望山（今八字山）、卢龙山（今狮子山）、鸡笼山（今北极阁）、覆舟山（今小九华山）、龙广山（今富贵山）筑城，因地基基础为山石，所以墙体本身用砖砌筑。其筑城技术的丰富性和因材适用的科学性，充分体现了南京城墙根据战术要求、合理利用地形的筑城指导思想。

外郭郭墙作为明南京城墙的最外一道城垣，是朱元璋战略防御思想中利用自然之势营建城池的再现，"都城既建，环以外郭。西北据山带江，东南则阻山控野。"[5] 外郭西北处未围合，直接延伸至江边，以长江为天然屏障。为扩大南京城纵深防御，将内城外围的一些制高点，包括俯瞰京城城池的钟山，北面的幕府山，南面的雨花台，全部囊括在郭城之内，以形成多个战略性的防御据点。外郭城垣大部分利用自然岗阜，培土修筑，节省资源和人力，"土城头"之名也由此而来。如今的大部分郭垣遗迹已成为郊区公路路基，高出路旁用地，既是界定南京城区范围的地标，也是南京城区外环林荫路。

The height of the walls was tuned to the setting of natural terrains. Different structures and materials were applied to meet local topographies. For example, the wall in the southern part of the city was erected on the older wall built in the South Tang Dynasty. The wall was built with rocks, taking into account the fact that this section of the city sat in the vicinity of the Qinhuai River. Meanwhile, the west section of the city walls was simply raised and widened on the older walls that were built to defend the Stone City in the Wu State Period. The wall stretching from the west to the north was mainly built borrowing the contours of neighboring mountains, including Qingliang, Ma'an, Siwang (today's Bazi), Lulong (today's Shizi), Jilong (today's Beiji Ge), Fuzhou (today's Xiaojiuhua), and Longguang (today's Fugui). The wall body was built with bricks, using mountain rocks as the foundation. Apparently, the walls were built with applicable techniques and materials to accommodate specific topographies in the locality, in line with the principle of building the walls: meet the tactical needs of defense while tailored to the terrains in the locality.

As the outmost enclosure on the outskirts of the city walls, defensive walls were built in line with the strategies laid out by Emperor Zhu for defense, namely the walls and moats should be built taking advantage of natural fortifications. "When building the city, folks encompassed it with an external wall. In the northwest, the external walls were built along the mountains and rivers, while in the southeast, the walls were built to block the mountains and fence off the wildness."[5] The external walls built at the time did not meet in the northwest, but rather simply stretched to the river side, making the Yangtze River a natural barrier. To deepen the defense, major strategic heights on the outskirts of the city were enclosed, including Mount Zhong overlooking the city walls and moats, Mount Mufu in the north, and Mount Yuhuatai in the south. Most part of the external walls were built with earth, taking advantage of the backing of natural hills and mounds, in an attempt to save manpower and resources. Therefore, the external wall was also referred to as the "earth wall". Today, most remains of the external walls have become the foundation of the roads on the outskirts of the city. They were raised higher than the level of adjacent lands, serving as a landmark to tell the border of a district. Meanwhile, they have been built into a belt boulevard with lines of trees on sides on the outskirts of the city.

注释

1. 《初学记》卷二十四，城郭第二："《吴越春秋》曰：鲧筑城以卫君，造郭以守民，此城郭之始也。"
2. 《明史》志，第七十五，艺文四，余光《两京赋》二卷
3. 南京市文化局（市文物局），中国民主同盟南京市委员会，杨新华主编．南京明城墙．南京：南京大学出版社，2006：123
4. （民国）国都设计技术专员办事处．首都计划．南京：南京出版社，2006：70
5. 陈作霖．上元江宁乡土合志：卷一．雕版印行．江楚编译书局，宣统二年

参考书目

1. （明）明实录·太祖实录．台北影印本卷，1962
2. （民国）国都设计技术专员办事处．首都计划．南京：南京出版社，2006
3. 南京市文化局（市文物局），中国民主同盟南京市委员会，杨新华主编．南京明城墙．南京：南京大学出版社，2006：123
4. 杨国庆，王志高．南京城墙志．南京：凤凰出版社，2008
5. 东南大学建筑设计研究院．全国重点文物保护单位南京明城墙保护总体规划，2008

Notes

1. *Chu Xue Ji* (Beginners Mind), Vol. 24, *External walls*, part II: "*Wuyue Chunqiu* says: Folks built the city walls to defend the king, and erected the external walls to guard the city, which makes the beginning of building city walls and external walls."
2. *Ming Shi* (History of the Ming Dynasty), Vol. 75, *Yi Wen Si*, Yu Guang, *Lianjing Fu* (Odes to Two Capital Cities), Vol. 2
3. Nanjing Municipal Culture Bureau, etc, ed. *Nanjing Ming Chengqiang* (Nanjing Ming City Wall). Nanjing: Nanjing University Press, 2006:123
4. Capital City Design Office (Republic of China). *Shoudu Jihua* (Capital Plan). Nanjing: Nanjing Press, 2006: 70
5. Chen Z L. *Shangyuan Jiangning Xiangtu Hezhi* (Local History: Shangyuan Jiangning): Vol. 1. engraved ed. Jiangchu Publishing House, 1910

Reference

1. *Ming Shilu: Taizu Shilu* (Authentic Records of the Ming Emperors: Emperor Taizu) Taibei, photocopy ed, 1962
2. Capital City Design Office (Republic of China). *Shoudu Jihua* (Capital Plan). Nanjing: Nanjing Press, 2006
3. Nanjing Municipal Culture Bureau,etc, ed. *Nanjing Ming Chengqing* (Nanjing Ming City Wall). Nanjing: Nanjing University Press, 2006:123
4. Yang G Q, Wang Z G. *Nanjing Chengqiang Zhi* (Annals of Nanjing City Wall). Nanjing: Phoenix Press, 2008
5. Architectural Design and Research Institute of Southeast University. The Conservation Master Plan for the Nanjing Ming City Wall (National Cultural Heritage), 2008

第三节 罗马城墙、城门及道路的发展和演变
1.3 The History and Evolution of the Rome City Walls, Gates and Roads

绘理奈·平田　Erina Hirata
费德里科·斯卡洛尼　Federico Scaroni

1. 城市的第一个边界（顺城圣区）（公元前 8 世纪）（图 1）

罗马城墙的概念始于一个传说，罗马的第一位国王罗慕路斯（Romulus），用犁拉出了城墙最初的轨迹。此边界的建成可能更多出于宗教目的，而不是防卫目的。它称为顺城圣区（Pomerium），这个词语源于拉丁语的"pone murum"或"post moerium"，由菲利波·科雷利（Filippo Coarelli）翻译过来，意思是城墙之外。在顺城圣区建立后的数个世纪里，沿城墙的内外区域逐渐成为圣地空间。城墙周边竖

1. First borders of the city (Pomerium) VIII century BC (Fig.1)

The concept of the Rome City Walls was born with the legend of the tracks made by the plough of Romulus, the first king of Rome. This border was probably realized for a religious purpose rather than a defensive one. It was called Pomerium from the Latin pone murum (or post moerium) that translated, according to Filippo Coarelli, meant out of the wall. In the centuries after the Pomerium, became an

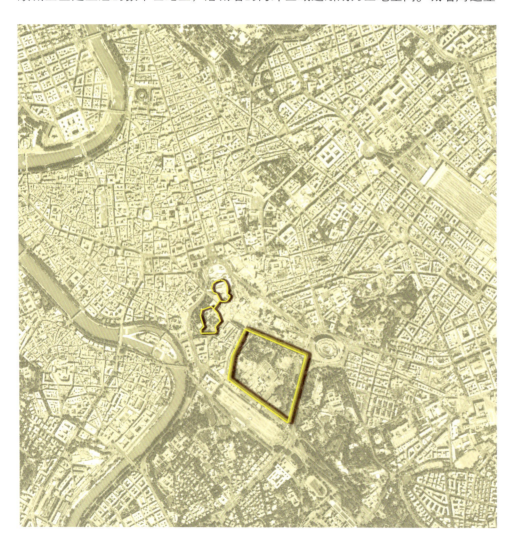

图 1　顺城圣区（引自：《罗马考古手册》）
Fig.1　First borders of the Rome city (Pomerium)
(from: Guida Archeologica di Roma)

立了几块写着"terminali"的石碑,在石碑规定的界限以内,不允许建造房屋、墓地,也不能用作耕地。最终它成为城市的神圣防御屏障,而不是用于军事目的。顺城圣区出现在帕拉蒂诺山(Palatinum)周围,也是罗马第一块居住区。朱庇特神庙(Capitolium)周边的圣地也有城墙包围,在城市中形成了类似于雅典卫城的形态。

2. 塞维安(Servian)城墙(公元前 6 世纪—公元前 1 世纪)(图 2)

这部分城墙形成于君主时期,最早的遗迹可追溯到公元前 6 世纪中叶。城墙名为塞维安(Servian),以纪念其第一位建造者,罗马第六位国王塞尔维乌斯·图利乌斯(Servius Tullius)。第一座城市之墙的建造几乎没有留下任何遗迹。这部分城墙大部分是由古罗马军营外的土堤——一种土方工程组成的,有大约 6 m 高,部分用石砌筑,采用的是一种在罗马地区很普遍的、叫作 cappellaccio 的石头。城墙系统保护着罗马广场帕拉蒂诺山和朱庇特神庙——城中第一块居住区,但是,很有可能延伸到大约 7 km,部分包含了维米那勒山(Viminale)、阿文提诺山(Aventino)、埃

holy ground space inside and outside all the way along the walls. It was forbidden to build houses or cemeteries and make cultivations along its borders, signed with stones called "terminali". Finally was an holy defense to the city rather than a military one. The First Pomerium was the one that surrounded the Palatinum, first inhabited area of Rome. The sacred area of Capitolium, was surrounded by walls as well, becoming a sort of Acropolis for the city.

2. Servian walls VI – I century BC (Fig.2)

Those walls were realized in the monarchic period, and the first traces go back to the half of the VI century BC They are known with the name of "Servian" in reference to their first constructor, the sixth king of Rome Servius Tullius. Of this first town-walls construction does not remain nearly any trace. It was mostly constituted of an agger, or earthwork, approximately 6m high with parts in masonry of cappellaccio, a stone common to find in the Roman area. This wall system surely protected the hills of

图 2 塞维安城墙(引自:《罗马地图集》)
Fig.2 Servian walls
(from: Le piante di Roma. Roma: Pianta LVIII, Tav. 118)

斯奎利诺山（Esquilino）、奥庇乌斯（Oppio）、奎利那雷山（Quirinale）和西里欧（Celio）等地区。

在公元前4世纪，古老的塞维安城墙得到了修复，并且用从奥斯古拉洞穴（Grotta Oscura）地区运来的凝灰石进行了替换。城墙依然部分沿着旧时遗留的轨迹修建，范围延伸至新的居住区。直到今天，我们仍能观赏到一小部分那一时期遗留下来的城墙。在公元前378年，历史学家利维姆（Livium）记录了这些用方砖砌筑技术（Saxo Quadrato）建造的新城墙的诞生时间，据推测，这部分城墙在公元前390年高卢人占领罗马之后，为这座城市提供了更为强大的防御工事。这种建造技术完整地运用于整个城墙上。它采用一排排长为60cm的砖块砌筑而成。城墙总高度大约有10m，有些部分厚度超过4m。城墙全长接近11km，包围了426 hm² 的城市区域，成为当时当之无愧的意大利最大的城市。城墙的建造利用了沿线不同的建造遗址，还雇佣了希腊工人。城墙分别在公元前353年、217年、212年和87年进行过维修，并且在共和时期仍然在修建。

3. 奥勒良城墙（公元4世纪至6世纪）（图3）

公元3世纪，当时严重的经济和政治危机清楚地显露出帝国的日渐衰微，建造一圈新城墙的需求日益明显。

蛮族入侵罗马的可能性增加，迫使奥勒良（Aurelian）皇帝建造更新更强大的防御工事。这项迫在眉睫的工程在217年开工，经过5年的时间建成，当时奥勒良皇帝已过世。城墙由砖砌筑成，约6m高，3.5m厚；每隔30m便建造方形平面的塔楼，上面建有更高的平台用来放置投石器。在最为重要的城门处，采用双扇的尖拱大门，用被称为"travertine"的石灰石加固表面，两边建造两个半圆形的塔楼。而较为次要的城门就采用一扇较为简易的拱门，而不是双扇门，直接嵌入位于两个方形塔楼之间的城墙中部。将现有建筑物嵌入城墙表明了建造城墙时的匆忙：古罗马禁卫军兵营（Castra Praetoria）、马焦雷城门（Porta Maggiore）、卡斯特兰塞圆形剧场（Castrense Amphitheater）、切斯提乌斯金字塔（Cestia Pyramid）和托尔托城墙（Muro Torto），便是匆忙建造城墙的例证。位于台伯河（Tevere）东北部的城墙（地图中加阴影的部分）有可能建成了，但是如今已找不到任何遗迹。

城墙全长大约19km。早在公元4世纪，从马森齐奥（Massenzio）皇帝（306—312年）开始兴建新的防御工事起，新的防御工事就显现出不足：加建的部分可以根据不同的砌筑技术很容易地分辨出来，即由横向的一排排由"tuff"凝灰石制成的砖（opera listata）砌筑而成。在霍诺里乌斯（Honorius）和阿尔卡狄乌斯（Arcadius）

Palatinum (the Square Rome) and Capitolium, first inhabited areas of the city, but probably was extended to partly cover the areas of Viminale, Aventino, Esquilino, Oppio, Quirinale and Celio reaching an approximate length of 7km.
During the IV century BC, older Servian walls were restored and replaced with those composed of tufo stone coming from the area of Grotta Oscura that partly followed the old tracks with extensions on new inhabited areas. Still today we can admire some little parts of these walls. The date of birth of these new walls realized with Saxo Quadrato technology (square brick) is reported by the historian Livium in the year 378 BC and were supposed to provide a greater defense to the city after the Gaulish occupation of the 390. The construction technology is the same for its entire length. It is composed by lines of 60cm length bricks. The total height was approximately of 10m and the thickness exceeded, sometimes, the 4m. The length of the walls was nearly 11km and surrounded an urban area of 426hm², surely the largest city of Italy in that period. The walls were realized with the use of different building site in the same moment and with the use of Greek workers. Restorations to the walls were executed in 353, in 217, in 212 and in 87 BC, still in the Republican period of the city.

3. Aurelian walls   IV – VI century AD (Fig.3)

The necessity of a new circle of walls appeared obvious during the III century AD when the serious economic and political crisis showed clearly the weakness of the empire.
The possibility that the Barbarians could arrive to Rome became possible and forced the emperor Aurelian to provide Rome with a new and more powerful fortification. The fast works begun in 217 and were finished 5 years later, after the death of the emperor. These walls were constituted of bricks and were approximately 6m high and 3.5m thick; the walls were reinforced every 30m with one square plant tower, with higher platform for ballistas. The most important gates were constituted of two twin doors surmounted with arcs, covered in travertine stone and completed with two semicircular towers, while the secondary gates had a simple arc instead of two and were directly inserted in the center of a section of wall, between two of the square towers. The insertion of already existing buildings in the walls is a confirmation of the haste around the building activities: Castra Praetoria, Porta Maggiore, Castrense Amphitheater, Cestia Pyramid and the Muro Torto are some examples of this hurry. The wall section

第一章 历史演变　1 – Historical Evolution

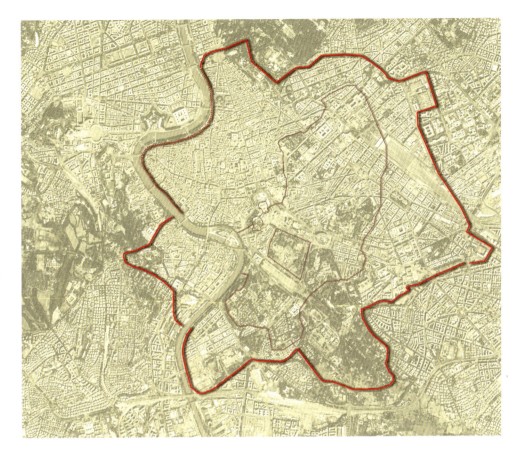

图3　奥勒良城墙，阴影部分待定（引自：《罗马地图集》）
Fig.3 Aurelian walls. The hatched section of the wall is still hypotetic
(from: Le piante di Roma. Roma: Pianta LVIII, Tav. 118)

on the north-east side of Tevere river (hatched in the map) was probably realized, but no traces arrived to nowadays.
The length is almost 19km. Already in the IV century the new fortification appeared insufficient, since the emperor Massenzio (306–312) supplied with new fortifications: it is easy to recognize those addings for the different building technique, constituted of horizontal lines of bricks of tuff stone, called opera listata. Some restorations were made during Honorius and Arcadius reign in the years 401–402, in order to make forehead to eventual attacks from Gothic invaders. This work was inspired by the famous general Stilicone and basically consisted in doubling the height of the wall. The previous patrol way became a covered gallery, in which many slits were opened. Above it, was created a new patrol way, fortified with merlons. Some of the double doors were reduced to a simple one and even the towers were doubled and reinforced: each gate became a sort of real fortress, self-sufficient in necessity occasion. Other restorations were realized during the VI century by Belisario in the period of the Gothic-wars. The walls became a powerful fortress with 383 towers, 7,020 merlons, 5 minor gates, 116 toilette services and 2,066 great windows.

4. Leonian walls (Leo the Fourth)　IX century AD (Fig.4)

Realized during the IX century, starting from 847 AD they are mostly important from an historical point of view.
They were in fact the first walls realized for protection of the Vatican area and the Constantinian church of St. Peter. Inside of these walls there was room for a village, latter "Spina di Borgo", one of the most inhabited areas of the Rome of the High Middle Ages. The walls were demolished in the 400 following years for the increasing of the Rione area. Renovated in XV century, a piece of wall survived connecting the Vatican buildings with Castel Sant'Angelo (former Mausoleum of Adrian). These section of wall is called "Passetto di Borgo". In the period of Leo the Fourth there was even the first general restoration of Aurelian

王朝期间（401—402 年）进行了多次修复，这是为了增加工作面，用以抵挡哥特侵略者的可能的攻击。修复工程从著名的史迪利柯（Stilicone）将军那里得到启发，将城墙的高度升高成为原来的两倍。之前的巡逻道改成了有顶篷的走道，上开许多狭长的箭孔。在其上形成了一个新的带有雉碟墙进行防御的巡逻道。有些双扇门简化成了单门，甚至建造了成倍数量的塔楼，并进行了加固：每个城门都或多或少成为真正的堡垒，在必要的情况下可自给自足。其余的修复工程在 6 世纪由贝利萨里奥（Belisario）在哥特战争期间主持完成。修复后的城墙成为强有力的要塞堡垒，总共有 383 个塔楼、7 020 个城垛、5 个辅门、116 个厕所和 2 066 扇大窗。

4. 利奥（Leonian）城墙（利奥四世，公元 9 世纪）（图4）

城墙于 847 年动工，建成于公元 9 世纪，从历史的角度看大部分城墙都非常重要。
这实际上是第一个为保护梵蒂冈地区和康斯坦丁圣彼得大教堂建造的城墙。城墙包围的区域有足够的空间容纳一个村落，后来成为博尔戈区的骨架（Spina di

图 4 利奥城墙（引自：《罗马地图集》）
Fig.4 Leonian walls
(from: Le piante di Roma. Roma: Pianta CLXXIII, Tav. 446)

Borgo），是罗马在中世纪鼎盛时期时居住人口最多的地区之一。在接下来的400年里，随着行政区（Rione）的发展，城墙被拆除。15世纪翻新后，一小段城墙得以幸存下来，它连接着梵蒂冈的建筑物与圣天使堡（Castel Sant'Angelo）——其前身是哈德良（Adrian）皇帝的陵墓。这段城墙被称作行政区密道（Passetto di Borgo）。在利奥四世期间，从查士丁尼（Justinian）公元6世纪开始，对奥勒良城墙进行了第一次整体修复，并对最重要的城门进行了重建。在教皇尼古拉五世（Pope Niccolo the Fifth）时期（1447—1455年），利奥城墙进行了一次大规模的修复，加固了几段城墙，建造了最少三座新的塔楼。

5. 保罗三世（Paul the Third）城墙（公元16世纪）（图5）

大约在1537年，罗马教皇保罗三世下令小安东尼奥·桑加罗（Antonio da Sangallo the Younger）加固城市的防御工事系统。这个计划注意到了台伯河两岸的城市堡垒的全面翻新。遗憾的是，在基督教舰队阿尔及尔海战战败之后，教皇被迫重

walls since the times of Justinian (VI century), with the reconstruction of the most important gates. Under the Pope Niccolo the Fifth (1447–1455), Leonian walls received a strong restoration with the reinforcement of some sections and the construction of, at least, three new towers.

5. Walls of Paul the Third　XVI century AD
(Fig.5)

Around 1537 the Pope Paul the Third ordered Antonio da Sangallo the Younger to strengthen the defensive system of the city. The plan regarded the complete renovation of urban fortifications from both sides of the river Tevere. Unfortunately, after the defeat of the Christian fleet in the sea battle of Algeri, the Pope was forced to reorganize the great program reducing it to the defense of Borgo area and few other restorations. Sangallo looked after the new fortifications until its death, when he was replaced by Meleghino, then for a single year, by Michelangelo, and finally by Castriotto. The unfinished gate, Santo Spirito and

第一章 历史演变　1 – Historical Evolution

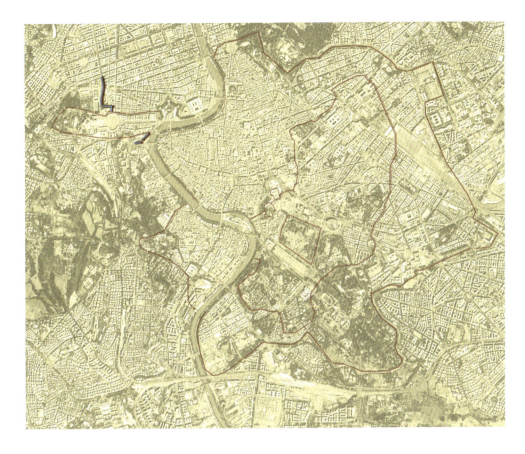

图5　保罗三世城墙（引自：《罗马地图集》）
Fig.5　Walls of Paul the Third
(from: Le piante di Roma. Roma: Pianta CLXXIII, Tav. 446)

新安排这项宏大的修复计划，缩减为仅在防卫博尔戈区（Borgo）和少量其他地区的修复工程。桑加罗负责新堡垒的建造，直至其去世，其后由麦莱基诺（Meleghino）接替他的工作，一年后由米开朗基罗（Michelangelo）接替，最终由卡斯特里奥托（Castriotto）负责。未完工的城门、圣灵（Santo Spirito）和美景宫（Belvedere）堡垒便是这些部分干预的结果。从 1536 年到 1539 年，桑加罗对城墙南部靠近阿尔代阿提那（Ardeatina）路附近区域 300 m 长的奥勒良城墙进行拆除并负责重建项目。这段新的城墙叫作桑加罗堡垒（Sangallo）或阿尔代阿提诺堡垒（Ardeatino）。这座堡垒是专为抵御加农炮的炮弹而设计建造的。在同一时期，安东尼奥·桑加罗紧接着重建了阿文提诺山下一段很长的城墙，并建造了科隆内拉（Colonnella）城堡，今天这座城堡就位于新罗马风的圣安塞尔莫（Sant' Anselmo）教堂的基础之下。

6. 皮乌斯四世（Pius the Fourth）城墙（公元 16 世纪）（图6）

皮乌斯四世也非常关注围绕着梵蒂冈地区的防御工程体系。该计划在米开朗基罗

Belvedere bastions are part of those interventions.
By 1536 and until 1539, in the south area of the walls near Ardeatina road, a big restoration was brought on by Sangallo with the demolishing and reconstruction of 300m of Aurelian walls. This new section, called Sangallo (or Ardeatino) Bastion was designed for resisting to cannon balls. In the same period, Antonio da Sangallo followed the rebuilding of another long line of walls under the Aventino hill, with the realizing of the Colonnella Bastion that nowadays lies under the base of Neo-Romanic church of Sant'Anselmo.

6. Walls of Pius the Fourth　XVI century AD
(Fig.6)

Pius the Fourth also attended to the defense system around the Vatican area. The plan was realized by the Cortonese architect Francesco Laparelli under guidance of Michelangelo. The fortification was based on a linear curtain system, realized almost 300m outside of the Leonian walls that were destroyed

图6 皮乌斯四世城墙（引自：《罗马地图集》）
Fig.6 Walls of Pius the Fourth
(from: Le piante di Roma. Roma: Pianta CLXXIII, Tav. 446)

的指导下，由来自科尔托纳（Cortonese）的建筑师弗朗西斯科·拉帕莱利（Francesco Laparelli）着手实施。防护工事采用线性的护墙体系，在利奥城墙外围大约300 m 的范围内建造，与此同时，利奥城墙被拆除。这一构筑物的上部用被称为"travertine"的石灰石，自圣天使堡开始，一直延续到所谓的米开朗基罗堡。这项工程始于16世纪。大部分城墙还遗存在普拉蒂（Prati）地区周边。在同一时期，米开朗基罗接受委托设计建造新的庇亚门（Porta Pia）（1561—1565年），以取代旧的诺曼塔纳门（Porta Nomentana）和需要重修的弗拉米尼亚门（Porta Flaminia）——后来称为人民门（Porta del Popolo）。这项工程开始由米开朗基罗主持，后来在1561年到1565年间由南尼·第·巴乔·比基奥（Nanni di Baccio Bigio）继续负责。城门的内侧在教皇亚历山大七世（Pope Alexander the VII）时期，由吉安·洛伦佐·贝尼尼（Gian Lorenzo Bernini）于1655年设计建造。

同样在1574年，受教皇格列高利十三世（Pope Gregorius the XIII）的指派，贾科莫·德拉·波尔塔（Giacomo della Porta）或贾科莫·杜克（Giacomo del

in the meantime. This structure, surmounted with a travertine marble cover, started from Castle Sant'Angelo, and arrived to the so called Bastion of Michelangelo. The works started during the XVI century. Most of the walls still exists near the borders of Prati area. In the same period, Michelangelo was commissioned to create the new Porta Pia (1561–1565) in order to replace the old Porta Nomentana and the restoration of Porta Flaminia, then called Porta del Popolo. This work was started by Michelangelo and continued by Nanni di Baccio Bigio between 1561 and 1565. The inner side of the gate was designed and realized by Gian Lorenzo Bernini in 1655, under the Pope Alexander the VII.
Also in 1574, under Pope Gregorius the XIII, Giacomo della Porta or Giacomo del Duca (cfr. Sandro Benedetti, Giacomo Del Duca e l'architettura del Cinquecento. Roma: Officina, 1973) realized the new gate of Porta San Giovanni, in order to replace the old Porta Asinaria on the southeast side of the Aurelian walls.

第一章 历史演变　1 – Historical Evolution

图 7　乌尔班八世城墙（引自：《罗马地图集》）
Fig.7　Walls of Urbanus the Eighth
(from: Le piante di Roma. Roma: Pianta CLXXIII, Tav. 446)

Duca）建造了新的圣乔凡尼门（Porta San Giovanni），用以取代奥勒良城墙东南部的阿西那里亚门（Porta Asinaria）。

7. 乌尔班八世（Urbanus the Eighth）城墙（公元 17 世纪）（图 7）

乌尔班八世的计划，通过建造一座新的堡垒工事，取代奥勒良建造的堡垒，拉开了全城防卫体系加固的序幕。但是这个类似于桑加罗的计划，因建设工程规模过大而未能实现。整个计划只在雅尼库伦山（Gianicolo）地区得到实施，这个地区紧邻台伯河岸区（Trastevere）和梵蒂冈。此段城墙是教皇乌尔班八世巴贝里尼（Barberini）因所谓的卡斯楚之战（War of Castro）而建的，这场战争爆发在巴贝里尼和法尔内塞（Farnese）这两大权力家族之间。由于惧怕奥多阿尔多·法尔内塞（Odoardo Farnese）公爵在托斯卡纳（Tuscany）、摩德纳（Modena）和威尼斯（Venice）等公国的支持下发起反攻，教皇通过建造雅尼库伦城墙（Gianicolensi wall）来加强雅尼库伦山地区的防御能力。无论如何，这场战争并未解决任何现实问题，1644 年在

7. Walls of Urbanus the Eighth   XVII century AD (Fig.7)

The plan of Urbanus the Eighth previewed the strengthening of the defense system of the entire city through the construction of a new fortification that would have replaced Aureliano's one. As for the analogous Sangallo's plan, the excessive bigness of the work stopped its realization. So, the plan was completed only for Gianicolo area, next to Trastevere and Vatican. These walls were realized under the Pope Urbano VIII Barberini in occasion of the so called War of Castro, burst between the two powerful families of Barberini and Farnese. The fear for a counteroffensive by Duke Odoardo Farnese, helped by Tuscany, Modena and Venice, pushed the Pope to realize a defense system on Gianicolo area with the construction of Gianicolensi Walls. Anyway, the war resolved with a nothing fact and was concluded in 1644 in Venice with the mediation of France that reestablished the pre–war situation.
The new fortification, realized with length of 2,500m,

威尼斯经过法国方面的调停双方达成协议，一切又恢复到战前的状况。

新的防御工事建成长度达 2 500 m，沿线有 12 个城堡和 2 个城门：新建的波图恩塞门（Portuense）和修复的圣潘克拉齐奥门（San Pancrazio）——之前的奥里利亚门（Porta Aurelia）。负责的建筑师是卡斯特里（Castelli）和博纳齐尼（Bonazzini），他们受雇于教廷，当时的军事建筑师是朱利奥·布拉蒂（Giulio Buratti）和马尔坎托尼奥·德·罗西（Marcantonio de Rossi）。雅尼库伦城墙得名于其环绕着的雅尼库伦山。城墙建造十分迅速，大约只用了三年时间于 1643 年基本竣工。他们以多种方式取代了奥勒良城墙跨越台伯河的部分，那些用处不大的城墙也分成很多部分被拆除了。这地区三座古老的城门：赛第米亚那门（Settimiana）、奥里利亚门（Aurelia）和波图恩塞门，也被迫进行了许多改造。第一座城门失去了它的战略价值，被新建的城墙包围在内；第二座被重建；第三座则被波尔泰赛（Portese）城门取代了。

雅尼库伦城墙当初为保卫皇廷而建造，恰在两个世纪后的 1849 年，就受到了严峻的考验，被用作相反的目的，不得不说是一种讽刺。这部分城墙被用于保护世俗的罗马共和国抵御教皇支持的法国军队的入侵。

8. 城墙的现状（21 世纪）（图 8）

城墙的现状与意大利统一过程结束后的情形并无太大差别。1870 年后，部分城墙因为这个新首都城市的扩建而被拆除。一些地区，如泰斯塔乔（Testaccio）和萨拉利亚门（Porta Salaria）地区，由于新建道路和广场而被破坏了。中央火车站（Termini）地区或许损失最严重。幸运的是，遗留下来的部分受到公众保护，直到如今依然作为历史遗产保留着。

1）铁路环线（图 9）

铁路环线与平行和邻近的次级道路体系一起，组成了围绕城市的更大的城墙环路。在某种程度上，铁路环线终止了 20 世纪初期到中期的城市扩张。附带着，很多现代堡垒沿着铁路线建造起来，用以守护意大利统一后的这座城市。

火车站点系统和次级城市公路的出口，都是对历史城门的古老系统的理想利用。

2）GRA（环城公路）——城内免费公路（图 10）

罗马城最外围的一道环路，到目前为止是包围了大部分现代城区的公路系统。环路周长 68 km，大约有 50 个出口，大部分出口与罗马的执政官道路是一致的，与城市从建造之初就开始的发展保持着完美的连续性。甚者，铁路环线的出口系统演化成了城门的新系统。不仅如此，GRA 是整个意大利公路系统的中心节点，与古罗马道路曾经的作用类似。

is equipped with twelve bastions and two gates, the Portuense, ex-novo built and the restored one of San Pancrazio (former Porta Aurelia). The architects were Castelli and Bonazzini, employed at the Apostolic Room, Giulio Buratti and Marcantonio de Rossi as military architects. Gianicolensi walls, thus called from the Gianicolo hill that the walls enclosed, were finished fast, and in 1643, barely three years of work, were almost completed. In various way they replaced the trans-tiberino side of Mura Aureliane, and those ones, useless, were demolished in many parts. Also the three ancient gates of this area, Settimiana, Aurelia and Portuense, were forced to many changes. The first one lost its strategic value, enclosed inside of the new walls, the second one was reconstructed and the third one was replaced with Portese gate. Gianicolensi walls, create for the defense of the Pope city, had the fire baptism only two centuries after, in 1849 but for irony, served for the opposite purpose. Those walls were used in defense of the secular Roman Republic against the French army that came in aid of the State of the Church.

8. Walls, the situation today XXI century AD (Fig.8)

The situation of the walls today is not so different from the one after the reunification of Italy process. After 1870, some parts of the walls were demolished to allow the expansion of the new capital city. Areas like the ones of Testaccio or Porta Salaria were destroyed for the creation of new streets and squares. Probably the area of Termini Station suffered the worst losses. Luckily, the remaining areas were subdued to public protection and still today resist with their historical inheritance.

1) The railroad ring (Fig.9)

The railway ring, together with the parallel and nearby system of tangential roads, composes a sort of further circle of walls around the city. It stopped in some way the expansion of the city between the beginning and the half of the XX century. Incidentally many modern fortresses realized in defense of the city after the unification of Italy were built all along the railway route. The same railway station system as well as the exits from the tangential urban highway are an ideal prosecution of the ancient system of the old city gates.

2) The G.R.A. (Grande Raccordo Anulare) – Urban Toll-free Highway (Fig.10)

Last ring (for the time being) of the city of Rome is the highway system that encloses the most part

第一章 历史演变　1 – Historical Evolution

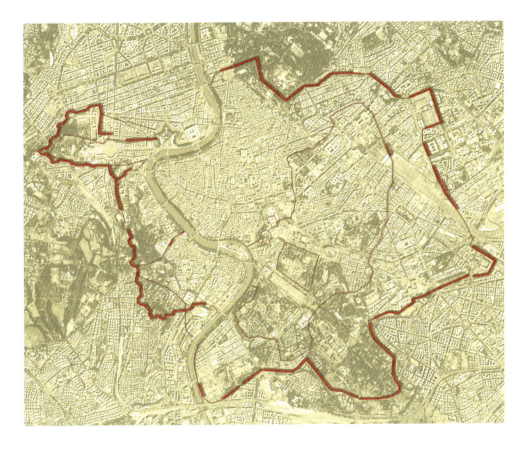

图 8　城墙的现状（引自：《罗马地图集》）
Fig.8　Walls, the situation today, Century. XXI AD
(from: Le piante di Roma. Roma: Pianta CLXXIII, Tav. 446)

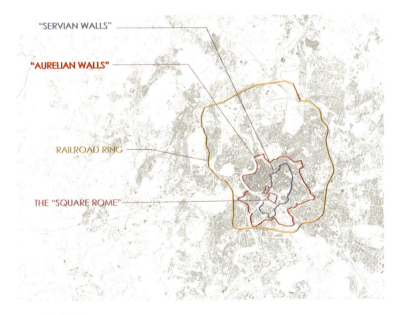

图 9　铁路环线
Fig.9　The railroad ring

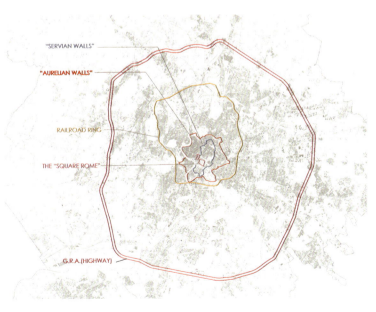

图 10　GRA（环城公路）
Fig.10　The G. R. A. (Grande Raccordo Anulare–Urban To 2011)

39

3）主要城门（图 11）

1 弗拉米尼亚门（Porta Flaminia），现在的人民门（Porta del Popolo），公元3世纪建成，公元16世纪和17世纪间修复。

2 平扎那门（Porta Pinciana），公元5世纪初建成。

3 萨拉利亚门（Porta Salaria）公元3世纪建成，5世纪修复，1921年拆除。

4 庇亚门（Porta Pia）建成于16世纪。1870年，意大利军队从此门进入攻占罗马。

5 诺曼塔纳门（Porta Nomentana）建成于3世纪，5世纪修复，1564年关闭。

6 克劳萨门（Porta Clausa）建于1世纪，5世纪修复，可能在公元8世纪关闭。

7 第布勒蒂纳门（Porta Tiburtina）现在的圣洛伦佐门（Porta San Lorenzo），建成于1世纪至3世纪之间，5世纪修复。

8 普雷内斯蒂纳门（Porta Prenestina）和拉比卡纳门（Porta Labicana），均被马焦雷城门（Porta Maggiore）取代。建于1世纪至3世纪间之间，5世纪修复，在6世纪至11世纪期间关闭，20世纪再次修复。

9 圣乔凡尼门（Porta San Giovanni），建成于1574年。

10 阿西那里亚门（Porta Asinaria），建成于3世纪，5世纪修复，1574年关闭，1956年重新开启。

11 曼特罗尼亚门（Porta Metronia）建成于5世纪，12世纪关闭，20世纪中叶重新开启。

12 拉丁纳门（Porta Latina）建成于3世纪，5世纪修复，11世纪到20世纪期间通常关闭。

13 阿皮亚门（Porta Appia）现在的圣塞瓦斯蒂安门（Porta San Sebastiano），建成于3世纪，5世纪和16世纪修复。

14 奥斯提安塞门（Porta Ostiense），现在的圣保罗门（Porta San Paolo），建成于3世纪，5世纪修复，1920被孤立起来。

15 波图恩塞门（Porta Portuense），现在的波尔泰赛门（Porta Portese），建成于3世纪，5世纪修复，1644年被取代。

16 奥里利亚门（Porta Aurelia），现在的圣潘克拉齐奥门（Porta San Pancrazio），建成于3世纪，5世纪修复，1644年和1854年被取代。

17 赛第米亚那门（Porta Settimiana），建成于3世纪，1498年重建，1798年修复。

18 安吉莉卡门（Porta Angelica），1563年在利奥城墙的基础上建成，1888年被拆除。

of the modern city area. It has a circumference of 68m and approximately 50 exits, many of which in correspondence with the consular Roman roads and in perfect continuity with the development of the city since its origin. Even more than the railway ring, the system of the exits is shaped as a new system of city gates. Moreover, the G.R.A. is the central knot of the Italian highway system as well as the ancient Roman road system once was.

3) Main gates (Fig.11)

1 – Porta Flaminia (now Porta del Popolo), realized in the III century., restored between the XVI and the XVII century.

2 – Porta Pinciana, realized in the early V century.

3 – Porta Salaria, realized in the III century., restored in the V century. and finally demolished in 1921.

4 – Porta Pia, realized in the XVI century. From this gate, the Italian army conquered Rome in 1870.

5 – Porta Nomentana, realized in the III century., restored in the V century. and finally closed in 1564.

6 – Porta Clausa, realized in the I century., restored in the V century. and probably closed in VIII century.

7 – Porta Tiburtina (now Porta San Lorenzo), realized between the I and the III century., restored in the V century.

8 – Porta Prenestina and Porta Labicana, both replaced by Porta Maggiore. Realized between the I and the III century., restored in the V century, closed between the VI and the XI century. Finally restored in the XX century.

9 – Porta San Giovanni, realized in 1574.

10 – Porta Asinaria, realized in the III century., restored in the V century., closed in 1574 and finally reopened in 1956.

11 – Porta Metronia, realized in the V century and closed in the XII century. Reopened in the mid XX century.

12 – Porta Latina, realized in the III century., restored in the V century., mostly closed between the XI and the XX century.

13 – Porta Appia (now Porta San Sebastiano), realized in the III century., restored in the V and in the XVI century.

14 – Porta Ostiense (now Porta San Paolo), realized in the III century, restored in the V century. and isolated in 1920.

第一章 历史演变　1 – Historical Evolution

4）主要道路（图12）

名称中带有"Via"（拉丁语为Viae）的道路，叫作以罗马为起点的城外道路。这些道路通常自发形成，基本上以通往的目的地而命名，例如阿尔代阿提那路（Via Ardeatina），其余的有些以服务功能来命名，例如盐路（Via Salariaor），或是以到达的聚居族群的名字来命名，例如拉丁纳路（Via Latina）。从公元前4世纪初开始，罗马人就开始建造新的道路，通往新征服的地区，主要用于军事目的，并以修建此路的地方行政官的名字来命名，主要是监察官和执政官，弗拉米尼亚路（Via Flaminia）便是例证。有些城外的道路直接通往意大利各省，比如奥里利亚路（Via Aurelia）。而许多其余的道路相互连接，例如凯斯亚路（Cassia），最

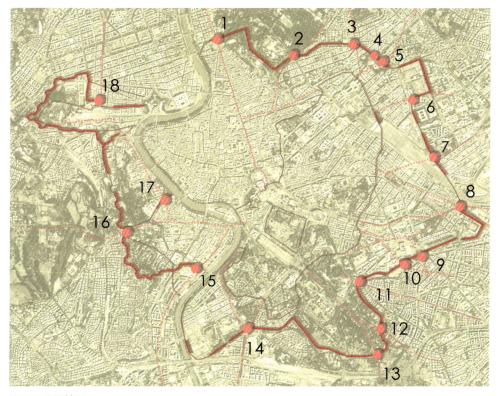

图11　主要城门
Fig.11 Main gates

1　弗拉米尼亚门　Porta Flaminia

2　平扎那门　Porta Pinciana

3　萨拉利亚门　Porta Salaria

4　庇亚门　Porta Pia

15 – Porta Portuense (now Porta Portese), realized in the III century, restored in the V century. and replaced in 1644.
16 – Porta Aurelia (now Porta San Pancrazio), realized in the III century, restored in V century and replaced in 1644 and 1854.
17 – Porta Settimiana, realized in the III century, rebuilt in 1498 and finally restored in 1798.
18 – Porta Angelica, realized on the Leonian walls in 1563 and demolished in 1888.
The gates were realized and restored in different periods and had many different names during the centuries.

4) Main Roads (Fig.12)

With the name of Via (Viae in Latin) were called the extra-city roads starting from Rome; their creation was usually spontaneous and took normally the name of the city to which they lead (Via Ardeatina f.e.), while others had the names of the functions to which they served (Via Salaria or road of the salt) or of the populations that was to catch up (Via Latina). From the beginning of the IV century BC the Romans started the construction of new roads, directed towards the new conquered regions, having mainly military purposes and took the name from the

5 诺曼塔纳门　Porta Nomentana

7 第布勒蒂纳门　Porta Tiburtina

8 马焦雷门　Porta Maggiore

9 圣乔凡尼门　Porta San Giovanni

10 阿西那里亚门　Porta Asinaria

11 曼特罗尼亚门　Porta Metronia

12 拉丁纳门　Porta Latina

13 圣塞瓦斯蒂安门　Porta San Sebastiano

14 圣保罗门　Porta San Paolo

15 波尔泰赛门　Porta Portese

16 圣潘克拉齐奥门　Porta San Pancrazio

17 赛第米亚那门　Porta Settimiana

终汇合到通往达尔马提亚（Dalmatia）的波斯托伊纳路（Via Postumia）上。罗马的道路从来没有被废弃，从中世纪晚期开始，直到今天仍在不断重修。道路名称被沿用至今，大多数名称甚至与早前古罗马时期的名称是相同的。

1 弗拉米尼亚路（Via Flaminia），通往威尼斯附近的里米尼（Rimini），始于人民门。

2 旧萨拉利亚路（Via Salaria Vetus），与安特姆奈（Antemnae）市连接，之后与新萨拉利亚路（Via Salaria nova）相交。始于平扎那门。

新萨拉利亚路通往亚德里亚海边的阿斯科利（Ascoli）市，始于萨拉利亚门（Porta Salaria）。

3 诺曼塔纳路（Via Nomentana），始于诺曼塔纳门，通往诺曼图姆城（Nomentum）——曼塔纳（Mentana）。

4 第布勒蒂纳路（Via Tiburtina），通往蒂沃利（Tivoli），一直延续到阿布鲁佐（Abruzzo）的佩斯卡拉（Pescara）。

5 科拉蒂纳路（Via Collatina），始于城墙外的普雷内斯蒂纳路（Via Prenestina）。

6 普雷内斯蒂纳路（Via Prenestina），通向普勒尼斯特（Praeneste）——帕莱斯特里纳（Palestrina），始于马焦雷门。

7 卡斯利纳路（Via Casilina），通往乔恰里亚（Ciociaria），始于马焦雷门。

8 图斯科拉纳路（Via Tuscolana），通往图斯库卢姆（Tusculum）——弗拉斯卡蒂（Frascati），始于阿西那里亚门。

9 阿纳尼纳路（Via Anagnina），通往阿纳尼城（Anagni），起点在图斯科拉纳路（Via Tuscolana）。

10 拉丁纳路（Via Latina），通往坎帕尼亚（Campania）地区的那不勒斯附近的卡普阿（Capua），始于拉丁纳门。

11 阿皮亚古道（Via Appia Antica），通往位于意大利南端的布林迪西（Brindisi），始于圣塞瓦斯蒂安门。

12 阿尔代阿提那路（Via Ardeatina），通往阿尔蒂阿（Ardea）城，始于阿尔代阿提诺（Ardeatino）小城门。

13 劳伦提那路（Via Laurentina），通往劳兰图姆（Laurentum）城，起点位于奥斯提安塞路（Via Ostiense）。

14 奥斯提安塞路（Via Ostiense），通往罗马最主要的港口奥斯提亚（Ostia），起点为奥斯提安塞门（圣保罗门）。

15 波图恩塞路（Via Portuense），通往罗马另一个港口波尔图斯（Portus）——

magistrates who realized them, mainly censors and consuls, like in the case of Via Flaminia. Some of the external roads linked directly the provinces to Italy like the Via Aurelia, while many others were joined to others like the Cassia, then continuing in the Via Postumia which could reach the Dalmatia. The Roman roads were never been abandoned completely and, starting from the late Middle Ages were restored to nowadays. The name of the roads is the one used today. Most of the names are even the same formerly used in Roman period.

1 – Via Flaminia brought to Rimini, near Venice and started from Porta del Popolo.
2 – Via Salaria Vetus joined the city of Antemnae and then the Via Salaria nova, started from Porta Pinciana.
Via Salaria Nova brought to the city of Ascoli on the Adriatic Sea and started from Porta Salaria.
3 – Via Nomentana started from Porta Nomentana and brought to the city of Nomentum (Mentana).
4 – Via Tiburtina brought to Tivoli and then continued to Pescara in Abruzzo.
5 – Via Collatina started from Via Prenestina outside the walls.
6 – Via Prenestina brought to Praeneste (Palestrina) and started from Porta Maggiore.
7 – Via Casilina brought to Ciociaria and started from Porta Maggiore.
8 – Via Tuscolana brought to Tusculum (Frascati) and started from Porta Asinaria.
9 – Via Anagnina brought to the city of Anagni and had the start on Via Tuscolana.
10 – Via Latina brought to Capua, near Naples in Campania and started from Porta Latina.
11 – Via Appia Antica brought to Brindisi in the estreme south of Italy and started from Porta San Sebastiano.
12 – Via Ardeatina brought to the city of Ardea and had the start from the little gate Ardeatino.
13 – Via Laurentina brought to the city of Laurentum and had the start on Via Ostiense.
14 – Via Ostiense brought to Ostia, the main harbour of Rome and started from Porta Ostiense (San Paolo).
15 – Via Portuense brought to Portus (Fiumicino) another harbour of Rome and started from the actual Porta Portese.
16 – Via Aurelia brought to Arles in the south of France and then in Spain. Started from Porta Aurelia (Porta San Pancrazio).
17 – Via Trionfale brought to the city of Veio and started from the Vatican hill.

菲乌米奇诺（Fiumicino），起点为波尔泰赛门。

16 奥里利亚路（Via Aurelia），通往位于法国南部的阿尔勒（Arles），当时位于西班牙境内。始于奥里利亚门（圣潘克拉齐奥门）。

17 帖奥法莱路（Via Trionfale），通往维伊奥（Veio）城，始于梵蒂冈山。

18 科妮莉亚路（Via Cornelia），始于埃利奥大桥（Elio Bridge），最终到达卡西里（Caere）——切尔韦泰里（Cerveteri）的伊特鲁里亚（Etruscan）城。

19 凯斯亚路（Via Cassia），通往佛罗伦萨，在基督教时期，安吉莉卡门是其起点。

18 – Via Cornelia started from Elio Bridge and arrived to the Etruscan city of Caere (Cerveteri).
19 – Via Cassia brought to Florence and in the christian period Porta Angelica was the starting point.

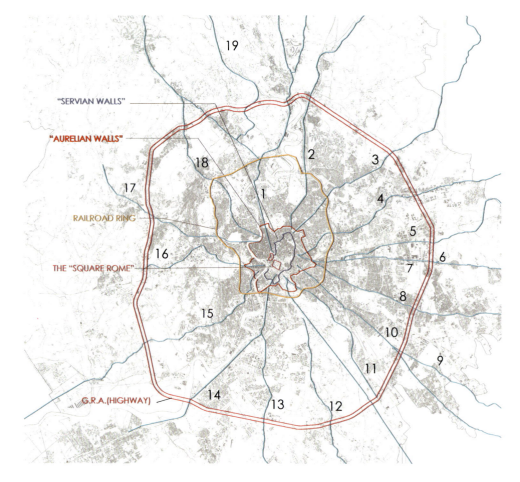

图 12　主要道路
Fig.12　Main roads

第一章　历史演变　1 – Historical Evolution

1　弗拉米尼亚路　Via Flaminia

11　阿皮亚古道　Via Appia Antica

2　旧萨拉利亚路　Via Salaria Vetus

14　奥斯提安塞路　Via Ostiense

参考书目

1. 佛鲁塔兹. 罗马地图集. 罗马：罗马研究学院，1962
2. 贝内代蒂 S. 贾科莫·德尔杜卡与十六世纪的建筑. 罗马：奥菲齐纳出版社，1973
3. 斯塔乔利 R A，利韦拉尼 P G. 奥勒良城墙. 罗马：卡皮托利出版社，1974
4. 卡萨内利 L，德尔菲尼 G，丰蒂 D. 罗马城墙. 罗马：布尔佐尼出版社，1974
5. 奎尔乔利 M. 罗马的城墙和城门. 罗马：牛顿康普顿出版社，1982
6. 夸雷利 F. 罗马考古手册. 米兰：拉泰尔扎出版社，1985
7. 德卡洛 L，夸特里尼 P. 罗马城墙，现实与图像之间. 罗马：牛顿康普顿出版社，1995
8. 德古特利 I. 现代罗马游览手册（1870 年至今）. 罗马：德卢卡艺术出版社，2001
9. 莱斯基乌塔 F E. 思考罗马的一种方法. 罗马：卡帕出版社，2002
10. AA VV. 罗马，TCI 指南. 米兰：TCI，2004
11. 巴尔贝拉 M R，马尼亚尼·恰内蒂 M. 罗马中央火车站考古. 维罗纳：伊莱克塔出版社，2008

Reference

1. Frutaz. Le Piante di Roma. Roma: Istituto di Studi Romani, 1962
2. Benedetti S. Giacomo Del Duca e l'architettura del Cinquecento. Roma: Officina, 1973
3. Staccioli R A, Liverani P G. Le mura Aureliane. Roma: Capitolium, 1974
4. Cassanelli L, Delfini L, Fonti D. Le mura di Roma. Roma: Bulzoni, 1974
5. Quercioli M. Le mura e le porte di Roma. Roma: Newton Compton, 1982
6. Coarelli F. Guida archeologica di Roma. Milano: Laterza, 1985
7. De Carlo L, Quattrini P. Le mura di Roma, tra realtà e immagine. Roma: Newton Compton, 1995
8. De Guttry D. Guida di Roma Moderna dal 1870 a oggi. Roma: De Luca Editori d'Arte, 2001
9. Leschiutta F E. Una maniera di pensare Roma. Roma: Kappa, 2002
10. AA VV. Roma, guida TCI. Milano, TCI, 2004
11. Barbera M R, Cianetti M M. Archeologia a Roma Termini. Verona: Electa, 2008

第二章　城墙、景观与城市肌理

2　City Walls, Lanscape and Urban Fabric

第一节　南京明城墙环境

2.1 The Environment of the Nanjing Ming City Wall

钟行明　Zhong Xingming
薛　垲　Xue Kai

1. 南京城墙与护城河及环境

南京以长江为天险，秦淮河则自方山流至城外，分为内外两支，外秦淮河作为护城河沿西部城墙达于长江，长江与外秦淮河组成的"人"字形水系界定了南京城市外部环境轮廓。明洪武二十六年（1393年）胭脂河开通后，沟通了石臼湖和秦淮河，从而使得漕船可从太湖经胥溪河、固城湖、石臼湖、胭脂河、秦淮河，到达南京[1]。东南部有破岗渎与苏南运河衔接，东部青溪自钟山而下，与城内水系相通。

1）明代南京护城河的构成（图1）

（1）宫城护城河

明宫城始筑于1366年，位于京城东隅，坐北朝南，平面略呈长方形。城周开壕，即明御河，明《金陵古今图考》载"国朝开御河"[2]。御河之水源于应天府城东的护城河及青溪、前湖，青溪"经明故宫之后（当年引为宫城护城河）"[3]。明御河在柏川桥下注入杨吴城壕，其地在该壕的复成桥以南[4]。

（2）皇城护城河

皇城护城河，亦称金水河、御河，位于皇城外侧，环绕皇墙而置。皇城护城河的水源，来自京城东面和东北面的护城河及后湖（今玄武湖），水流通过京城太平门等地段城墙下的涵闸，穿垣入潮沟、青溪等水系，汇入城壕而成[5]。

（3）京城护城河

①东段、北段（朝阳门至神策门）护城河：明初的宫城和皇城是在填燕雀湖的基础上兴建的。当时所填之湖只是其大部，尚存的部分湖面因临近皇城东垣，朝廷为节约建设成本，遂使新建的城垣穿于二者之间，成了护城河之一部分（图2），此段亦免除了修建护城河的额外开支。东部城墙在向北延伸后至龙广山（即今富贵山）又折向西行，其北则为玄武湖，此湖的水域面积在南京诸湖中最大，以其作为天然护城河在当时实乃上策，既节省了建设费用又有了天然的军事屏障，城垣的走向沿玄武湖的南岸与西岸，与湖岸平行（图3），一直向北修筑，"缘湖水以北，至直渎山而西八里"[6]。明初南京的护城河在城东北的太平门段没有开挖山体使之成壕，是因当时认为此处的龙广山（今富贵山）为龙脉中的"龙脖子"所在，开挖山体将破坏南京城的风水。

1. City walls' moats and associated environment

Nanjing, when initially built, was designed to take advantage of the fortification role played by the Yangtze River in the northern part of the city. The QinhuaiRiver stretched to the outskirts of the city via Mount Fang, split into two tributaries. The external part of the river became the moat guarding the west part of the city walls, up to the Yangtze River. The Yangtze River and the external part of Qinhuai River formed up a " 人 "–shaped water system, which defined the outline of the city's external environment. In 1393, the Yanzhi River was opened, channeling through both Shijiu Lake and the Qinhuai River, allowing the food supply boats to reach Nanjing from Taihu Lake, via the Xuxi River, Gucheng Lake, Shijiu Lake, Yanzhi River, and Qinhuai River [1]. In the southeast, the Pogang waterway was connected to the Sunan Canal, and in the east the Qing Stream flew down from Mount Zhong. All the waterways were connected to the city's internal water system.

1) Composition of the moats (Fig.1)

(1) The moat of Palace

The Ming imperial palace was built in 1366, in the east corner of the city, sitting north and facing south, in a quasi rectangular shape. The palace was guarded by an artificial river named the Imperial River. A map atlas published in the Ming Dynasty showed that the Imperial River was dug out when the palace was built [2]. The river borrowed the water mainly from the moat defending the east section of the Yingtian City, and from the Qing Stream and Qian Lake as well. The Qing Stream passed by the rear part of the palace (the river was the palace's moat at the time) [3]. The Imperial River flow into the moat of the Yangwu City under the Bochuan Bridge, to the south of the Fucheng Bridge associated with the moat [4].

(2) The moat of Imperial city

The moat guarding the imperial city was also named the Golden Water River, or the Imperial River, circling around the outskirts of the imperial city. The moat got its water mainly from the moats in the east and northeast part of the city and a Hou Lake (today's Xuanwu Lake). The water was diverted into the moat through a water tunnel under Taiping Gate, via ditches and streams [5].

(3) The moat of capital city

第二章 城墙、景观与城市肌理　2 – City Walls, Landscape and Urban Fabric

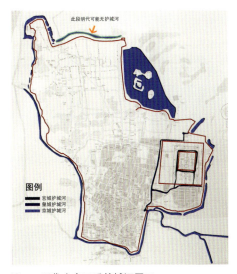

图 1　明代南京三重护城河图示
Fig.1　Three lines of moats built in the Ming Dynasty

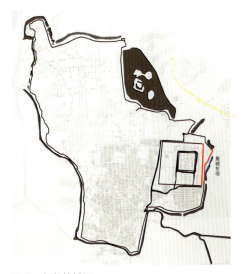

图 2　东段护城河
Fig.2　East section of the moat

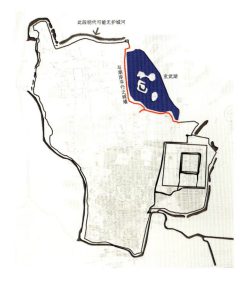

图 3　玄武湖段护城河与城墙
Fig.3　Xuanwu Lake section of the moat and city walls

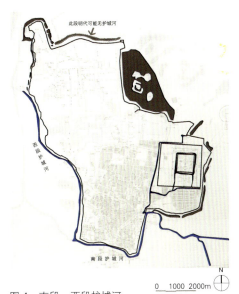

图 4　南段、西段护城河
Fig.4　South and west section of the moat

② 东南段（朝阳门至通济门）护城河：城东南角护城河则引钟山之水，《肇域志》载："城濠绕城，阔二十五丈，周四十五里。其水引钟山南源，在朝阳门外，折南入正阳门，外达外濠。"[7]

《道光上元县志·山川》载："明城濠，自通济门外，东经正阳门，北折，绕朝阳门，上有平桥、夔角桥。"[8]

③ 南段、西段（通济门至仪凤门）护城河：南段和西段利用外秦淮河作为护城河，

① East and north: In the early Ming Dynasty, both the palace and imperial city were built by filling up a lake named Yanque. However, the lake was not filled up to the full. To save the costs of construction, the unfilled part of the lake was taken as part of the moat (Fig.2), allowing the city walls to run in between, thanks to its close range to the east part of the city walls. The east part of the walls stretched north, before turning west at Mount Longguang (today's Mount Fugui). On the northern side of the walls stood Xuanwu Lake, the largest lake in the city. Apparently, letting the lake be the moat was the most desirable solution at the time, saving the costs of construction while keeping a natural fortification. The walls went in parallel to Xuanwu Lake in the southern and west banks (Fig.3), stretching out north, or "stretching out along the lake to the north till Mount Zhidu and turning west by four kilometers"[6]. In the early Ming Dynasty, the moat ceased to go further at Taiping Gate in the northeast part of the city, as it was believed that the site (today's Mount Fugui) was the neck of the dragon, and digging out a moat here would mean to cut off the neck of the dragon, which would bring bad luck to the city.

② Southeast (from Chaoyang Gate to Tongji Gate):The moat defending the southeast part of the city borrowed the water diverted from Mount Zhong. According to *Zhao Yu Zhi* (a local annals), " The moat, 25 zhang wide and 22.5 kilometers long, circles the city. It gets its water from Mount Zhong in the south. The water flows into the moat via Chaoyang Gate, before stretching to Zhengyang Gate in the south ."[7]

Daoguang Shangyuan Xian Zhi: Shanchuan (the Annals of Shangyuan County in the Daoguang times) described the moat as follows: " The moat, built in the Ming Dynasty, started its course on the outskirts of Tongji Gate, traveling through Zhengyang Gate in the east, before turning north and circling Chaoyang Gate, through the Ping Bridge and the Kuijiao Bridge."[8]

③ South and west (from Tongji Gate to Yifeng Gate): The south–west section of the moat was the Qinhuai River, the longest successive water body among the moats(Fig.4).

Chongkan Jiangningfu Zhi (The Annals of Jiangning fu) described the moat at the time as: " The river on the outskirts of the city walls was made a moat starting from Zhengyang Gate in the west, circling the city, before turning west and north, and stretching into the river via Yifeng Gate. The city wall had no moat in the northeast, as it was built against the mountains and hills. There was the Hou Lake in the northern part of the city. However, it could not serve as a moat for its zigzagged course ."[9]

④ Northwest (from Shence Gate to Yifeng Gate via

这也是护城河中最长的一段连续水体（图4）。

《重刊江宁府志》对当时的护城河作了这样的描述："其城外之河，自正阳门西因杨吴所凿淮流，绕城为池，西流北转抱城至仪凤门外流入江；城之东北倚山冈无城河，而正北则后湖，当其曲限矣。"[9]

④西北段（神策门经狮子山至仪凤门）护城河：自玄武湖至卢龙山（今狮子山）段护城河的开凿情况，文献资料记载较少，笔者结合诸文献对此段护城河情况作一推测，得出的结论是此段可能无护城河。

在《洪武京城图志》之"京城山川图"、《金陵古今图考》之"明都城图"与"境内诸水图"[10]中标有其他各段护城河，独不见此段护城河。蒋绣岑所著《金陵诸山形势考》中的一段话，也许可以在一定程度上说明这一问题："后湖之水通秦淮，出西关，归大江，为钟山随龙养荫真正胎水，断不可旁泻"，"神策门外大龙正脉入城之处，当六朝时曾经凿断，引后湖通江，故百余年间屡遭杀戮，至明初建都，始得其旧，最忌开凿。"[11]

从这些记述中可以得知，明初为了保护风水，而没有在神策门处开渠泄湖。

清道光年间，城中积水为患，有人议开山凿脉，引湖入江。"并有河身深阔俱及五丈之说，拟自神策门外湖边起，循城西行十余里，以达下关。"[12]所描述的这一路线应是护城河的位置。结果因下至黎民百姓，上至同乡京官的反对，最终没有开挖。

另，《道光上元县志》则明确指出只有从朝阳门起，经正阳门、通济门、聚宝门等至仪凤门有护城河。"城东北山势延接，旧无濠。惟朝阳、正阳、通济、聚宝、三山、石城、清凉、定淮、仪凤九门外有濠。濠本为二，一自朝阳门外平桥东走夔角桥，抵通济门外，明初所凿也。一自东水关外通济桥分淮水，南走聚宝桥至西水关外，复会秦淮水，经三山桥绕石城、清凉、定淮、仪凤门入江，杨吴之遗迹也。今平桥一濠复断为二，分秦淮者，仍通舟楫焉。"[13]

这恰好说明明南京城的西北防御体系由于山脉连亘勿需开河筑壕的原由，也表达出南京城墙体系中的护城河因地制宜的建造特点。明代永乐中关闭金川门，以及后来关闭钟阜、定淮二门，则是迁都后北向交通减少而防御加深使然，从另一侧面加强了对北边的防御。

2) 明南京护城河的特色

(1) 利用自然水体与人工开凿水体相结合

明南京护城河是充分利用原有河道、湖泊等自然水体或以前的城河，稍加挖掘，串联而成的（表1）。这在客观上突破了传统的因城开凿护城河的惯例，甚至南京城墙依赖环境走向进行围城。同时，这一做法也符合当时的客观实际。时值明朝初建，

Mount Shizi): Little was said in ancient literatures about building a moat running from Xuanwu Lake to Mount Lulong (today's Mount Shizi). Having consulted relevant literatures, the author believed that there was possibly no moat built for the section.

According to the mountain and river maps shown in *Hongwu Jingcheng Tu Zhi* (Atlas of Imperial City under Emperor Hongwu), and the maps of capital city and associated water systems in *Jinling Gujin Tu Kao* (Atlas of the Jinling City: today and past)[10], all the sections but the northwest were built with moats. In his *Jinling Zhushan Xingshi Kao* (Mountains in the Jinling City), Jiang Xiucen depicted:" Hou Lake was connected to the Qinhuai River, and destined to the Yangtze River, via the West Pass. It was the major water source nourishing Mount Zhong, and could not be diverted. " He added that: " On the outskirts of Shence Gate sat a major water system that coursed its way into the city. It was cut off to feed Hou Lake in the Six Dynasties, so there were wars and fights repeatedly in the past 100 years. In the early Ming Dynasty when the capital was founded, it was reconnected, forbidden to be disrupted."[11]

One can see from the above description that there were no channels being dug up at shence Gate in order to protect Fengshui in the early Ming Dynasty.

During the times of Emperor Daoguang in the Qing Dynasty, the city proper frequently saw inundations. It was suggested that canals be built to divert the excessive water into the Yangtze Rive. For example, " people proposed to build a ditch 5 zhang wide and deep, starting from the lake on the outskirts of Shence Gate, stretching out 5 kilometers westwards, before reaching Xiaguan"[12]. The route proposed could be the one where the moat was to build. Unfortunately, the proposal was not materialized as it met with oppositions from both the authorities and people in the streets.

Additionally, according to the Annals of Shangyuan County in the Daoguang times, a moat was built from Chaoyang Gate to Yifeng Gate, travelling through Zhengyang Gate, Tongji Gate, and Jubao Gate: " The northeast part of the city was built along the mountains, without moats. Only 9 gates, including Chaoyang, Zhengyang, Tongji, Jubao, Sanshan, Shicheng, Qingliang, Dinghuai, and Yifeng, were built with moats. The moats were initially built in two major sections: one, built in the early Ming Dynasty, started from the Ping Bridge on the outskirts of Chaoyang Gate and ended up at Tongji Gate, via the Kuijiao Bridge; and the other, built under Yangwu Dynasty, started from Tongji Gate on the outskirts of the East Water Pass, and reached the West Water Pass via the Jubao Bridge in the south, meeting with the Qinhuai River,

图 5　利用玄武湖为城壕
Fig.5　Xuanwu Lake used as the moat

图 6　护城河与秦淮河相通
Fig.6　The moat meeting with Qinhuai River

where it passed through the Sanshan Bridge, snaking along Shicheng, Qingliang, Dinghai, and Yifeng, before flowing into the river. Today, the moat near the Ping Bridge was split again into two. The tributary that went with the Qinhuai River allows the passing of boats "[13]. The aforesaid accounts depicted the fact that the northwest part of the city was fenced by the mountains, rather than by the moats on the one hand, and that the moats in the city were built to meet with local terrains on the other. In the times of Emperor Yongle in the Ming Dynasty, Jinchuan Gate was closed. After that, two more gates, including Zhongfu and Dinghuai, were also closed, suggesting a deepened defense system was desired in the north to address the reduced traffic, after the capital was relocated to Beijing.

2） Highlights of the moats built in the Ming Dynasty
(1) Combo of natural and man–made water systems
In the Ming Dynasty, the moats in Nanjing were built by borrowing a string of natural water bodies in the city, including rivers and lakes, and the moats built before. The water systems were deepened, consolidated, and connected to one another to make the moats defend the city (Table 1). The practice was, unintentionally, a breakthrough to the traditional way of building a moat, namely digging out a moat along the city walls. In Nanjing, the walls built to encompass the city had also borrowed the contours of natural environment. Meanwhile, the practice met with the objective reality at the time. In the early Ming Dynasty, the society was not that stable yet, and state treasury was in a poor shape. In this context, making natural water systems part of the moats saved both labor and money (Fig.5, Fig.6).

社会尚未安定，国家财政紧张，利用自然水体并结合部分开凿，可以最大限度地减少工程量，经济合理（图5、图6）。

表 1 明代南京护城河各段形成情况表

护城河名称		形成类型	利用的水体
宫城护城河	东侧、北侧	利用以前河道	古青溪
	西侧	新开挖	
	南侧	新开挖	
皇城护城河		新开挖	
京城护城河	东段、北段（朝阳门至神策门）护城河	利用原有湖泊	燕雀湖、前湖、琵琶湖、玄武湖
	东南段护城河	新开挖	
	南段、西段护城河	利用自然河流	秦淮河

Table 1 Compositions of moats in the Ming Dynasty

Name of moat section		Composition	Water source
Palace moat	East & north	Previous waterway	Guqing Stream
	West	Newly dug	
	South	Newly dug	
Imperial city moat		Newly dug	
Capital city moat	East and north (from Chaoyang Gate to Shence Gate)	Lakes	Lakes of Yanque, Qianhu, Pipa, and Xuanwu
	Southeast	Newly dug	
	South and west	Natural rivers	Qinhuai River

（2）顺应地形，宽窄不一

南京护城河顺应自然地形，因地制宜，充分利用自然水体，表现在另一方面即护城河呈现出宽窄不一的特色。最宽处为东北部的玄武湖，宽约 2 600 m；在东部，利用已有的湖泊形成不连续的护城河，琵琶湖宽约 200 m，前湖宽约 160 m；东南部护城河宽约 80 m；西部护城河宽约 100 m；西北部护城河最窄，宽约 30 m。

(2) Irregular in width and borrowing the contours of natural terrains

In ancient times, the moats in Nanjing were built to respond to the natural terrains, taking full advantage of natural water bodies. As a result, the moats were uneven in width, with the widest part being at Xuanwu Lake (2,600m), in the northeast part of the city. The moats in the east part of the city were

（3）通过涵闸、水涵洞、水关等将护城河与城内水系连通

护城河还通过多处涵闸（洞）、水关与城内水系沟通，现存明代涵闸（洞）、水关有4处，分别是武庙闸、琵琶湖涵闸、东水关、西水关；考古发现3处，分别是草场门涵闸、太平门涵闸、铜管闸（图7）。城内水系与护城河相互贯通，共同构成了南京城市水网体系，使其在明代呈现出典型的江南城市特点和独特景观。同时，通过对文字资料的梳理并与古地图相对照，发现南京城内的水系最终都汇入秦淮河，即所谓"金陵之水以淮为经"[14]，沿石城西北流，达于江，与长江水系连通。

technically a string of lakes, with Pipa Lake being 200m wide, and Qianhu Lake 160m. The moats measured 80m wide in the southeast, and 100m in the west. The narrowest part of the moats was 30m wide in the northwest section.

(3) Linked by culvert gates, water tunnels, and water passes

In Nanjing, the moats were also connected to other water systems through culvert gates, water tunnels, and water passes. For example, four culvert gates or water tunnels built in the Ming Dynasty have survived the times, including Wumiao Culvert Gate, Pipahu Culvert Gate, East Water Pass, and West Water Pass. Archaeological excavations led to the discovery of 3 similar mechanisms, including Caochangmen Culvert Gate, Taipingmen Culvert Gate, and Tongguan Culvert Gate (Fig. 7). The internal water systems of the city, intertwined with the moats, formed up an urban water network enjoying the unique feature and landscape a typical southern city would had in the Ming Dynasty. Meanwhile, ancient literatures and old maps revealed that all the water systems in Nanjing found their destinations at the Qinhuai River, or "all the waters of the Jinling City found their way into the Qinhuai River"[14], which continued the course northwest via the Stone City, reaching the Yangtze River, before joining the water system of the Yangtze River.

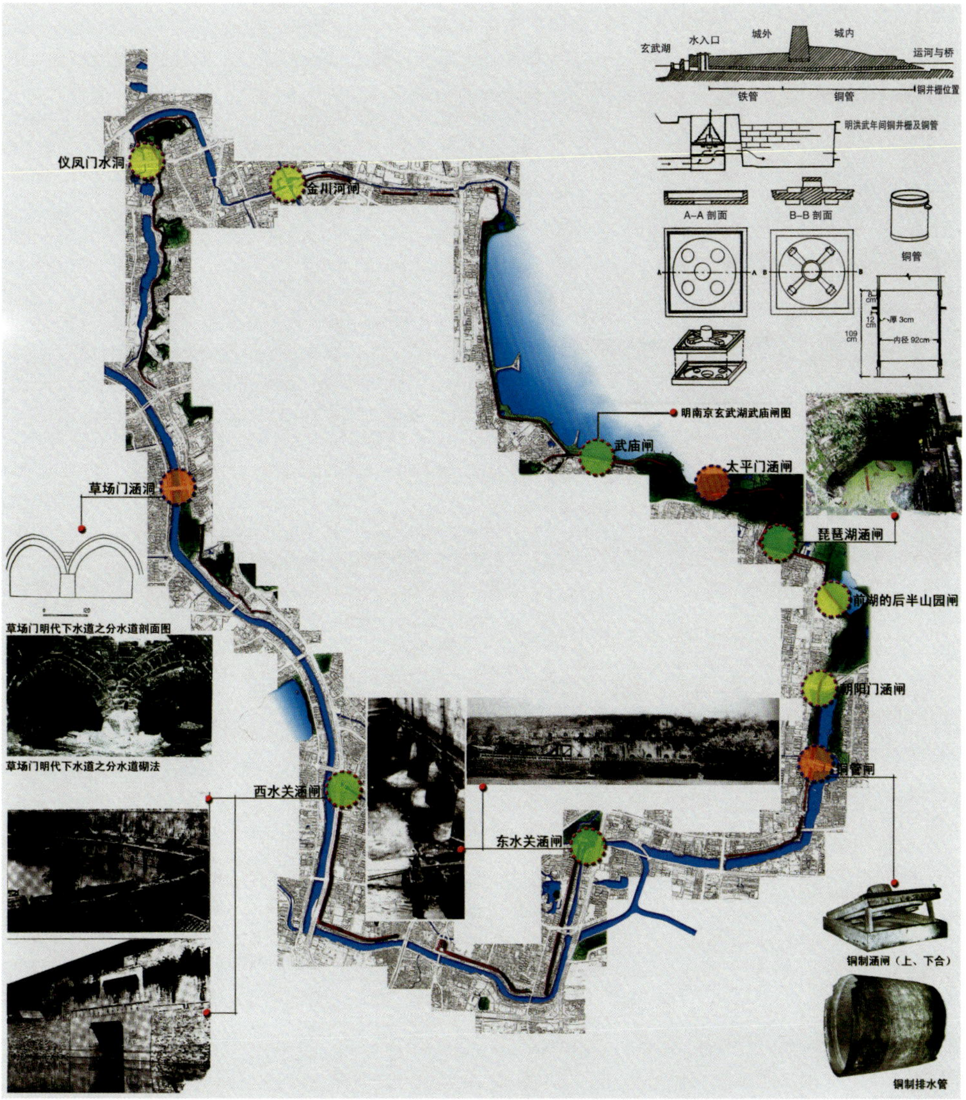

图例

● 现存明代涵闸
● 未发掘的明代涵闸
● 已发现的明代涵闸遗址

图7 明代护城河涵闸（洞）、水关图
Fig.7 Culvert gates, water tunnels, and water passes of moats in the Ming Dynasty

3）南京护城河上的桥梁

（1）明代南京护城河上的桥梁（图8）

历史上南京除北边，从城外至城内必经过护城河，而过护城河必有桥。因此明南京城主要城门外护城河上都有桥，而城内主要道路又与城门相连。因而护城河上的桥梁成了连接城内城外以及沟通陆路的关键所在。

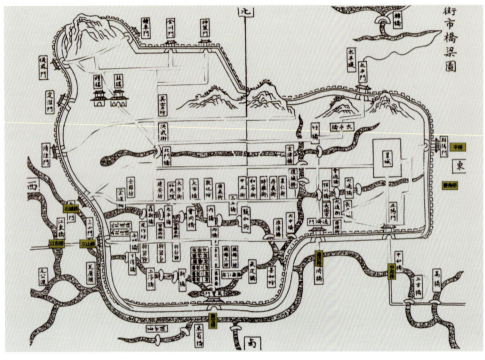

图8 明代护城河上的桥梁（引自《洪武京城图志》）
Fig.8 Bridges across the moats in the Ming Dynasty (from: *Hongwu Jingcheng Tu Zhi*)

明初护城河上的桥梁有："跨今城濠者，曰正阳、曰通济、曰聚宝、曰三山、曰石城"[15]，正阳桥，一称夔角桥，再加上平桥，一共七座桥梁。这些桥梁因主要城门而设，成为城内与城外交通的重要通道，也通过桥梁与城外的码头、驿站、市场等相连。

明时江东门外有江东市，是米麦商聚集之地，同时设有江东马驿，江东市附近上新河上设有"皇木厂"，从城内至这些江东市和上新河必须由三山门出，故于洪武二十九年（1396年），在三山门外造石桥，即三山桥。再譬如，明时去钟山祭祀必出正阳门，过正阳桥；而至来宾街市，则需出聚宝门，过聚宝桥。

（2）目前护城河上的桥梁

随着南京城市规模的扩大和发展，护城河的压力增大。为了沟通老城和外围，在护城河上增建了大量桥梁，整个护城河上目前建有29座大大小小的桥梁（表2），且有增加的趋势（图9）。

3) Bridges across the moats

(1) Bridges built in the Ming Dynasty (Fig.8)

In ancient times, one had to cross the moat when entering the town of Nanjing, except the northern part. That means there had to be a bridge above the moat for crossing. As a result, major moats built in the Ming Dynasty were associated with a bridge, leading to the city gates connecting to trunk roads. The bridges across the moats was a key land link between the internal and external part of the city.

In the early Ming Dynasty, an array of bridges were built above the moats facilitating people crossing, including Zhengyang, Tongji, Jubao, Sanshan, and Shicheng[15]. Plus the Kuijiao Bridge (the old name of Zhengyang Bridge) and the Shangping Bridge, the bridges built across the moats reached 7 in number. The bridges, designed to be a passage to the city gates, were associated with the trunk roads linking the internal and external part of the city, and leading to the ports, post-houses, and marketplaces on the outskirts of the walls.

In the Ming Dynasty, on the outskirts of Jiangdong Gate sat a town named Jiangdong, where people traded rice and wheat. In the vicinity of Jiangdong, there was a place called Shangxinhe popular for a bazaar fair opened on a regular basis, a posthouse, and a wood plant. One had to cross Sanshan Gate when visiting Jiangdong and Shangxinhe. In 1396, a stone bridge was built on the outskirts of Sanshan Gate to facilitate the crossing. Another example is one had to cross Zhengyang Gate when doing worships at Mount Zhong in the Ming Dynasty So, there you go with a Zhengyang Bridge. Additionally, one had to cross the Jubao Bridge on the outskirts of Jubao Gate, when visiting the street fair in Laibin.

(2) Moat bridges in today's Nanjing

The expansion and development of Nanjing has turned the moats into pressure transmitter. To improve the traffic from the old town to the outskirts, a string of new bridges have been built across the moats, reaching 29 in number (Table 2), and the number could go up in the future (Fig. 9).

表2　护城河桥梁现状表

类型	桥名	数量（座）	比例
现存明代桥梁	九龙桥	1	3%
在明代桥梁遗址上的桥梁	石城桥、三山桥、长干桥、御道街桥	4	14%
新增桥梁	中央门桥、钟阜桥、金川桥、新民桥、建宁桥、醒狮桥、卢龙桥、静浮桥、兴中桥、桃园桥、三汊河桥、定淮门桥、草场门桥、国防大桥、清凉门、凤凰桥、集庆门桥、凤台桥、饮马桥、雨花桥、红旗桥、秦虹大桥、紫金桥、月牙湖堤桥	24	83%

Table 2　Moat bridges in today's Nanjing

Type	Name	Number	%
Built in Ming Dynasty	Jiulong Bridge	1	3%
Built on the remains of Ming bridges	Shicheng, Sanshan, Changgan, Yudaojie	4	14%
Newly built bridges	Zhongyangmen, Zhongfu, Jinchuan, Xinmin, Jianning, Xingshi, Lulong, Jingfu, Xingzhong, Taoyuan, Sanchahe, Dinghuaimen, Caochangmen, Guofang, Qingliangmen, Fenghuang, Jiqingmen, Fengtai, Yinma, Yuhua, Hongqi, Qinhong, Zijin, and Yueyahudi	24	83%

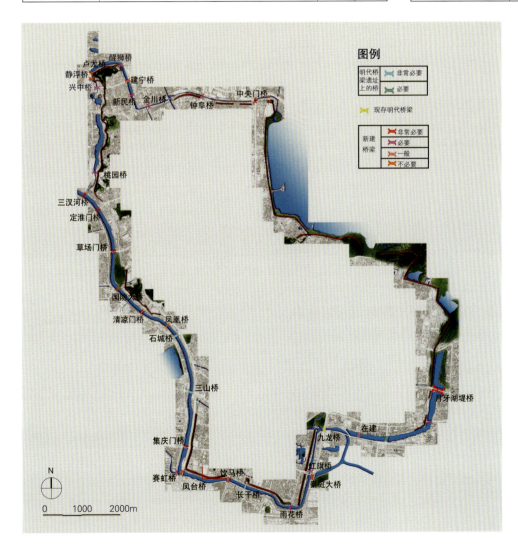

图9　护城河桥梁现状
Fig.9　Present condition of moat bridges

从以上图表中可以看出，护城河现存 29 座桥梁中，仅有一座是明代遗存；在明代桥梁遗址上的桥梁也为数不多，共 4 座，占总数的 14%；而绝大多数是新建桥梁，占总数的 83%。

（3）目前护城河上桥梁存在的问题

部分河段桥梁过多，使得护城河水域视觉空间断裂：

南京向外秦淮以西（河西）发展，从而使得昔日的外秦淮河西段交通流量较大，目前自通济门至三汊河口已建有 16 座桥梁，而这虽然能缓解交通压力，但破坏了护城河的整体性，使得护城河水域视觉空间产生不流畅的断裂感。

多数桥梁仅出于满足交通需要，没有考虑形象及景观品质：

目前护城河上的许多桥梁建设时仅出于解决交通的目的，而没有考虑桥梁的形象及景观品质，而桥梁作为护河上的重要环境要素，其较差的形象必然使得护城河的景观大打折扣。如护城河上多数桥梁造型单一，多为钢筋混凝土平桥，缺少变化。

4）南京护城河的休闲时代

南京多年来一直致力于护城河的整治，并取得了显著成绩，使得护城河的水质和环境都得到了很大改善（图 10、表 3），也迎来了休闲的护城河。

It won't be difficult to see from the table and figure that of the 29 bridges, there is only one surviving moat bridge that was built in the Ming Dynasty, with 4 bridges (or 14% of the total) rebuilt on the remains. Most bridges were newly built, or 83% of the total.

(3) Problems

Excessive numbers of bridges broke the successive view of moats in some sections.

Nanjing has stretched its urban development to the west of the External Qinhuai River, which brought up more traffic in this part of the Qinhuai River. As a result, new bridges were added to improve traffic, with the bridges sitting across the section from Tongji Gate to the Sancha River Mouth reaching 16 in number. The excessive numbers of bridges compromised the integrity of the moats, and made the successive view of moat landscapes broken.

Most bridges were built merely to accommodate traffic needs, without taking into account the style they go with the environment, and possible effects on the landscape. In modern times, people built bridges across the moats mainly to improve traffic, without much thinking of letting the bridges be part of the moat landscape. Unfortunately, bridges, a major element in the moat landscape, could jeopardize the landscape if they were poorly built. Most moat bridges people see today were built in a monotonous style, simply the reinforced concrete bridges, without much difference in outlook.

4) Entertainment function

Municipal authorities has worked hard to protect the moats for many years, and achieved laudable results. The water quality and environment of the moats have witnessed noticeable improvements (Fig.10, Table 3). Moats have become more popular for their entertainment.

图 10　中华门东南段拐角护城河整治前后对比（引自《古城一瞬间》第 36 页）
Fig.10　Before and after the renovation of the moat at southeast corner of Zhonghua Gate (from: *Gucheng Yishunjian*: 36)

表3 2000年以后护城河环境整治工作表[16]

时间	整治内容	投资金额
2000年	整治东水关段护城河,进行景观绿化,建成东水关遗址公园	4 127万元
	拆除集庆段城墙与护城河之间建筑	5 100万元
2001年	整治狮子山周边环境,拆除城墙与护城河周边16 628.55 m² 建筑,进行景观绿化,建成狮子山公园	
2002年	《外秦淮河综合整治总体规划纲要》正式出台	
2002—2005年	整治从入江口至武定门节制闸长约12.5 km的外秦淮河	25亿元
2003年	恢复小桃园段护城河,并对沿岸进行绿化	1.8亿元
2004年	对绣球公园段城墙两侧的护城河边的环境进行整治	875万元

Table 3 Moats' environment control since 2000 [16]

Time	Environment control efforts	Investment
2000	Built a park on the remains of East Water Pass with greenery landscape	RMB 41.27 million
	Dismantling the structures between the city walls and the moats (Jiqing section)	RMB 51 million
2001	Dismantling the structures (16,628.55m²) between the city walls and the moats, and built a park named after Mount Shizi	
2002	Published the outlines for preparing the master plan to facelift the external Qinhuai River in a comprehensive manner	
2002–2005	Facelift the External Qinhuai River, from the mouth of the Yangtze River to Wudingmen gate valve (12.5 km)	RMB 2.5 billion
2003	Rebuilt the moats of the Xiaotaoyuan Section, with greeneries	RMB 180 million
2004	Facelift the environment along the sides of the moats at the Xiuqiu Park	RMB 8.75 million

通过对南京护城河的整治,前湖、琵琶湖、月牙湖、武定门至东水关以及狮子山、乌龙潭、小桃园等护城河现已建成公园,环境质量大大提高,已经成为南京市民重要的休闲场所。武定门至三汊河口段外秦淮河已开发为水上旅游路线,成为南京的特色旅游路线。明南京城护城河在历史上的许多功能已不复存在,如军事、运输等,但一些基本功能如防洪、排水等仍然发挥作用,同时,南京护城河今天已成为南京的生态环境和城市景观的重要组成部分,并承担着城市休闲的功能,为城市增添着亮丽的色彩和风景(图11、图12)。

2. 城墙与相关植物

1)南京明城墙与相关植物的历史情况

南京明城墙的一大特色是因地制宜和利用旧城,所以在形态上表现为平面上和高度上的不规则,同时有诸多种变化,如包山墙、架山墙、石砌墙、砖砌墙等。与此相对应的植物也在建造初期和发展过程中有如下几种情形。

Nanjing municipal authorities launched a campaign to facelift the old moats, which turned the sections at Qianhu Lake, Pipa Lake, Yueya Lake, Wudingmen–East Water Pass, Mount Shizi, Wulongtan, and Xiaotaoyuan into public parks. The greatly improved environment allowed the moats to be a major entertainment ground for citizens. The External Qinhuai River section running from Wuding Gate to the Sancha River Mouth has become a special tourist route. The moats built in the Ming Dynasty have lost some of the originally designed functions, including defense and transport. Fortunately, their other utility functions, such as flood control and drainage, remained applicable. Meanwhile, moats have become a major component of the city's ecological environment and urban landscapes, with newly developed entertainment functions. Moats makes a beautiful landscape in today's Nanjing City (Fig. 11, Fig.12).

2. City walls and associated plants

1) Plants associated with the walls in the past

The Nanjing Ming City Wall were built borrowing the contours of local terrains, and utilizing the old city. As a result, the walls looked irregular in terms of both plane and height. Meanwhile, the walls were built in diversified styles, including the walls built to enclose or ride across the mountains, stone wall, and brick wall. The plants grown with the walls were basically in the following forms.

图 11　西北段城壕景观
Fig.11　Landscape of the moats at the northwest section

图 12　西南段城壕景观
Fig.12　Landscape of the moats at the southwest section

（1）新建砖城墙

这是南京明城墙的主体。主要是用大约高 10 cm、宽 20 cm、长 40 cm 的砖砌造，城墙的砌垒黏合剂主要由石灰、黄沙、黏土、糯米汁或高粱汁以及桐油掺和而成的"夹浆"。这种黏合剂凝固后有很强的黏着力和耐蚀能力。可想而知，当年明城墙初建时应该是咬合紧密、砌筑平整的城墙，再加上守城士兵的巡查清理，城墙上应该不会杂草丛生，更不可能长出会严重破坏城墙的树木来。《大明会典》载："凡京师城垣，洪武二十六年定：皇城、京城墙垣，遇有损坏，即便丈量明白，见数计料，所有砖、灰，行下聚宝山黑窑等处关支，其合用人工，咨呈都府，行移留守五卫差拨军士修理。"[17] 可见明代是有兵士定期对城墙进行修理维护的。

（2）包山或架山的城墙

主要体现在由西而北连接或包山、跨山于清凉山、马鞍山、狮子山、鸡笼山、小九华山、富贵山等。如此在城墙内山体上原有的植物就会形成丰富的景观，而城墙外也风景无限。如《金陵图咏》的"鸡笼云树"描绘的"孤峰高枕帝城隅，南望纷纶列九

(1) New brick walls

This part of the walls constitutes the main body of the Nanjing Ming City Wall. The walls were built with the bricks of a size of 10cmx20cmx40cm. The bricks of were bonded together using a mixed plaster made of lime, sands, clay, glutinous rice juice or sorghum juice, and wood oil. The powerful plaster, when becoming hardened, presents a strong adhesiveness and erosion resistance. One can assume that the walls, when initially built, were piled up firmly and smoothly, without the growth of weeds. Soldiers' frequent inspection would not allow trees to grow out of the walls either. According to an ancient literature named *Da Ming Hui Dian* (Regulations and By-laws) in the Ming Dynasty, "Emperor Hongwu stipulated in 1393 that the walls of imperial city and capital city, once broken or damaged, shall be measured and calculated for mending or repairing. All the bricks and plaster needed shall be supplied by the Black Kiln at the foot of Mount Jubao. The labor used in producing the needed materials should be reported to the authorities. Spared soldiers shall be dispatched to repair the broken or damaged walls."[17] Apparently, in the Ming Dynasty, soldiers were supposed to take care of the walls on a regular basis.

(2) Walls built to enclose or ride across the mountains

This part of the walls includes the one linking or enclosing the mountains from the west to the north, and the one riding over a range of mountains, including Mount Qingliang, Ma'an, Shizi, Jilong, Xiaojiuhua, and Fugui. Evidently, the plants originally grown on the enclosed mountains constituted a rich landscape, matching the beautiful landscape on the outskirts of the walls. In an ancient book named *Jinling Tu Yong* (Odes to Jinling Landscape), the beautiful landscape created by the enclosed Mount Jilong was described like this: " the isolated mountain peak makes a raised pillow for the corner of the walls, with nine crossings in the south. Clouds drifted by, together or individually, above hundreds and thousands of trees in the distance. "[18] It spoke about what looked like on the enclosed Mount Jilong (Fig. 13). One can feel that Mount Jilong was a green landscape densely grown with trees at the time.

(3) External walls

In the Ming Dynasty, an external wall as long as 60 km was built on the outskirts of the city walls. The wall was also called "earth wall" for the materials it was built of. The external walls enclosed extensive

衢。联合流云三五片，凄迷远树万千株"[18]，说的就是鸡笼山墙内的情形（图13），由此可知鸡笼山处树木郁郁葱葱。

（3）外郭土墙

在南京明城墙外围，明代还修筑了长达60 km的外郭土墙，俗称"土城头"。它把钟山、玄武湖、幕府山等大片郊区都围入郭内。这些山水当然也是城墙不可分割的一部分，历史上这些地方草木繁盛。

城墙之外的诸山更是被广袤的树木所覆盖。东晋即规定"刺史罢官还都，种植白株，郡守五十株"于钟山。明洪武年间，朱元璋命驻军在钟山南麓植树，还下令百姓、驻军广植桑、栎、胡桃等树，明孝陵也曾植树10万株。经过60多年，至宣德三年（1428年），朝阳门外钟山南麓，所建桐、漆、棕树园植树达200余万株[19]。

南京这座城市一向就有植树的传统。民国时期，政府创办林场，出现了完全开放的近代公园，广泛植行道树，设置绿化带。民国政府为了纪念孙中山，把他的逝世纪念日3月12日定为植树节。在《首都计划》中，还曾经规划沿城墙设置林荫道路："所拟定之林荫大道，有特别足以引起市民之兴趣者，即在城内之墙角下，筑道以环绕一周也。"[20]（图14）虽然后来没有实现，但是近年的沿南京城墙整治，也部分地实现了这一景观。

图13 "鸡笼云树"（引自《金陵图咏》第27页）
Fig.13 Mount Jilong with the clouds and trees (from: *Jinling Tu Yong*: 27)

suburban areas, including Mount Zhong, Xuanwu Lake, and Mount Mufu. The mountains and rivers enclosed became, of course, an inalienable part of the walls. In the past, said places were flourished with trees and grasses.

Mountains sitting on the outskirts of the walls were covered by dense trees. In the East Jin Dynasty, it was stipulated that "when an ousted governor returned to the capital, he shall grow 50 trees on Mount Zhong ". Emperor Hongwu ordered the troops to plant trees at the southern foot of Mount Zhong, and asked citizens and soldiers to grow mulberry, Quercus serrata, and walnut trees. Some 100, 000 trees were planted on the Ming Xiao Mausoleum. Thanks to more than 60 years' efforts, the tung, toxicodendron vernicifluum, and palm trees planted across the southern foot of Mount Zhong on the outskirts of Chaoyang Gate had reached more than 2 million in number in 1428 [19].

Nanjing has a long history of planting trees. In the Republican times, authorities founded forestry farms, and built modern parks completely open to the public. Trees were planted along the sides of avenues, and greenery belts were created. To memorize Dr. Sun Yat-sen, the authorities made March 12, the passing day of Dr. Sun Yat-sen, the tree planting day. In the Capital Plan, it was proposed to build boulevards shaded by trees along the city walls: "the proposed tree-shading boulevards, or the boulevards circling the city walls, would be special enough to attract people's attention ." [20] (Fig. 14) The proposal was partially materialized through a campaign to facelift the city walls launched in recent years, though it failed to come true at that time.

图14 南京林荫大道系统图（引自《首都计划》第110页）
Fig.14 Boulevard systems of Nanjing in the Capital Plan (from: *Shoudu Jihua*: 110)

2）南京明城墙与相关植物的现状（图 15）

数百年的时间使得南京明城墙本体与周围的相关植物和历史上比起来发生了较多变化。

南京明城墙本体上据统计，"共有维管植物 81 科、198 属、266 种。区系地理成分分析表明南京明城墙植物具有温带性质。明城墙植物所反映的气候特征与明城墙特殊的环境特点造就了多年生草本和一年生草本在城墙植物中占优势。这些草本大多为颖果、瘦果，种子较小，很容易通过风力或动物的传播带到城墙上。"[21] 现今城墙上的植物杂生的状况是由于城墙失去其城防作用后，城砖和黏结材料风化又年久失修造成的（图 16）。

2) Plants associated with the walls today (Fig.15)

In the past hundred years, the body of the Nanjing Ming City Wall and associated plants have undergone noticeable changes.

Statistics show that the Nanjing Ming City Wall has been grown with 266 varieties of vascular plants under 198 genuses in 81 families, mostly temperate plants. The climate in Nanjing, and the special environment where the walls sit are desirable for the growth of perennials and annuals. The plants usually bear cariopside and thin fruits. The seeds, in tiny size, are easily carried away by birds or blown by winds to the walls . The mixed growth of plants on the walls people see today is the result of the weathered and broken bricks and plaster materials, after their defensive functions got lost (Fig.16).

图 15 南京明城墙本体上相关植物的现状图
Fig.15 Plants associated with the noumenon of the city walls today

第二章 城墙、景观与城市肌理　2 – City Walls, Landscape and Urban Fabric

图16　南京明城墙各段绿化现状照片
Fig.16　Photos of greenery condition of several sections of the city walls

据调研，武定门至雨花门段城墙上长满了爬山虎。东水关至武定门段城墙石缝中长有杂草和爬藤类植物，墙体顶部植物较多。中山门至后标营路段城墙墙体表面长满藤类植物，局部城墙顶面长有木本植物。前湖至中山门段城墙石缝中长有杂草和藤本植物，局部墙体植物较茂盛粗壮。太平门至前湖段城墙墙体表面大部分长有杂草和爬藤类植物，局部砖缝中生有木本植物，城墙顶面生有木本植物。台城至太平门段城墙墙顶面砖缝中生有杂草，雉堞和与墙上有爬藤类植物。神策门至玄武湖隧道入口处段未经维修的墙体上，砖、石缝中长有杂草和爬藤类植物，墙体顶部植物较多，部分植物对墙体产生了严重破坏。黑龙江路遗址段城墙遗迹土芯上生长了大量的高大柏树。定淮门至狮子山段城墙墙体上生有爬藤类植物，局部比较茂盛。石头城段城墙局部墙面砖缝中生有植物。

具体城墙上相关植物现状见表4。

According to the author's investigation, the wall section running from Wuding Gate to Yuhua Gate was covered with Parthenocissus trcuspidata. The walls stretching from the East Water Pass to Wuding Gate were grown with weeds and climbing vines, with a lot of plants on the top. One can see the walls covered with vines from Zhongshan Gate to Houbiaoying Road, with some trees on top of the walls. The section between Qian Lake and Zhongshan Gate was teemed with weeds and vines, with some walls having flourishing plants. One may see weeds and vines in the walls running from Taiping Gate to Qian Lake, with woody plants on top of the walls. Weeds could be spotted on wall top running from Taicheng to Taiping Gate, and climbing vines on the battlements and walls. The broken walls between shence Gate and the entrance of Xuanwuhu Tunnel were teemed with weeds and vines, with numerous plants on top. Some plants have caused serious damages to the wall body. For example, large cypress trees have grown out of the wall remains over Heilongjiang Road. The walls stretching from Dinghuai Gate to Mount Shizi were grown with climbing vines. Some part of the walls has been covered with dense vines. The walls of Stone City section were partially grown with plants in brick seams.

The plans associated on the walls can be seen in Table 4.

表 4 城墙上相关植物现状

城墙段		现　状
中华门—东水关	中华门瓮城	中华门瓮城上长有茂盛的爬藤植物
	中华门—东水关	局部城墙墙体长有爬藤植物
东水关—月牙湖老墙南端	月牙湖老墙南端	这段城墙是在遗址的基础上做了一段演示矮墙，城墙遗址上长满了茂密的树木
月牙湖—太平门	月牙湖公园段	墙体上生长了很多乔木
	铜管闸段—中山门	这段城墙属于包山墙，城墙顶上植被茂盛，并有部分用于附近居民菜地
	中山门—琵琶湖东侧	城墙上长了很多植物，树根对于城墙破坏很大
	琵琶湖—太平门	经过近期维修清理，城墙上没有危害大的乔木，长有爬藤植物和草本植物
太平门—台城	太平门—九华山西端	城墙顶部长了茂密的杂草
	九华山西端—台城	城墙顶部长了稀疏的杂草，台城段城墙侧面长有树木和爬藤类植物
解放门—神策门	解放门—神策门	经过近期维修清理，城墙上没有危害大的乔木，局部长有爬藤植物和草本植物
	神策门	利用原山体在城墙顶部建有一个绿地，成片的薰衣草是其一大特色
神策门—狮子山东大门	神策门—钟阜路	这段城墙只有夯土墙基，上面长有高大的乔木，乔木的根系能保持水土，对城墙有保护作用
狮子山—定淮门	狮子山风景区	这段属于包山墙，植物茂盛，狮子山西部区域树木根系对城墙有很大的破坏
	仪凤门—定淮门	局部段是包山墙，城墙上的植物过于茂密，部分大的乔木根系对城墙产生破坏
定淮门—汉西门	清凉山段	这段属于包山墙，清凉山上植物茂盛，城墙墙体上也有很多较小的树木，对墙体有不利影响
汉西门—中华门	汉西门	被茂密的爬山虎覆盖着
	三山桥—中华门	这段城墙属于新近砌筑，局部段的爬山虎能让城墙显得年代久远些

Table 4　The plants associated on the walls

Section		Current Status
Zhonghua Gate–East Water Pass	Zhonghua Gate Fortress	Flourishing climbing vines on the fortress
	Zhonghua Gate– East Water Pass	Climbing vines on some walls
East Water Pass–S. End of Yueya Lake old walls	S. End of Yueya Lake old walls	The wall is a showcase of parapet walls built on the remains, grown with dense trees
Yueya Lake – Taiping Gate	Yueya Lake Park	Numerous trees on the walls
	Tonguanzha – Zhongshan Gate	Walls built to enclose the mountains. Dense vegetations grown on top of the walls, with some vegetables plots grown by residents in the vicinity
	Zhongshan Gate – E. Pipa Lake	Numerous plants grown on the walls. Plant roots caused great damages to the walls
	Pipa Lake–Taiping Gate	After clean-up, no large trees can be seen on the walls, though there are some climbing vines and weeds
Taiping Gate –Taicheng	Taiping Gate– W. End of Mount Jiuhua	Dense weeds on wall tops
	W. End of Mount Jiuhua–Taicheng	Some weeds on wall tops, with trees and climbing vines on the side of Taicheng wall section
Jiefang Gate–Shence Gate	Jiefang Gate– Shence Gate	After clean-up, no large trees can be seen on the walls, though there are some climbing vines and weeds
	Shence Gate	A greenery was built on the wall top, which was originally a hill, dominated by lavender
Shence Gate–E. Gate, Mount Shizi	Shence Gate– Zhongfu Rd.	Earth walls, grown with large tress. Tree roots keep soil moisture, protecting the walls
Mount Shizi– Dinghuai Gate	Mount Shizi Park	Walls built to enclose the mountains, with flourishing plants. Tree roots in the west part of Mount Shizi caused great damages to the walls
	Yifeng Gate–Dinghuai Gate	Partial walls built to enclose the mountains, excessive plants on the walls, some large tree roots caused damages to the walls
Dinghuai Gate– Hanxi Gate	Mount Qingliang	Walls built to enclose the mountains, plants are flourishing on Mount Qingliang, some undesirable small trees in the walls
Hanxi Gate–Zhonghua Gate	Hanxi Gate	Covered with dense Parthenocissus tricuspidata
	Sanshan Bridge–Zhonghua Gate	Newly built, partially covered with Parthenocissus tricuspidata, in an attempt to make the wall look older

另一方面，现在南京明城墙周围的绿化也发生了很大变化，由过去城墙外围为防御而禁种乔木，已转变为城墙与周围绿地植被多数有机结合，甚至成为南京主城区重要的绿地系统。据有关部门统计，沿南京明城墙周边现有大树95棵，品种有梓树、杨树、槐树、石榴、梧桐等等（图17）。

On the other hand, the walls have been affected by the changed policies on growing greeneries in the vicinity, from forbidding to grow trees for the sake of defense to the systematic combination of the walls and green vegetations. Some walls have become major greeneries in the main port of the city. According to statistics, the Nanjing Ming City Wall has 95 large trees in the vicinity, including catalpa, poplar, locust tree, megranate, phoenix tree among others (Fig.17).

图17 南京明城墙周边植被现状照片
Fig.17 Photos of greenery condition around the city walls

尽管如此，问题依然存在，围绕对城墙的基础影响、视觉影响等，据调研，城墙周围相关植物现状见表5。

表5 城墙周围相关植物现状

城墙段			现　状	景观风貌	对城墙视线的影响程度
中华门—东水关	中华门—长乐路		多为密集建筑和道路，绿化很少	差	—
	长乐路—东水关	城墙外侧	主要是建筑和道路，绿化很少	差	—
		城墙内侧	内侧有白鹭洲公园，景色优美，绿化好	好	低
东水关—月牙湖老墙南端	东水关—御道街		多为比较新的住宅小区，小区内环境都还可以，绿化也比较好	一般	—
	御道街—月牙湖老城墙南端	城墙外侧	主要是一些杂乱的建筑，很少有绿化	差	—
		城墙内侧	内侧是一批年代较久的住宅，整体环境较差，绿化也较少	差	—
月牙湖—太平门	月牙湖—中山门	城墙外侧	主要是一些新建小区，虽然高楼林立，但是绿化率很高，景观较好	好	—
		城墙内侧	主要是住宅，绿化较少	一般	—
	中山门—北安门街	城墙外侧	属于紫金山风景区，植被茂密	好	高
		城墙内侧	内侧有部分是住宅小区，还有军事区，小区有零星绿化	差	—
	北安门街—太平门		属于紫金山风景区，植被茂密，并有白马公园，景观较好	好	高
太平门—台城	太平门—九华山西端		外侧为玄武湖，内侧为九华山，绿化较好，都有不错的风景	好	高
	九华山西端—台城	城墙外侧	外侧为玄武湖，景观较好	好	高
		城墙内侧	城墙内侧多为建筑，绿化较少	差	—
解放门—神策门	解放门—玄武门	城墙外侧	外侧为玄武湖，景观较好	好	高
		城墙内侧	内侧主要是住宅小区，环境比较差，缺乏绿化	差	—
	玄武门—神策门	城墙外侧	外侧为玄武湖，景观较好	好	高
		城墙内侧	城墙内侧只有一些零星的绿化，整体环境较差	差	—
	神策门		外侧有一些高楼大厦，绿化很少	差	—
神策门—狮子山东大门	神策门—钟阜路	城墙外侧	有很多杂乱的建筑，很少有绿化	差	—
		城墙内侧	有几个小区，整体环境尚可	一般	—
	钟阜路—狮子山东大门		主要是道路和建筑，只有零星绿化	差	—
狮子山—定淮门	狮子山风景区	城墙外侧	有一条交通主干道，绿化很少	差	—
		城墙内侧	内侧属于狮子山风景区，环境较好	好	高
	仪凤门—挹江门		主要是密集的建筑，绿化较少	差	—
	挹江门—定淮门	城墙外侧	主要是密集的建筑，只有部分段有绿化	差	—
		城墙内侧	主要是住宅小区和一些山体，绿化率较高	一般	—
定淮门—汉西门	定淮门—石头城	城墙外侧	有沿河的景观带和小区绿化，景观较好	好	—
		城墙内侧	主要是建筑，绿化率比较低	差	—
	石头城—汉西门	城墙外侧	有沿河的景观带和小区绿化，景观较好	好	低
		城墙内侧	清凉山上植被茂密，但是过于杂乱	一般	高
汉西门—中华门	汉西门—集庆门大桥		有密集的建筑，绿化很少	差	—
	集庆门大桥—赛虹立交桥	城墙内侧	有密集的建筑，绿化很少	差	—
		城墙外侧	有沿河的景观带和小区绿化，景观较好	好	低
	赛虹立交桥—中华门		有密集的小型建筑和大型厂房，绿化较少	差	—

The plants grown with the walls may affect the wall foundation, and compromise the landscape view of the walls. The following information was derived from the investigations made by author on the plants associated with the walls (Table 5).

Table 5 The plants associated with the walls

Section			Current status	Landscape	Impact on view
Zhonghua Gate– East Water Pass	Zhonghua Gate–Changle Rd.		Dominated by dense structures and roads, little greeneries	Poor	—
	Changle Rd.–East Water Pass	Outside	Dominated by structures and roads, little greenery	Poor	—
		Inside	Bailuzhou Park, beautiful scenery and greeneries	Good	Low
East Water Pass –S. End of Yueya Lake old walls	East Water Pass–Yudao Ave.		New residential areas, fine internal environment and greeneries	Fair	—
	Yudao Ave.–S. End of Yueya Lake old walls	Outside	Messy structures, little greenery	Poor	—
		Inside	Old residential structures, poor environment, and limited greeneries	Poor	—
Yueya Lake – Taiping Gate	Yueya Lake–Zhongshan Gate	Outside	New residential areas with high rise buildings, fine greeneries	Good	—
		Inside	Mainly residential areas, with limited greeneries	Fair	—
	Zhongshan Gate–Beianmen Ave.	Outside	Park area with dense vegetations	Good	High
		Inside	Residential areas, and military zone, some greeneries	Poor	—
	Beianmen Ave.–Taiping Gate		Park areas with dense vegetations, fine landscape views	Good	High
Taiping Gate –Taicheng	Taiping Gate–W. End of Mount Jiuhua		Outside: Xuanwu Lake; inside: Mount Jiuhua, fine greeneries and landscape	Good	High
	W. End of Mount Jiuhua–Taicheng	Outside	Xuanwu Lake, fine landscape views	Good	High
		Inside	Mainly structures, with limited greeneries	Poor	—
Jiefang Gate– Shence Gate	Jiefang Gate–Xuanwu Gate	Outside	Xuanwu Lake, fine landscape view	Good	High
		Inside	Mainly residential areas, poor environment, and little greeneries	Poor	—
	Xuanwu Gate–Shence Gate	Outside	Xuanwu Lake, fine landscape view	Good	High
		Inside	Scattered greeneries, and poor environment	Poor	—
	Shence Gate		Numerous high rise buildings, little greeneries	Poor	—
Shence Gate –E. Gate, Mount Shizi	Shence Gate–Zhongfu Rd.	Outside	Messy structures, little greeneries	Poor	—
		Inside	Residential areas, fair environment	Fair	—
	Zhongfu Rd.–E. Gate, Mount Shizi		Mainly roads and structures, scattered greeneries	Poor	—
Mount Shizi– Dinghuai Gate	Mount Shizi Park	Outside	Trunk roads with little greeneries	Poor	—
		Inside	Park area, fine environment	Good	High
	Yifeng Gate–Yijiang Gate		Dense structures, limited greeneries	Poor	—
	Yijiang Gate–Dinghuai Gate	Outside	Dense structures, some greeneries	Poor	—
		Inside	Residential areas, mountains, fine greeneries	Fair	—
Dinghuai Gate –Hanxi Gate	Dinghuai Gate–Stone City	Outside	Riverside landscape, fine greeneries in residential areas	Good	—
		Inside	Mainly structures, little greeneries	Poor	—
	Stone City–Hanxi Gate	Outside	Riverside landscape, fine greeneries in residential areas	Good	Low
		Inside	Dense vegetation on Mount Qingliang, but too wild looking	Fair	High
Hanxi Gate –Zhonghua Gate	Hanxi Gate–Jiqingmen Bridge		Dense structures, little greeneries	Poor	—
	Jiqingmen Bridge–Saihong cloverleaf	Inside	Dense structures, little greeneries	Poor	—
		Outside	Riverside landscape, fine greeneries in residential areas	Good	Low
	Saihong cloverleaf—Zhonghua Gate		Dense small structures, large factories, limited greeneries	Poor	—

可以看出，经过多年整治，城墙沿线的绿化总的来说还是不错的。但问题有如下方面：①大树过于靠近城墙，有可能对城墙基础造成影响，如太平门城墙地段；②植被繁密且高大，部分遮挡城墙轮廓线的展示，如前湖地段；③没有绿化，厂房和居民房过于接近城墙本体。

3）南京明城墙与相关植物的未来

依据上述分析及南京总体规划的要求，我们对未来南京明城墙相关植物的规划目标是：对于南京明城墙本体上的植物，首先保证其品种不会危害到城墙本体的安全性（图18），其次是保留适当品种以彰显城墙的沧桑感；对于城墙周围的植物，既要保证植

Apparently, many years' facelifting efforts have improved the greeneries along the city walls. However, one has to bear in mind the following problems: ① the large trees that sit too close to the walls may harm the walls' foundation, e.g. Taiping Gate section; ② excessively grown vegetations would hide the contour lines of the walls, e.g. Qian Lake section; ③ lacking of greeneries, and factory/residential buildings were too close to the walls.

3）Walls and associated plants in the future

Based on the aforesaid analysis and the master development plan of Nanjing, the walls and associated plants shall be handled in the following manner: the plants grown with the walls shall not endanger the safety of the walls (Fig.18); vegetation

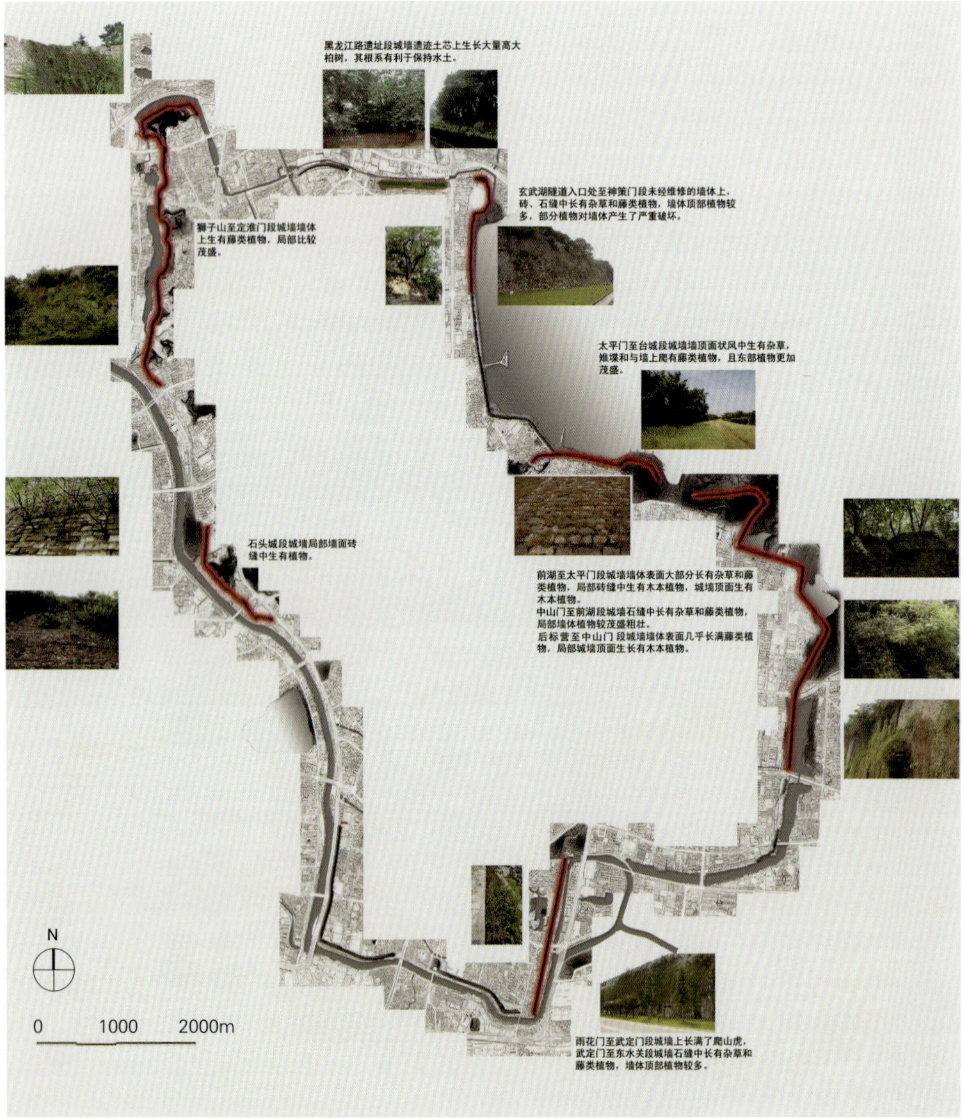

图 18 需要清除植物的城墙段
Fig.18 Sections of the city walls demanding clean up of plants

物绿化满足城墙安全性的必要距离要求，同时最好能起到烘托城墙的作用（图19）。

具体而言，对城墙危害最大的是乔木，多数乔木根系发达，具有强大的破坏力，长在城墙上的乔木能破坏夯土墙基和墙体，长在城墙附近的也会使墙基产生松动。过于高大密集的树木会对城墙产生遮挡，不利于人们发现和远距离观赏城墙。典型的树种有：青桐、梧桐、槐树。整治办法是清理城墙上的树木，对于离城墙太近的树木可以适当清除或移植，使其不会破坏城墙的墙基，也不会对城墙主体景观产生负面影响。一般树木的根系范围和树冠尺寸是1：1，所以城墙两侧的树木与城墙间的距离应大于树木树冠

species applied shall be able to enhance the walls' weathered look; and the plants grown in the vicinity of the walls shall keep a given distance from the walls for the sake of safety, while beautifying the environment(Fig.19).

Specifically, trees may cause serious damages to the walls, due to the development of root systems. The trees grown in the walls would damage the foundation as well as the body of the walls. Trees, even when grown in the vicinity of the walls, may cause the loosening of the foundations. Additionally,

图19 南京明城墙周围相关绿化等级图（左）；南京明城墙景观空间规划图（中）；南京明城墙分区域植物栽种规划图（右）

Fig.19 Greenery grades around the city walls (left); Landscape planning of the city walls (middle); Vegetation planning of the city wall (right)

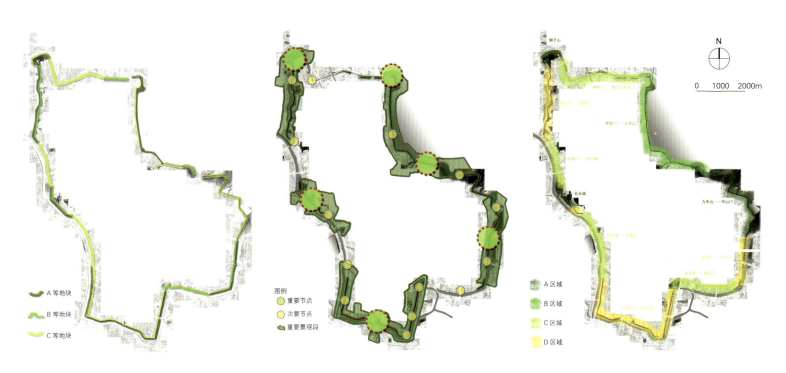

半径，且不小于 8 m。部分长得较快的树木不能种在城墙附近，如法国梧桐、枫杨。藤本植物和草本植物也会对城墙造成一定的破坏，它们的根系可能钻进明城墙的砖缝里，继而破坏原本已经脆弱的城砖。根据 1954 年的城墙勘察报告："惟各段多半损坏，雨水无法畅排，而墙顶杂草丛生，更使水流阻滞，以至渗入墙身，实为城墙损坏原因之一。"[22] 部分藤本植物的生长客观上会使明城墙的墙壁渗水，典型种类有爬山虎。具体整治办法就需要根据实际情况调查各段藤本植物对城墙的影响，控制藤本和草本植物的生长，经常修剪，生长久的老根破坏较大，要清除。

针对明城墙现有状况，可以形成以下几个绿色景观带：（1）结合护城河水体、山林等周边用地，重点形成狮子山—小桃园、石头城—汉中门、东水关—西水关、神策门—富贵山及中山门—光华东街 5 个主题段落；（2）结合现存城门及城门遗迹遗址形成 6 个重要节点；（3）结合现存城门及城门遗迹遗址形成 14 个一般节点；（4）使明城墙沿线既能为外地游客服务，又方便本市居民到达，成为一个有机的整体。

the tall trees with large canopy, such as phoenix tree and locust tree, would block the view of the walls, undesirable for people to enjoy the walls in the distance. In this context, it is desirable to clean up the trees grown in the walls. The trees standing too close to the walls shall be removed, preventing them from crippling the wall foundations. The area that tree roots stretch to shall be proportioned to its canopy at a ratio of 1:1. In this context, the distance between the trees and the walls shall be larger than the radius of tree canopy, and not less than 8m. Fast growing trees, such as phoenix tree, maple trees, and poplar, shall not be allowed to grow near the walls. Additionally, vines and herbals may cause damages to the walls by stretching their roots into the brick seams, and loosening the already weathered bricks. According to a survey report published in 1954, "Most of the wall sections had been damaged, and inundated with water. Weeds flourished on top of the wall, blocking the drainage of rainwater, and forcing rainwater into the body of the wall, which explained a cause for the damage."[22] The growth of some types of vines, e.g. Parthenocissus trcuspidata, may lead to the penetration of rainwater into the walls. In this context, vines shall be planted in the walls when allowed, and be pruned properly. The old roots of vines may impose damage to the walls, and should be cleaned up.

The following green landscapes can be created in line with the current status of the walls: (1) combining the moats and hills around to form 5 theme sections, Mount Shizi–Xiaotaoyuan, Stone city–Hanzhong Gate, East Water Pass–West Water Pass, Shence Gate–Mount Fugui, and Zhongshan Gate–Guanghua East Avenue; (2) combining the existing city gates and the remains of city gates to form 6 key areas; (3) combining the existing city gates and the remains of city gates to form 14 ordinary areas; (4) making the traffic alongside the city walls convenient both for tourists and for the citizens of Nanjing, to become a dynamic integration.

注释

1. 南京市地方志编纂委员会. 南京水利志. 深圳：海天出版社，1994：114
2. （明）陈沂撰. 金陵古今图考. 南京：南京出版社，2006：97
3. （民国）朱偰. 金陵古迹图考. 北京：中华书局，2006：36
4. 江苏省南京市公路管理处史志编审委员. 南京古代道路史. 南京：江苏科学技术出版社，1989：212
5. 杨国庆，王志高. 南京城墙志. 南京：凤凰出版社，2008：175-176
6. （明）陈沂撰. 金陵古今图考. 南京：南京出版社，2006：90
7. （民国）王焕镳. 明孝陵志. 南京：南京出版社，2006：7
8. 道光上元县志. 南京：江苏古籍出版社，1991：93
9. （清）吕燕昭修，姚鼐. 重刊江宁府志. 南京：江苏古籍出版社，1991：110
10. （明）王俊华纂修. 洪武京城图志. 北京图书馆古籍珍本丛刊. 北京：书目文献出版社，1990；（明）陈沂撰. 金陵古今图考. 南京：南京出版社，2006：15，89，98
11. （清）甘熙. 白下琐言. 南京：南京出版社，2007：171
12. （清）甘熙. 白下琐言. 南京：南京出版社，2007：172
13. 道光上元县志. 南京：江苏古籍出版社，1991：79
14. （清）金鳌. 金陵待征录. 台北：成文出版社有限公司，1983：17
15. （明）顾起元撰. 张惠荣校点. 客座赘语. 南京：凤凰出版社，2005：227
16. 南京市文化局（市文物局），中国民主同盟南京市委员会，杨新华主编. 南京明城墙. 南京：南京大学出版社，2006：297
17. 《大明会典》卷一八七
18. （明）朱之蕃. 金陵图咏. 台北：成文出版社有限公司，1983
19. 南京市地方志编纂委员会办公室. 话说南京. 南京：南京出版社，2006
20. （民国）国都设计技术专员办事处. 首都计划. 南京：南京出版社，2006：106-107
21. 龙双畏. 南京明城墙维管植物多样性的调查与分析：[硕士学位论文]. 南京：南京师范大学，2007：51
22. 南京市文化局（市文物局），中国民主同盟南京市委员会，杨新华主编. 南京明城墙. 南京：南京大学出版社，2006：297

Notes

1. Nanjing Local Annals Compilation Committee. *Nanjing Shuili Zhi* (Hydrology in Nanjing). Shenzhen: Haitian Press, 1994：114
2. Chen Y (Ming Dynasty). *Jinling Gujin Tu Kao* (A Review of Jinling Maps). Nanjing：Nanjing Press, 2006: 97
3. Zhu X(Republic of China). *Jinling Guji Tu Kao* (Historical relics of the Jinling City). Beijing: Zhonghua Book Company, 2006: 36
4. Nanjing Municipal Road Administration. *Nanjing Gudai Daolu Shi* (History of Ancient Roads in Nanjing). Nanjing: Jiangsu Science and Technology Press, 1989: 212
5. Yang G Q, Wang Z G. *Nanjing Chengqiang Zhi* (Annals of Nanjing City Wall). Nanjing: Phoenix Press, 2008: 175-176
6. Chen Y (Ming Dynasty). *Jinling Gujin Tu Kao* (A Review of Jinling Maps). Nanjing: Nanjing Press, 2006: 90
7. Wang H B (Republic of China). *Ming Xiao Ling Zhi* (Annals of Ming Xiao Mausoleum). Nanjing: Nanjing Press, 2006: 7
8. *Daoguang Shangyuan Xian Zhi* (Annals of Shangyuan County under Emperor Daoguang). Nanjing: Jiangsu Classics Publishing House, 1991: 93
9. Lv Y Z, Yao N (Qing Dynasty). *Chong Kan Jiangning Fu Zhi* (Annals of Jiangning City Reprint.) Nanjing: Jiangsu Classics Publishing House, 1991: 110
10. Wang J H (Ming Dynasty). *Hongwu Jingcheng Tu Zhi* (Capital City Atlas under Hongwu): Collections of Precious Ancient Books in the Beijing Library. Beijing: Bibliography and Document Publishing House, 1990; Chen Y (Ming Dynasty). *Jinling Gujin Tu Kao* （A Review of Jinling Maps). Nanjing: Nanjing Press, 2006: 15, 89, 98
11. Gan X(Qing Dynasty). *Baixia Suo Yan* (Folks' Miscellanea). Nanjing: Nanjing Press, 2007: 171
12. Gan X(Qing Dynasty). *Baixia Suo Yan* (Folks' Miscellanea). Nanjing: Nanjing Press, 2007: 172
13. *Daoguang Shangyuan Xian Zhi* (Annals of Shangyuan County under Emperor Daoguang). Nanjing: Phoenix Press, 1991:79
14. Jin A (Qing Dynasty). *Jinling Daizheng Lu* (A story Collection of Jinling City). Taibei: Chengwen Publishing Co. Ltd., 1983: 17
15. Gu Q Y, Zhang H R (Ming Dynasty). *Kezuo Zhui Yu* (Visitors' Verbosity). Nanjing: Phoenix Press, 2005: 227
16. Nanjing Municipal Culture Burean, etc. ed. *Nanjing Ming Chengqiang* (The Nanjing Ming City Wall). Nanjing: Nanjing University Press, 2006: 297
17. *Da Ming Hui Dian* (Regulations and By-laws in the Ming Dynasty). Vol. 187
18. Zhu Z F (Ming Dynasty). *Jinling Tu Yong*(Odes to Jinling Landscape). Taibei:Chengwen Publishing Co. Ltd, 1983
19. Nanjing Local Annals Compilation Committee. *Huashuo Nanjing* (A Story of Nanjing). Nanjing: Nanjing Press, 2006
20. Capital City Design Office (Republic of China). *Shuodu Jihua* (Capital Plan). Nanjing: Nanjing Press, 2006: 106-107
21. Long S W. Survey and analysis: diversity of vascular plants associated with the Nanjing Ming City Wall: [master's thesis]. Nanjing: Nanjing Normal University,2007: 51
22. Nanjing Municipal Culture Burean, etc. ed. *Nanjing Ming Chengqiang* (The Nanjing Ming City Wall). Nanjing: Nanjing University Press, 2006: 297

参考书目

1. （明）朱之蕃．金陵图咏．台北：成文出版社有限公司，1983
2. 南京市地方志编纂委员会办公室．话说南京．南京：南京出版社，2006
3. 南京市文化局（市文物局），中国民主同盟南京市委员会，杨新华主编．南京明城墙．南京：南京大学出版社，2006
4. 杨国庆，王志高．南京城墙志．南京：凤凰出版社，2008
5. （民国）国都设计技术专员办事处．首都计划．南京：南京出版社，2006
6. 龙双畏．南京明城墙维管植物多样性的调查与分析：[硕士学位论文]．南京：南京师范大学，2007
7. 东南大学建筑设计研究院．全国重点文物保护单位南京明城墙保护总体规划，2008

Reference

1. Zhu Z F (Ming Dynasty). *Jinling Tu Yong* (Odes to Jinling Landscape). Taibei: Chengwen Publishing Co. Ltd, 1983
2. Nanjing Local Annals Compilation Committee. *Huashuo Nanjing* (A Story of Nanjing). Nanjing: Nanjing Press, 2006
3. Nanjing Municipal Culture Burean, etc, ed. *Nanjing Ming Chengqiang* (The Nanjing Ming City Wall). Nanjing: Nanjing University Press, 2006
4. Yang G Q, Wang Z G. *Nanjing Chengqiang Zhi* (Annals of Nanjing City Wall). Nanjing: Phoenix Press, 2008
5. Capital City Design Office (Republic of China). *Shoudu Jihua* (Capital Plan). Nanjing: Nanjing Press, 2006
6. Long S W. Survey and analysis: diversity of vascular plants associated with the Nanjing Ming City Wall: [master's thesis]. Nanjing: Nanjing Normal University, 2007
7. Architectural Design and Research Institute of Southeast University. The Conservation Master Plan for the Nanjing Ming City Wall (National Cultural Heritage), 2008

第二节 "围"与"穿"——明城墙的城门与道路
2.2 "Enclosure" and "Traverse" — Gates and Roads under the Nanjing Ming City Wall

陈 薇 Chen Wei
杨 俊 Yang Jun

1. 新中国成立前南京城墙的"围"与"穿"（图1）

1）明初蜿蜒城墙上开拓十三门，为呼应交通

明初朱元璋在南京定都后，经过一段时间发展诏谕国策："生齿日繁，守备日固，田野日辟，商贾日通。"即既要加强防守，又要广通贸易。因此，一方面在城墙建设上，于历代基础上增建、加高原有城墙，并新建城墙，形成不规则的蜿蜒城墙；另一方面，配合都城建设，改建城门以及增设瓮城共计13处，自宫城南向城市正南门依次顺时

1. "Enclosure" and "traverse" before the P.R.C. (Fig.1)

1) Thirteen gates opened to improve traffic

In the early Ming Dynasty, Emperor Zhu Yuanzhang made Nanjing the capital city. Thanks to the sustained development efforts for many years, the city started to enjoy "an increased population, enhanced fortification, more arable land, and more economic activities". Evidently, the ruler wanted a fortified defense system and prosperous economic activities at the same time. As a result, the city walls were expanded, rebuilt, thickened, and raised in height on the foundations built in the past dynasties, snaking along the contours of natural terrains. Meanwhile, the city gates were rebuilt and added with 13 fortresses. The gates were stretching clockwise from the south of the imperial palace to the middle of the southern loop of the walls as follows: Zhengyang, Tongji, Jubao, Sanshan, Shicheng, Qingliang, Dinghuai, Yifeng, Zhongfu, Jinchuan, Shence, Taiping, and Chaoyang. 48 new streets were paved up to facilitate traffic. The efforts led to the establishment of a nationwide traffic system centered on Nanjing, intertwined with smooth and wide horizontal and vertical roads. The development heralded a new historical chapter in Chinese history. Inner streets were connected to the major trunk roads stretching to the external part of the city via the city gates. The gates in the Nanjing City Wall were built at the sites carefully chosen. In the sections vulnerable to attacks, the gates were built with fortified fortresses having multiple enclosures, like Jubao Gate and Tongji Gate [1], serving the dual purposes of enhanced fortification and easy traffic.

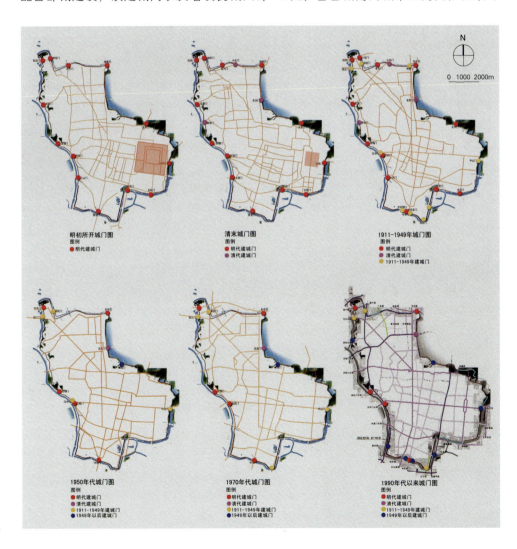

图 1　城墙城门增减与道路关系示意图
Fig.1　The relations between city gates and traffic system

针方向分别为：正阳门、通济门、聚宝门、三山门、石城门、清凉门、定淮门、仪凤门、钟阜门、金川门、神策门、太平门、朝阳门。同时辟建48条街道，建成了以南京为中心对外辐射的全国驿道网，纵横条陈、坦平宽阔，开辟了新的历史篇章，通过城门，市内大街也与向外辐射的主要大道相连。由于南京明代城门选址讲究，于通达难守处则设坚固的瓮城多重，如聚宝门和通济门[1]。从而较好地实现了坚固城防与便利交通并举的策略。

2）明末清初闭门封路仅存八门，是权宜之计

明代的十三门到清代有一定的变化，除了明末先后封闭的仪凤、钟阜和金川三座城门外，清初神策门、清凉门亦封闭，仅存八门。顺治十六年（1659年）复开仪凤、神策两门，但由于正阳与朝阳两座城门为清代驻城通道，一般百姓不得出入，故实为八门供居民进出。这种封闭大致是从由西而北的城门考虑，一方面由于明成祖迁都北京后南京对外城市交通需求减少，尤其北边地极僻静、人迹罕至[2]；另一方面则完全出于防御的需要，西侧临江，北边荒凉，难以把守。

3）清末至民国初城门增至十二，欲引路入城

1895年，两江总督张之洞开筑贯通南京城区南北的主干道"江宁马路"。1909年，开通贯穿全城的"宁省铁路"，复开金川门，引铁路入城，标志着南京近代交通的开始，也开创了明以来南京城墙与城市交通的新节点。此时城墙上先后开筑的草场门、海陵门、丰润门等也都与城防无关，主要满足城市交通发展的需求。尽管在20世纪上半叶战争中，城墙重新肩负起守卫的功能，但是，总体来说，新中国成立前南京城墙防御功能正在逐步退化，"围"与"穿"的矛盾开始。

2. 新中国成立后南京城墙的"围"与"穿"

1）1950年代中期对南京城墙有计划拆除

1949年在战火下幸存的南京城墙已破败不堪，1950年代中期开始进行有计划拆除。一是1954年，受到当时经济条件等方面的限制，在城墙年久失修、多处地段出现坍塌险情，同时基建急需用砖的情况下，南京市政府开始有计划地拆除城墙；二是1958年，全国"大跃进"风潮引致的"拆城大潮"，南京多处城门被拆除。这样南京城墙的围合界面多处被打破，"穿"的问题解决，但城墙保护岌岌可危。

2) Closing gates for expedience's sake

The thirteen gates saw some changes in number from the Ming Dynasty to the Qing Dynasty. In the late Ming Dynasty, three gates, including Yifeng, Zhongfu, and Jinchuan, were closed. In the early Ming Dynasty, two more gates (Shence and Qingliang) were closed. In 1659, Yifeng Gate and Shence Gate were reopened. However, the gates technically accessible to ordinary citizens remained 8 in number, as both Zhengyang Gate and Chaoyang Gate were the passages retained only for the military forces stationed in the city. The gates that had been closed mainly sat in the west and northern part of the city. The number of accessible gates in this part of the city was reduced to accommodate the fact that on the one hand, the city saw a reduced traffic volume after Emperor Ming Chengzu moved his capital to Beijing, making the northern part of the city a desolate place[2]. On the other hand, some gates had to be closed to make the west part (bordering a river), and the northern part (a desolate place) of the city easier to guard.

3) Increasing gates to improve traffic

In 1895, Zhang Zhidong, a governor taking care of the two river valleys, ordered to build a trunk road named Jiangning to run through the southern and northern part of the Nanjing City. In 1909, a citywide rail system was put into operation, which led to the reopening of Jinchuan Gate for the passage of the rails. The event heralded the beginning of a modern urban traffic system in Nanjing . The gate became a new node between the city walls and the urban traffic system. A range of new gates, including Caochang, Hailing, and Fengrun, were opened in the walls to meet traffic rather than defense needs, though the walls were employed to defend the city in the following civil wars and liberation wars in the 20th century. Overall speaking, Nanjing had a steadily reduced demand for the defensive functions of the walls, before the founding of the People's Republic of China. Consequentially, conflicts started to build up between closing and opening the gates in the walls.

2. "Enclosure" and "traverse" after the P.R.C.

1) Planned dismantling in the mid 1950s

In 1949, part of the city walls survived the wars was no longer in function. A planned dismantling was organized in the mid 1950s for two reasons: ① in 1954, the walls had collapsed or caved in in numerous places due to poor maintenance and economic constraints. At the same time, building new structures was short of bricks. In this context, authorities decided to dismantle the walls in a planned manner; ② in

2）1960—1970年代对南京城墙行掏墙防空

1960—1970年代中期，南京城墙多处因防空需要被掏作防空洞，如现中山门以北地段等仍存在防空洞及高处城墙上开设的透气风口。防空洞由于建造时也采用了现代建筑结构加固，目前没有发现因防空洞带来的城墙坍塌问题，但客观上由于防空洞的建造，改变了城墙原有的结构方式，特别是包山墙段的城墙下部山体的构造方式改变了，形成隐患。而且当时为了方便行走，也在城墙上开了一些小门进行穿越。

3）改革开放后破墙开路发展成增长趋势

虽然1970年代末已注重对南京城墙的考古发掘和保护，1982年7月5日，经南京市人大常委会第10次会议审议通过，同年7月29日南京市人民政府公布施行《南京市文物古迹保护管理办法》（其中第13条为南京明城墙制定）；1982年7月16日公布施行《南京市人民政府关于保护城墙的通告》；1982年8月2日公布施行《南京市人民政府关于保护城墙的通知》。但由于城市快速发展，破墙开洞已成增长趋势（图2）。这其中，有1990年新开的集庆通道，由东南大学潘谷西教授谨慎设计，坚持后开的通道不叫门，形式上也明确区分古今的差异，力保了城市交通与城墙保护的协调。但也有21世纪以来诸如察哈尔路西延、紫竹林路、芦席营路、鸣羊街实施或计划开墙破洞，结果于2007年因遭质疑而停工"深思"的实例。但总体来说，南京破墙开洞是慎重的，一些行而又止的"彷徨"，实质上体现出历史城市在保护和发展中的困惑。

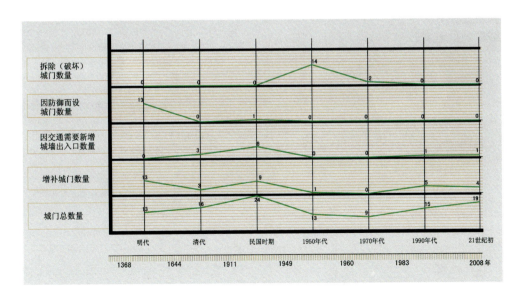

图2　南京明城墙各时期城门（洞）变化分析
Fig.2　Analysis of gates (doors) changing at different times

1958, a nationwide Great Leap Forward campaign fed a catalyst to dismantling the walls. Numerous gates were dismantled, allowing easier traffic in and out of the walls. The issue of "traverse" was solved for the time being at the sacrifice of protecting the walls.

2) Digging bomb shelters in the walls

In the 1960s and the mid 1970s, an array of bomb shelters were dug out in the walls to get prepared for an assumed war. Today, one still can see the bomb shelters in the northern wall section of Zhongshan Gate, and spot some air vent openings on the upper part of the walls. The walls built with bomb shelters have so far seen no cave-in or collapse, thanks to the reinforced structures applied when they were built. Unfortunately, bomb shelters, when built in the walls, have changed the original structures of the walls, especially the mountain part of the walls, left a hidden risk. Additionally, some small doors were opened in the walls at the time for the convenience of getting in and out of the walls.

3) Economic activities asking for more passages through the walls

Authorities has paid more attention to the archaeological excavation of ancient walls and associated protection, starting from the late 1970s. A by-law was adopted on July 5, 1982 at the 10th Nanjing Municipal People Congress Standing Committee to protect and take care of the cultural relics and historic sites in Nanjing. The Nanjing Municipal Government published and enforced the said by-law on July 29, 1982. In the by-law, Article 13 was written to protect the Nanjing Ming City Wall. Nanjing municipal authorities issued on July 16, 1982 a circular to protect the city walls. The circular went into effect on August 2 in the same year. However, the fast development of the city was asking for more passages through the walls (Fig. 2). For example, a Jiqing passage, designed by Prof. Pan Guxi at Southeast University, was opened in the walls. Prof. Pan insisted that the passages opened in the walls after the founding of the People's Republic of China shall not be referred to as "gates", as they are noticeably different from the old gates in form. The effort bridged a gap between improving traffic and protecting the walls. However, the city had ceased in 2007 a number of road projects that were supposed to open a new passage through the walls, including the west extension of Chaha'er Road, Zizulin Road, Luxiying Road, and Mingyang Avenue. Objectively speaking, municipal authorities are prudent to open a new passage through the walls. The hesitation shows the confusions municipal authorities had in keeping a historical city developing while protecting it.

3. 关于南京城墙"围"与"穿"的反思

区分南京城墙"围"与"穿"在 1949 年前后的两大时段，原因有二：

首先，两大时段的发展特征和动因存有差异。即自明代南京城墙形成基本格局后，在新中国成立前的漫长发展阶段，主要以"围"为主的城墙，是作为防御的一种主动态势存在的，"穿"为被动式；而新中国成立后（1949 年后）则以突破式的思路为主，"穿"为进行时，"围"是被动和静态的。这既反映出历史城市在中国不同阶段社会制度（封建制度和社会主义制度）下发生的根本变化，也反映出城墙在 1949 年后演变为文物或遗产的特质。

其次，两大时段理解城墙的性质、态度、做法不一样。我国关于文物保护的意识和相应保护手段开始较晚，1961 年才有文物保护管理相关规定出台。新中国成立前，保护的意识更是淡薄，南京城墙在民国时的改变，基本上没有将它作为文物进行思考。新中国成立后，虽然受政治、经济等因素的影响，并未对南京城墙进行有效保护，但将它作为文物的意识已逐渐形成。特别是中国改革开放后（1978 年后），已有了相应的保护法律法规。

但是总体来说，体现在城墙上"围"与"穿"的矛盾，特别是从近二、三十年城市高速发展以来形成的情形来看，还是因为不同领域沟通认识不同造成的，也是保护与发展在特定时期产生矛盾的必然反映。

同时，随着遗产保护意识的逐渐加强，关于和城墙相关的历史信息的完整性传承和真实性表达也日益成为保护的重点，包括近代（民国阶段）的遗存、历史上穿城形成的门洞、环境等（图 3）。这些复杂性都使得我们必须将南京城墙放在城市及其发展的平台上进行探讨（表 1），同时必须将其遗产保护的属性放在首位。

3. Some thoughts on "enclosure" and "traverse"

Theoretically, two periods, before and after 1949, constitute a watershed on keeping the city wall as it was, and on opening new passages to improve traffic.

First, the two periods are different in the pattern of development, as well as in the momentum behind the development. Specifically, the long period of development, from the Ming Dynasty where the city wall took its roots to the time before the founding of the People's Republic of China (1949), was featured with ambitions for breakthroughs. In this context, "traverse" was an action in the continuous tense, while "enclosure" a passive and static "door keeper", reflecting the fundamental changes a historical city has experienced under different social systems, and the changed nature of the city walls (cultural relics or heritages after 1949).

Second, people saw and acted differently on protecting and utilizing the walls. China started rather late to enhance people's awareness of protecting cultural relics, and to develop associated means of protection. China didn't have any by-laws available to protect cultural relics before 1961. People's awareness of cultural relics protection was even weaker before 1949. In the times of the Republic of China, the Nanjing City Wall had some changes but not as a cultural heritage. After 1949, people gradually enhanced their awareness to protect the walls, though the walls were not protected in a substantive manner due to political and economic reasons. Thanks to the reform and opening up campaign launched in 1978, the Nanjing City Wall has eventually been placed under the protection of applicable laws.

The conflicts between enclosure and traverse reflect the differences in understanding, especially in the past 20 and 30 years where Chinese cosmopolitan cities have witnessed an impressive development. It is also a natural reaction from the people who are keen on the protection and those who are enthusiastic about the development.

Meanwhile, the integrity of historical information and the authenticity of the city walls (including the relics from the Republican times), the gates, the tunnels, and the environment in different historical periods (Fig. 3) became the focus of protection, thanks to the increasingly enhanced protection awareness. The sophisticated nature of protecting the Nanjing City Wall has to be addressed in the context of a city and its development (Table 1).

图3 当代南京诸城门和道路关系一览
Fig.3 City gates and main roads in Nanjing today

表1 民国以来新开道路（铁路）穿越城墙处现状评估

分类		道路	相关城门或城门遗址	评估
道路直接通过城门	城市主干道	中山北路	挹江门	城墙的历史保护与城市交通发展得到良好的结合
		中山东路—中山门大街	中山门	
		集庆路—"集庆门"大街	"集庆门"（通道）	
	城市支路	玄武门路	玄武门	景观和抵达性较好，道路尺度与城门尺度相宜，一定程度上保留了城门的历史信息，同时也为城市景观增添了层次
		鸡鸣寺路	解放门	
道路跨越城墙，城门闲置一侧		清凉门大街—清凉门桥—广州路	清凉门	为历史城墙保护与城市交通协调发展提供了新方法，城门成为路侧景观
道路位于城门城墙遗址之上	明代遗址	建宁路	仪凤门和钟阜门遗址	遗址的覆盖、历史信息的流失、历史可读性的断裂，都是这些道路在修建过程中带来的问题
		定淮门大街—模范西路	定淮门遗址	
		水西门大街—升州路	三山门遗址	
		龙蟠中路	通济门遗址	
		御道街	正阳门遗址	
		龙蟠路	太平门遗址	
		金川门外铁路北街	金川门遗址	
	清代遗址	草场门大街—北京西路	草场门遗址	城墙历史信息有一定保留，但真实性受到损害
		钟阜路	小北门遗址	
	民国以后	汉中门大街—汉中路	汉中门遗址	
		江宁路—晨光路	雨花门遗址	
		中华路—雨花路	中华东、西门	
		新民路	新民门遗址	
		长乐路	武定门	
		中央北路—中央路	中央门遗址	
道路通过缺口穿越城墙	城市主干道	后标营路—锦湖路	—	城墙真实性、完整性、延续性都受到破坏
		光华东街—紫金路		
		察哈尔路西延		
	城市支路	广东路	—	城墙真实性、完整性、延续性都受到破坏
		富贵巷		

Table 1 New road and rail passages through the walls since the Republican times

Type		Roads	Associated gates or relics sessment	Assessment
Direct passing through	Trunk Roads	Zhongshan Rd. N.	Yijiang Gate	Fine combination of wall protection and traffic improvement
		Zhongshan Rd. E. – Zhongshanmen Ave.	Zhongshan Gate	
		Jiqing Rd.– Jiqingmen Ave.	Jiqing Gate (passage)	
	Branches	Xuanwumen Rd.	Xuanwu Gate	Fine landscape and accessibility, compatible size for both roads and gates, retaining some historical information while enriching the landscape
		Jimingsi Rd.	Jiefang Gate	
Roads striding across the walls, with the gate idled		Qingliangmen Ave.– Qingliangmen Bridge –Guangzhou Rd.	Qingliang Gate	A new approach to coordinate the wall protection and traffic improvement, making the gate a roadside landscape
Roads built on the top of the gates or wall relics	Ming relics	Jianning Rd.	Remains of Yigeng Gate and Zhongfu Gate	Covering the remains, loss of historical information, and breaking up a readable historical line, all these are the problems appeared in building a traversing road
		Dinghuaimen Ave.– Mofanxi Rd.	Remains of Dinghuai gate	
		Shuiximen Ave. –Shengzhou Rd.	Remains of Sanshan Gate	
		Longpan Rd. Middle	Remains of Tongji Gate	
		Yudao St.	Remains of Zhengyang Gate	
		Longpan Rd.	Remains of Taiping Gate	
		Jinchuanmenwai Tielu St. N.	Remains of Jinchuan Gate	
	Qing relics	Caochangmen Ave. –Beijing Rd. W.	Remains of Caochang Gate	Retaining some historical information with compromised authenticity
		Zhongfu Rd.	Remains of Xiaobei Gate	
	After ROC	Hanzhongmen Ave.– Hanzhong Rd.	Remains of Hanzhong Gate	
		Jiangning Rd.–Chenguang Rd.	Remains of Yuhua Gate	
		Zhonghua Rd. –Yuhua Rd.	Zhonghua Gates, E. & W.	
		Xinmin Rd.	Ruins of Xinmin Gate	
		Changle Rd.	Wuding Gate	
		Zhongyang Rd. N. –Zhongyang Rd.	Ruins of Zhongyang Gate	
Roads traversing the walls through indents	Trunk Roads	Houbiaoying Rd.–Jinhu Rd.	—	Jeopardized authenticity, integrity, and continuity of the walls
		Guanghua Rd. E. –Zijin Rd.		
		Cahaer Rd. W. Exten.		
	Branches	Guangdong Rd.	—	Jeopardized authenticity, integrity, and continuity of the walls
		Fugui Rd.		

4. 解决南京城墙"围"与"穿"矛盾的探讨

1）从整体的观念入手，认识南京诸城门和相关道路的关系和价值

首先，是对南京城门和通道进行价值评估，并参照世界遗产的真实性、完整性和延续性的要求开展，从而依此对城门（通道）在价值上分出等级。其次，对南京和诸城门（通道）联系的道路进行价值评估，尤其重点考察南京在都城建设时期形成的重要的、对南京格局有重要影响的道路，如中华路、御道街、中山大道（中山北路、中山路、中山东路、陵园路）等。在此基础上，形成最具重要价值的城门（包括遗址）和重要道路的相关联系。依此类推，可以得到城门和道路作为遗产的一张网络等级图（图4），在"围"和"穿"的节点上，形成解决问题的判断基础。

4. Potential solutions to "enclosure" and "traverse"

1) Understand the linkage between the gates and roads and associated values as a whole

First, an assessment shall be made to understand the values of gates and passages, based on the criteria of authenticity, integrity, and continuity. Second, Each gate or passage shall be graded according to its values. Efforts shall be made to evaluate the traffic utilities of each gate and passage, especially its contributions to the trunk roads, including Zhonghua Road, Yudao Street, and Zhongshan Avenue (Zhongshan Road N., E., and Lingyuan Road), defining the accessibility between the gates (including the remains) having most important values and major roads. In doing so, one can work out a map to show the grated values of gates and their contributions to the roads, as a heritage (Fig. 4). This will serve as a basis to judge the rationality of pro-enclosure or pro-traverse.

图4 南京城门和道路作为遗产的网络等级分析图
Fig.4 Analysis of grades of city gates and historical roads

2）在这个判断基础的平台上，为解决由于城市不断发展带来的交通与城墙的"围"与"穿"的矛盾，建立基本原则

对于重要历史道路和保护较好的城门节点形成的道路网，建议严格保护，基本不作为城市交通发展的线路，虽然其中有些道路在历史上是宽阔的主要道路；反之，今天或将来可以拓展或延伸的道路，从历史上不重要的、价值等级最低的开始选择。这种成逆反的关系也可以依此类推，即遗产价值比较低的道路以及在相应城墙节点上已不存遗迹的路线，可以作为道路发展的参考。

3）在具体做法上，解决南京城墙和道路"围"与"穿"的关系，提出几种借鉴方式

（1）"富贵山"平交隧道模式

富贵山是南京紫金山的龙头，也是自然山体比较靠近历史城市的部分，在明代，富贵山是明宫殿轴线出城北延的终点，形成背倚之势，也成为后来明清北京宫殿背靠镇山的形制先河，因此对富贵山的山峰和轮廓线的保护非常重要。而南京历史城市和北部区域的联系又十分必要，因此富贵山隧道形成道路和富贵山脚的平交通道模式（图5、图6）。由于富贵山有足够的高度，所以这种模式既解决了交通，同时不破坏原来城墙遗址的构造，也没有影响山体及轮廓线。而南京城墙的一大特点就是因地制宜而形成许多段骑山、架山的筑城方式，如果在"穿"的选择上，选择在骑山和架山的一些地段，在有足够的山体高度保证下，采用"富贵山"通道模式，便能在保护城墙不破坏基础、不涉及墙体的结构和外观的情形下，有效解决道路的

2) Establish a basic principle to address pro-enclosure and pro-traverse, based on the said judgment

A special road network made up of major historical roads and relatively well preserved city gates shall be placed under a strict protection, not subject to the future call of traffic improvements, though some of the roads, historically, used to be a wide major trunk line. The roads to be built or extended in the future shall be the one with the lowest historical importance or values. The principle can be applied accordingly. For example, the roads with a low heritage value and traffics line that will pass through a site of the city wall having no traces of relics can be considered to tap up in the future road development.

3) Alternatives for addressing pro-enclosure and pro-traverse

(1) Mount Fugui model

Mount Fugui is the head of Zijin Mountain in Nanjing. It is also a historical part of the city sitting near the natural mountains. In the Ming Dynasty, Mount Fugui was an external terminal that the axial line of the Imperial Palace would reach in the north. It set an example to build an imperial palace against the mountains, which was later copied by emperors in the Ming and Qing dynasties when building their imperial palaces in Beijing. In this context, it is extremely important to protect the peaks and contours of Mount Fugui. Taking into account the fact that it is necessary to improve the traffic between the historical and the

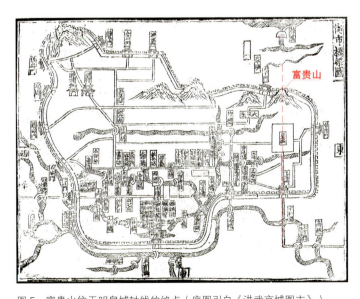

图5 富贵山位于明皇城轴线的终点（底图引自《洪武京城图志》）
Fig.5 Mount Fugui at the end of the imperial axis in the Ming Nanjing (from: *Hongwu Jingcheng Tu Zhi*)

图6 今富贵山隧道
Fig.6 Tunnel running through Mount Fugui today

发展问题。

（2）隧道下穿模式

在解决穿越城墙时，这是一种常见的思路和模式。问题有两方面，一是要充分保证城墙基础不受影响，二是"入地"和"出地"要有足够的坡道长度，所以在选择路线时要精心、慎重，同时施工方案要充分论证，以保证城墙安全不受到影响。南京的"通济门"隧道应该属于这种类型（图7、图8），只是通济门比较特殊，隧道入口选择也应更加考究。通济门在古代为交通要道，《南都察院志》称为"冲要"，通济门还是南京当时最大的内瓮城，为交通要道，可惜1950年代被拆除，地面无存。2002年，随着建设需求，被动考古进行过遗址勘探，发现有1~5层条石不等的城墙西垣基础，残长25.8m，以及城墙的土芯、包砖等。这些历史真实信息在后来进行通济门下穿隧道建设时，没有保留和标识出来，以至于现在世人无从知晓，甚为遗憾。但下穿式隧道对于南京历史文化名城的城墙保护十分必要，在解决"围"与"穿"的关系时，是我们编制《全国重点文物保护单位南京明城墙保护总体规划》时倡导的一种方式。

（3）局部环路模式

南京城墙比较特殊，因地制宜建设，从而形成平面和高度上的不规则形态。突出表现在：自西而北依山而建，筑墙有包山墙、架山墙、骑山墙及于平地高耸的城墙结合的多种形式（图9、图10）；而自东而南由于地势平缓又水系充沛，所以顺

northern part of the city, it is desirable to build a tunnel road running through Mount Fugui and joining the road at the foot of Mount Fugui (Fig. 5, Fig. 6). Thanks to the height of Mount Fugui, the road design proposed above makes a desirable solution to improving traffic without compromising the structure of the wall relics or affecting the mountain and its contours. One of the major features enjoyed by the Nanjing City Wall is it was built borrowing the contours of local topography, and allowing the walls sitting across or over the mountains. When traversing a city wall built on the mountains with a desired height, the Mount Fugui Model can be applied to address the road issue without compromising the foundation, structure, and outlook of the old city walls.

(2) Tunnel model

Tunneling is an approach frequently employed to allow the road to traverse the walls. When building a tunnel, one has to take into account two issues: first, a design shall be made without affecting the foundation of the walls; and second, a sufficient slope length shall be secured for both in and out of the tunnel. Additionally, the route shall be selected in a careful and prudent manner, with a thoroughly discussed and reviewed work plan, ensuring the safety of the walls. The tunnel built under Tongji Gate makes a good example (Fig. 7, Fig. 8). The tunnel was built with a special entrance, taking into account the special nature of the gate. In ancient times, Tongji Gate was a busy juncture, as it was mentioned in *Nan Du Cha Yuan Zhi*. The gate also had the largest internal fortress in the city. It was dismantled in the 1950s, left no traces

图7 通济门瓮城旧影（引自：《古城一瞬间》）
Fig.7 Old picture of Tongji Gate Fortress (from: *Gucheng Yishunjian*)

图8 今通济门下穿隧道
Fig.8 Tunnel named Tongji Gate today

势而建，且多用砖石砌（图11、图12）。这样的情形不同于平原城市的城墙相对独立的状态，南京城墙与地形和地势有着密不可分的关系，这也增加了在道路组织中的难度。尤其在内侧，形成环路几乎没有必要，也不可行。目前上述两种方式比较适用于城北，而于城南比较适宜形成局部内环路或内外平行路以成局部外环路，以便进行引导和疏解，在有效利用历史形成的门和通道的同时，在不另行增加门道的情形下，解决"围"与"穿"的问题。同时，在城墙边开辟道路，并与绿化隔离带结合，能够有利于维护城墙的环境和本体保护，在这次保护规划中，我们还对环路车行道路等级规定为不得高于支路，对通行的车辆进行控制（以小车为主），以减少由于振动给城墙带来的隐患，现在部分实施地段效果较好（图13）。

on the ground. In 2002, a passive archaeological investigation was made upon the call of construction activities. The investigation led to the discovery of the west foundation of the city walls made up of stone slabs up to five layers, with a residual length at 25.8m. The investigation also unearthed some earth cores and bricks. The historical information unveiled in the investigation was, unfortunately, not preserved nor marked in the course of building the tunnel traveling under the remains. As a result, nobody knows the details of the historical information uncovered. When preparing the conservation master plan for the Ming City Wall, we encourage people to apply underground tunneling as an effective means to address the enclosure and traverse issue.

(3) Local loops

In Nanjing, the city walls were built borrowing the contours of topography. As a result, the walls are irregular in both shape and height. For example, the section running from the west to the north was built against the mountains, though in diverse forms, including the walls built to enclose, across, or ride the mountains, and the walls simply erected from the ground(Fig.9, Fig.10). Meanwhile, the section stretching from the east to the south was built in an area with gentle topography and rich water ways. The walls, therefore, were built mainly with rocks along the smooth contours of topography (Fig.11, Fig.12). However, such design was different from the walls built in a plain city that was relatively an independent structure. In Nanjing, the city walls were built closely associated with topography, which made traverse more sophisticated. For example, it is meaningless and infeasible to build a belt road inside the walls. The aforesaid two alternatives are desirable for the northern part of the city. However, in the southern part of the city, it is more desirable to build a local belt road, or a road system running in parallel inside and outside of the walls. It is desirable to improve traffic taking advantage of the existing gates and passages rather than adding new gates or passages. Meanwhile, the new roads built along the city walls shall be separated by a greenery belt, protecting both the walls and environment. In the protection plan, the belt road is defined with a grade not higher than branch roads, mainly for sedan cars, in an attempt to reduce the vibration effects on the walls. The practice has been proved effective in the selected roads (Fig. 13).

图 9　清凉山段包山墙
Fig.9　City wall built to enclose the Mount Qingliang

图 10 石头城段架山墙
Fig.10 City wall built to across the Mount Stone

图 11 琵琶湖段砖砌城墙
Fig.11 City wall built by bricks beside the Pipa Lake

图 12 中华门段石砌城墙
Fig.12 City wall built with rocks in Zhonghua Gate section

图 13 台城段内环道路及其环境
Fig.13 Loop and environment from Taicheng view

注释

1. "聚宝门，建有内瓮城三座，设有瓮洞（今人称藏兵洞）二十七个，门垣共四道。"
   "通济门，建有内瓮城三座，内设瓮洞若干，门垣共四道。"见南京市文化局（市文物局），中国民主同盟南京市委员会，杨新华主编．南京明城墙．南京：南京大学出版社，2006：39
2. "鸡鸣寺之阴，近台城一带，有胥家大塘，蓄水冬夏不涸，环塘有田近百亩……地极僻静，人迹罕至。"见南京市文化局（市文物局），中国民主同盟南京市委员会，杨新华主编．南京明城墙．南京：南京大学出版社，2006：12
   "查神策门口，大路仅宽三尺有奇，街之西即系低洼处。由神策门而西为钟阜、金川诸门，久经闭塞，城外沿城一带都是荒地……"（清）甘熙．白下琐言．南京：南京出版社，2007：168

参考书目

1. 《明史》卷二百二十二，列传第一百十
2. （清）甘熙．白下琐言．南京：南京出版社，2007
3. 江苏省南京市公路管理处史志编审委员．南京古代道路史．南京：江苏科学技术出版社，1989
4. 南京市文化局（市文物局），中国民主同盟南京市委员会，杨新华主编．南京明城墙．南京：南京大学出版社，2006
5. 东南大学建筑设计研究院．全国重点文物保护单位南京明城墙保护总体规划，2008

Notes

1. "Jubao Gate was built with an internal fortress with three enclosures, 27 vaults, and 4 arches." "Tongji Gate was built with an internal fortress with three enclosures, several vaults, and 4 arches." Nanjing Municipal Culture Burean, etc. ed. *Nanjing Ming Chengqiang* (The Nanjing Ming City Wall). Nanjing: Nanjing University Press, 2006: 39
2. "In the north of Jiming Temple, and near Taicheng, there was a large pond, never dried up in both winters and summers. There were nearly a hundred mu of land surrounding the pond. The area is a desolate place, rarely visited. " Nanjing Municipal Culture Burean, etc. ed. *Nanjing Ming Chengqiang* (The Nanjing Ming City Wall). Nanjing: Nanjing University Press, 2006: 12
   "Shence Gate gave way to a road 1 meter wide, with a low land in the west. In the west of Shence Gate stood Zhongfu Gate and Jinchuan Gate that have been blocked for a long time. One can see wildness everywhere in this part of the city." Gan X (Qing Dynasty). *Baixia Suo Yan* (Folks' Miscellanea). Nanjing: Nanjing Press, 2007:168

Reference

1. *Ming shi* (History of the Ming Dynasty), Vol.222, Biography 110
2. Gan X (Qing Dynasty). *Baixia Suo Yan* (Folks' Miscellanea). Nanjing: Nanjing Press, 2007
3. Nanjing Municipal Road Administration. *Nanjing Gudai Daolu Shi* (History of Ancient Roads in Nanjing). Nanjing: Jiangsu Science and Technology Press, 1989
4. Nanjing Municipal Culture Burean, etc. ed. *Nanjing Ming Chengqiang* (The Nanjing Ming City Wall). Nanjing: Nanjing University Press, 2006
5. Architectural Design and Research Institate of Southeast University. The consevation Master Plan for the Nanjing Ming City Wall (National Cultural Heritage),2008

第三节　奥勒良城墙和城市肌理的关系
2.3　The Relation between the Aurelian Walls and the Urban Fabric

亚历桑德拉·德·塞萨里斯　Alessandra de Cesaris

在意大利及全世界的城市之中，奥勒良城墙是少数未被拆除的城墙之一（图1）。这给我们提供了一个分析城墙及其相关城市价值以及现代城市生长方式的机会。受制于现存实体的限制形成的城市发展，也使得这个实体越来越远离它原初的价值。

我们的研究对象是一个周长为约19 km的环形城墙，是按照奥勒良的命令建造的，用以抵御蛮族的入侵。它的建设过程相当匆忙，仅仅持续了三年时间。实际上，在这座城市的历史中，该城墙从未真正用于防御，而是承担了城市象征的角色（图2、图3），而它的另一个重要作用则是定义了城市的形态（forma urbis）。

The Aurelian Walls are amongst the few city walls in Italy, and the world, not to have been demolished(Fig.1). This offers us an opportunity to analyze the architectural-urban value of the walls and the methods of growth of the modern city. (A growth conditioned by the physical presence of a limit that, what is more), has lost its original value. We are speaking of a ring of walls measuring some 19km in length, constructed in great haste – only three years – by Aurelius to defend the city against invasion by the Barbarians. In reality, in the history of the city, the Walls never played a truly defensive role, but rather assumed an important symbolic value(Fig.2, Fig.3) and a crucial function in defining the forma urbis of the city.

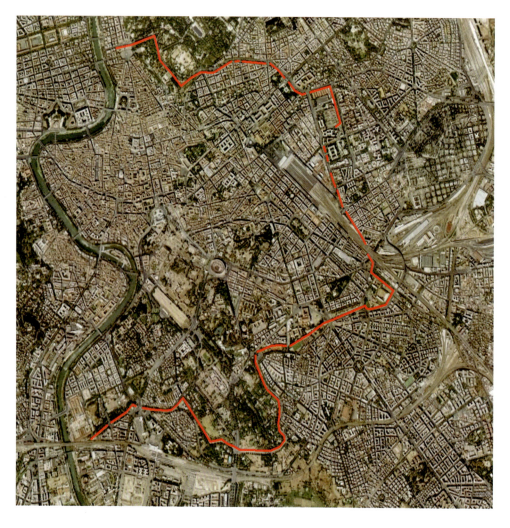

图1　奥勒良城墙
Fig.1　The Aurelian Walls

第二章　城墙、景观与城市肌理　2 – City Walls, Landscape and Urban Fabric

图 2　切斯提乌斯金字塔
Fig.2　Pyramid of Cestius

图 3　坎帕尼亚路
Fig.3　Via Campania

实际上，城墙和穿过城门的众多执政官道路（Consular Road）一起，一方面成为限制和定义这座历史城市的元素；另一方面，在定义这座当代城市结构的过程中扮演着重要的角色。由一圈城墙外放射式执政官道路的相互连接形成外圈的环城公路（GRA）——一条自 1950 年代开始建造的环形高速公路，长约 70 km。

在欧洲的一些主要城市中，拆除城墙代表着一次改造空间的机会，用于新建公共服务设施。从更广泛的角度来说，拆除城墙提供了一次城市形态现代化的契机。事实上，城墙曾经占用的区域可以用于兴建公园、花园、林荫步道、服务设施、博物馆、剧院、火车站、机动车道路和铁路。维也纳利用这个环形区域创建了一组城市基础设施，服务于新的社区。巴黎在 20 世纪初开始在梯也尔城墙（Thiers Wall）所在的区域建设廉价住房(HBM, Habitations Bon Marché)。柏林利用拆除城墙所产生的地面面积，建了一条高架有轨电车线路 (S Bahn)。那些小一些的城市，例如博洛尼亚和佛罗伦萨，也把拆除城墙看作是一个重新考虑未来城市结构的机会：消除了城墙的限制，新的扩张就可以没有障碍地进行规划了。

罗马在近几百年的发展过程中，反映出一种很强的趋势：抵制变革。在设计这座首都城市的未来时，它放弃了城市转型的激进方案，选择适应，与城墙友好并存。

In fact, the walls, together with the Consular Roads that pass through its gates, on the one hand represented the element that establishes confines and identifies the historical city; on the other hand, they have played an anything but secondary role in defining the structure of the contemporary city. The ring of city walls reverberates on the exterior and, based on the radial pattern of the historical Consular Roads, is moved all the way out to the G.R.A – Grande Raccordo Anulare, the high-speed ring road, approxi-mately 70km in length, constructed beginning in the 1950s.

In Europe's primary cities, the demolition of city walls represented an opportunity to reclaim space for the construction of new services and, in more general terms, provided an occasion to modernize the forma urbis. In fact, areas once occupied by city walls were used to create parks, gardens, tree-lined promenades, services, museums, theatres, railway stations, vehicular roads and rail lines. The city of Vienna used the ring to locate a series of fundamental urban services for a new society; in the early 20th century Paris began constructing the Habitations Bon Marché (HBM) in the area of the Thiers Wall;

不仅如此，城墙并没有阻碍城市的发展，不像其他城市那样因城墙内人口稠密而寻找新的空地。实际上，在19世纪末，罗马以城内有大量空地和可用地而自豪，尤其是一系列贵族别墅和花园。此外，从建造一开始，奥勒良城墙就被赋予了某种民用性的特性，从来没有呈现出其他城墙防御结构所暗含的纪念价值。这归因于城墙的尺度和缺少护城河的设计，最重要的是，它们有一种可以从某种意义上来说"混杂的"构筑物的特点：在建造过程中，出于节约时间和成本的目的，它们吸收了已经存在的一些纪念物和建筑物（图2，图4～图7）。

这种兼容并包的品质无疑是奥勒良城墙最为特殊的性格之一（图8）。

图4　卡斯特兰塞圆形剧场（a）
Fig.4　Castrense Amphitheatrer (a)

图5　卡斯特兰塞圆形剧场（b）
Fig.5　Castrense Amphitheater (b)

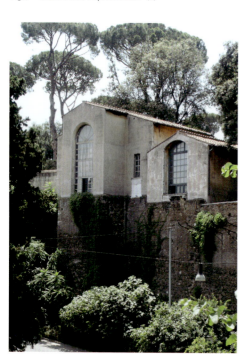

图6　托尔托城墙——美第奇别墅
Fig.6　Muro Torto – Villa Medici

图7　桑加罗堡
Fig.7　Bastione di Sangallo

Berlin utilized the area resulting from the demolition of its walls to construct an elevated rail line (S Bahn). Minor cities such as Bologna and Florence also saw the demolition of their city walls as an occasion to reconsider the structure of the future city where the absence of a limit allowed for the obstacle-free planning of new expansions.

When designing the future of the capital city, Rome, which during the recent centuries of its existence has demonstrated a strong resistance towards change, renounced radical works of urban transformation and chose to adapt to living with the defensive walls. What is more, the walls did not constitute an obstacle to development, as in other cities that are densely inhabited inside the walls and searching for open land. In fact, at the end of the 19th century Rome boasted a vast quantity of void areas and available lands inside the city walls, in particular a series of patrician villas and gardens. What is more, since their construction the Aurelian Walls were characterized by a certain domesticity and never assumed the monumental value that connotes other defensive wall structures. This is a result of their scale, the absence of a moat and, above all, their characteristic of being a construction that is, in a certain sense,

第二章 城墙、景观与城市肌理　2 – City Walls, Landscape and Urban Fabric

从城墙建造的时期开始，城墙的布局就显示出战略决策与经济选择之间的妥协。据估计，大约有十分之一的城墙是由整合原有构筑物而形成的：例如切斯提乌斯金字塔（Pyramid of Cestius）（图2）、禁卫军兵营（Castra Praetoria）、卡斯特兰塞圆形剧场（Castrense Amphitheater）（图4、图5）、诺曼塔纳路和萨拉利亚路之间的一些陵墓，以及马尔乔（Marcio）与克劳狄（Claudio）输水道的一部分。

在历史的时间长河中，这座城市在城墙的周围和墙顶上生长，对城墙进行新陈代谢、再利用甚至占用，创建了住所、办公室、博物馆、小圣堂。这些建筑物就像是被写入城墙的基因序列似的。拉古齐尼（Raguzzini）1750 年设计的詹蒂利 – 多米尼奇（Gentili-Dominici）别墅（图9），在城墙和费利切（Felice）输水道之间寻找空间，吸收了一个防御塔楼并把一部分输水道转化成了敞廊。不仅如此，在花园里，水

"promiscuous" : during their erection, in order to reduce time and cost, they absorbed existing monuments and buildings(Fig.2, Fig.4 ~ Fig.7).
This quality of inclusiveness undoubtedly remains one of the most peculiar characteristics of the Aurelian Walls(Fig.8).
Since the era of their construction, their layout represented a compromise between strategic decisions and economic choices; it is estimated that approximately one tenth of the walls were constructed by incorporating existing structures: the Pyramid of Cestius(Fig.2), Castra Praetoria, the Castrense Amphitheater(Fig.4, Fig.5), a number of sepulchres situated between the Via Nomentana and the Via Salaria and sections of the Marcio and Claudio aqueducts.

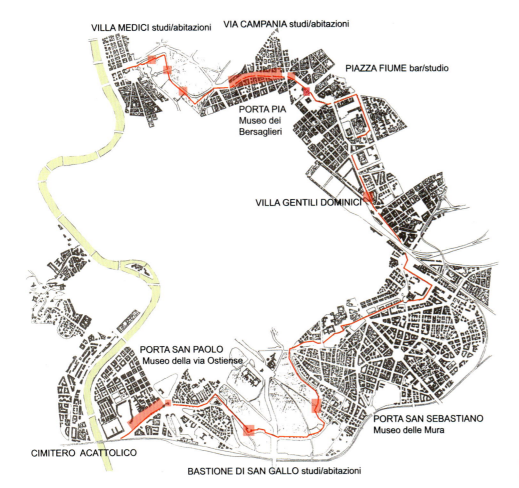

图8　容包的城墙 / 居住的城墙
Fig.8　Inclusive walls / Inhabitable walls

道的出口紧靠着城墙，刻入墙体内部。在人民广场，瓦拉迪耶（Valadier）1822年在设计海关大楼和兵营的时候，不动声色地把奥勒良城墙和塔楼整合到新建筑的北翼中。而在几个世纪以前，桑加罗接受保罗三世的委托设计建造阿尔代阿提诺堡时，整合了一个中世纪的塔楼。今天这个堡垒的内部则陈列着拆除博尔戈区的"骨架"时收集到的古代遗物。1894年，公共教育部长将位于坎帕尼亚路（Via Campania）的39号塔楼委托给雕塑家弗朗西斯科·兰多内（Francesco Randone），他将其改造为一个烧制陶瓷砖的窑，用于免费学校的艺术教育。几个世纪以前的1672年，13、14和15号塔楼被当作红衣主教费德里科·鲍罗麦欧（Cardinal Federico Borromeo）的私人书房。在1950年代，城墙内可居住部分曾被托付给罗马市政府，当作艺术家的工作室。现在庇亚门是狙击兵历史博物馆的所在地，圣塞瓦斯蒂安门容纳着城墙博物馆，而圣保罗门成了奥斯提安塞路博物馆。

城墙多用并且可居住。城墙从其建造开始，就被证实可以适应不规则的地形系统，根据沿途的各种障碍进行调整，改变自身的形式和功能。

Over the course of its history the city grew around and on top of the walls, metabolizing, reusing and appropriating them, creating dwellings, offices, museums, sacred aedicules and mascheroni, as if they were written in its genetic code. The Villa Gentili-Dominici(Fig.9), attributed to Raguzzini (1750), winds its way between the walls and the Felice Aqueduct, absorbing a defensive tower and transforming a part of the aqueduct into a loggia; in the garden, moreover, the nymphaeum is set against the walls, carving into them. In Piazza del Popolo, when designing the Customs House and the Barracks (1822) Valadier incorporated the Aurelian Walls and towers within the north wing of the new building with great nonchalance. Centuries earlier, Sangallo absorbed a medieval tower when constructing the defensive bastion commissioned by Paul III. Today, their interior of the bastion is filled with the remains of the demolition of the Spina di Borgo. In 1894, the Minister of Public Education entrusted the XXXIX Tower in Via Campania to the sculptor Francesco Randone, who used it to create an oven for baking ceramic tiles for the Scuola gratuita d'Arte Educatrice. Centuries earlier (1672), towers 13, 14 & 15 were occupied by the private study of Cardinal Federico Borromeo. During the 1950s, the inhabitable portions inside the walls were entrusted to the city of Rome as artists' studies. The Porta Pia is now home to the Museo Storico dei Bersaglieri, while Porta San Sebastiano hosts the Museo delle Mura and Porta San Paolo the Museo della via Ostiense .

The walls are inclusive, inhabited and inhabitable and, since their origins, have proven capable of adapting to the irregularity of the topographic system, to

图9　詹蒂利－多米尼奇别墅
Fig.9　Villa Gentili-Dominici

在这段历史中，标志着从执政官道路进入城市的入口的城门，以及每隔 30 m 出现的防御塔楼，确定了城墙的节奏。这座现代城市则以一种相当无序的方式在城墙内外两侧被组织和生长起来。

现在，人们可以识别出与城墙的轨迹相连、一系列带有强烈自治特点的系统和组成部分，譬如各个历史时期遗留下来的公园和历史别墅系统、基础设施系统、城市公共服务系统、居住系统以及纪念性建筑与特殊元素系统。它们基本都分布在城墙周界的内侧（图 10）。

城墙在与其他系统相交叉关联的时候，呈现出多重角色、象征意义、隐喻意味。

1. 绿地系统：波各赛别墅（Villa Borghese）和阿皮亚古道考古公园（Appia Antica Park）

这两个区域分别位于城市的北部和南部，城墙在该区域中具有很强的景观价值。由于没有建成区，人们可以依稀看到它们曾经与城墙外的罗马乡村建立起来的历史关系。

沿着托尔托城墙（Muro Torto），我们可以再次发现这座城墙的兼容并包的特点，

impediments along their path, modifying form and function.

In the midst of this history, whose rhythm is defined by the gates that mark the entrances to the city from the Consular Roads and the defensive towers located every 30m, the modern city is organized and grows, inside and outside, in a rather disorderly manner.

It is now possible to recognize a series of systems and urban sectors with a strong autonomy, connected to the path of the walls: the system of parks and historic villas, the infrastructural system, the system of public urban services, the residential system and the system of monumental and specific elements from different periods in history, situated primarily inside the perimeter of the walls(Fig.10).

The walls assume different roles, symbolic values and figurative meanings in relation to the different systems crossed.

1. The natural system: the Villa Borghese and the Appia Antica Park

In these two sectors, situated in the northern and southern parts of the city, the walls assume a strong

美第奇别墅—托尔托城墙
Villa Medici – Muro Torto

萨拉利亚路—阜姆广场
Via Salaria – Piazza Fiume

萨拉利亚路—阜姆广场
Via Salaria – Piazza Fiume

坎帕尼亚路
Via Campania

坎帕尼亚路
Via Campania

新教墓地
Cimitero Acattolico

图 10　城墙沿线的元素
Fig.10　Elements along the walls

也就是根据与它所跨越的不同环境而改变。在这里，城墙也发挥着美第奇别墅高地花园的挡土墙的功能，而很多塔楼依然被居住在法兰西学院的艺术家们当作工作室。

在南段，沿着阿皮亚古道考古公园的边缘，城墙保持了它原有的防御品质。该区域超越了其他任何地区，提供了城墙—城市—领土三者之间原始关系的概念。此处城墙仍然像一个被孤立的元素，也就是一个考古学的构筑物，和它的周边空地形成了鲜明的反差，呈现出一种与周边环境分离的形而上学的姿态。

2. 基础设施与交通系统（图11）

城墙与执政官道路所呈现的"环状—放射状"的结构，在城市的公路和铁路交通组织方面依然发挥着决定性的作用，继续代表着这座当代城市的结构骨架。机动交通的第一个环路沿着城墙的边缘发展起来，从未像其他城市规划的那样成为一条真正的林荫大道。道路基本上沿着城墙的外侧，除了在圣洛伦佐和中央火车站附近的道路是在内侧。这种颠倒的布局让人感觉到城墙的外部就像城墙的内部一样，而

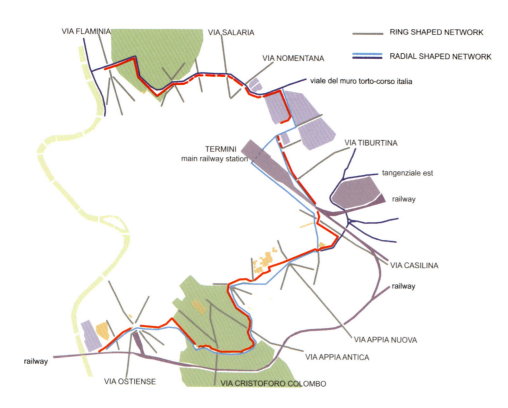

图11 奥勒良城墙与基础设施及交通系统
Fig.11 The Aurelian Walls and the system of infrastructure and transport

landscape value. The absence of built areas allows for a glimpse of the historical relationship they once established with the landscape of the Campagna Romana, outside of the city walls.

Along the Muro Torto, confirming the characteristics of an inclusive ring of walls that transforms in relation to the different contexts crossed, the walls also function as a retaining structure for the hanging gardens of the Villa Medici, while a number of towers are still utilized as studios for artists in residence at the French Academy.

In the southern sector, along the edges of the Appia Antica Park, the walls maintain the original qualities of a defensive ring. This sector, more than elsewhere, offers an idea of the original relationship between wall–city–territory. The walls continue to resemble an isolated element, an archaeological structure, in opposition to the surrounding void space, in a condition of metaphysical alienation from context.

2. The system of infrastructure and transport (Fig.11)

The radial–annular structure of the walls and Consular Roads still plays a decisive role in the organisation of road and rail transport and continues to represent the structural backbone of the contemporary city. A first ring of vehicular transport develops along the edge of the walls, without ever becoming a true boulevard, as those planned in many other cities. The road runs primarily along the external perimeter, with the exception of the route in proximity to San Lorenzo and the Termini Rail Station. The condition of inversion is such that the exterior of the walls feel like an interior and vice versa.

The annular structure of the walls, as mentioned, is reflected initially in the anello ferroviario (rail ring) and further out in the Grande Raccordo Anulare, which currently represents the edge of the contemporary city.

The radial system, instead, is structured by the system of the historic Consular Roads with their access gates, and by the rail lines that lead to the terminus stations of Ostiense and Termini, the latter being one of the most important national stations, realized inside the city walls.

At the intersections between the radial roads and the walls we find the most evident contradictions between historical pre-existences and the structure of the contemporary city.

In a number of sectors the opening of new gates

内部又像外部。

城墙的环状结构，正如所提到的那样，最初在铁路环线中也反映出来，后来在环城公路中以更向外围扩展的一圈反映出来，环城公路目前代表了这座当代城市的边界。

与之相反的是，放射状系统是由古老的执政官道路和道路上的城门以及通往奥斯提安塞火车站和中央火车站的铁路线形成的，后者建在城墙之内，是最重要的国家火车站之一。

在放射状道路和城墙的交接处，我们发现在历史遗存和当代城市的结构之间存在着最明显的冲突。

在很多地段，新建城门的开口已经打断了城墙的延续性，而周围的空间无法呈现出清晰的自身形式，尤其是在城墙的外围。城墙内外空间品质方面的差异被同一个地名的内外分别所强调，"piazza (plaza)"表示在城墙内部的广场，"piazzale (square)"表示在城墙外部的广场，后者未必是城市组织的结果。

3. 公共服务系统：政府部门、军事城、医院、大学和国家图书馆

首都罗马的大部分公共服务建筑以一种相当随意的方式，建造于19世纪末和20世纪初。公共设施和军事设施沿着城墙建造，主要是在东段，缺乏为这座现代城市的建造提供战略性参照点的实力与雄心。它们构成了一系列飞地，证明其缺乏与现有要素之间的关联性。此外，在大多数情形中，它们与城墙的尺度不符。

4. 居住系统

居住系统也被组织成相当具有自治性质的城市核心，尺度各不相同，以不同的建筑类型（合院住宅、街区、大型公寓楼、小别墅、小型多户住宅）为特征。在城墙之内，各种各样的居住地块与城墙边缘的空地相适应，最终把这些空地都填充起来。在城墙之外，新的居住地块沿着道路的轴线被组织起来，这些道路都汇聚在城门处：人民门外的规整棋盘格布局沿着弗拉米尼亚路展开，圣洛伦佐的工人住区跨越第布勒蒂纳路的两侧布置。与之不同的是，阿皮奥—拉丁诺（Appio-Latino）处的城市扩张以放射轴体系来组织，其中心点位于城门外的开放广场。这些广场曾经提供了通往这座历史城市的入口：在圣乔凡尼门外的阿皮奥广场（Piazzale Appio）以及曼特罗尼亚门外的曼特罗尼奥广场（Piazzale Metronio）。

卢多维西（Ludovisi）邻里是这座城市中唯一一个以统一的方式在城墙内外发展起来的部分，在正交街道形成的格网中将城墙放置进去，这些街道界定了地块分割。

has interrupted the continuity of the walls and the surrounding spaces are unable to assume a formal clarity and autonomy, above all along the external perimeter. The qualitative difference between internal and external spaces is underlined by the same toponomastic that distinguishes between piazza (plaza) in the first case, and piazzale (square) in the second, where the latter is not necessarily the result of an urban organization.

3. The system of public services: ministries, the military city, the hospital, the university and the national library

The majority of the services for Roma capital were realized in the late 19th and early 20th century, in a rather casual manner. The civil and military facilities constructed alongside the walls, above all in the eastern sector, lack both the strength and the ambition to create strategic points of reference for the construction of the modern city; configured as a series of enclaves, they demonstrate a scarce capacity to relate to pre-existing elements. In the majority of cases, what is more, they are out of scale with respect to the dimensions of the walls.

4. The system of settlement

The system of settlement was also organized in rather autonomous urban nuclei, contained in scale and characterized by different building types (courtyard houses, blocks, large apartment buildings, small villas and small multi-family dwellings). Inside the city walls the various lot divisions adapted to the perimeter of the void areas, eventually saturating them. Outside, new lots were organized along the road axes converging on the access gates: the regular checkerboard of blocks outside the Porta del Popolo is structured along the Via Flaminia, while the working class neighbourhood of San Lorenzo straddles the Via Tiburtina. The urban expansions of the Appio-Latino are organized instead by a system of radial axes, whose centre is located in the open squares outside the gates that once provided access to the historic city: Piazzale Appio outside the Porta San Giovanni and the Piazzale Metronio outside the Porta Metronia.

The Ludovisi neighbourhood is the only part of the city to have developed in a unitary manner, inside and outside the walls, absorbing them within the grid of orthogonal streets that define the lot divisions.

城墙在蜿蜒着穿越整个城市的过程中，呈现出不同的用途、意义和角色，与之相关联，可以将 19 km 长的城墙按同类特性被分为 9 段（图 12）。

In relation to the different uses, meanings and roles assumed by the walls as they wind through the city, their 17km length has been subdivided into 9 intervals with homogenous characteristics(Fig.12).

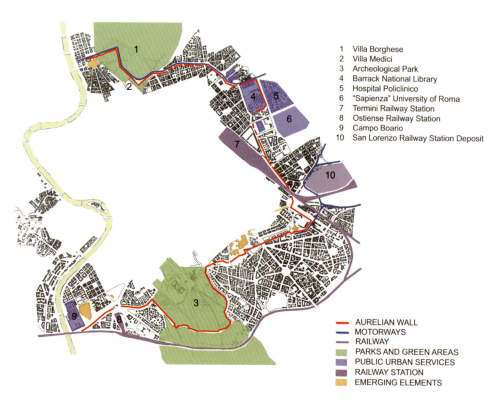

1 Villa Borghese
2 Villa Medici
3 Archeological Park
4 Barrack National Library
5 Hospital Policlinico
6 "Sapienza" University of Roma
7 Termini Railway Station
8 Ostiense Railway Station
9 Campo Boario
10 San Lorenzo Railway Station Deposit

— AURELIAN WALL
— MOTORWAYS
— RAILWAY
  PARKS AND GREEN AREAS
  PUBLIC URBAN SERVICES
  RAILWAY STATION
  EMERGING ELEMENTS

图 12　奥勒良城墙与城市体系
Fig.12　The Aurelian Walls and the urban system

第二章 城墙、景观与城市肌理　2 – City Walls, Landscape and Urban Fabric

第一段　人民门至平扎那门段 — Sector 1　Porta del Popolo – Porta Pinciana

城墙作为景观要素 — The walls as an element of the landscape

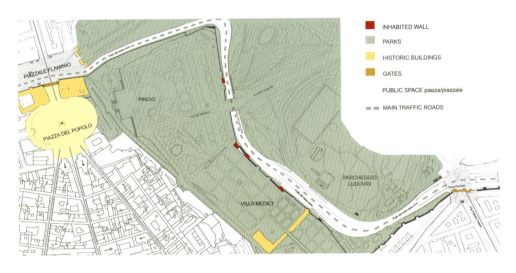

在这一段，城墙呈现出很强的景观价值，尽管有托尔托城墙，却有一条通往波各赛别墅的沿着城墙外围建设的高速路。与美第奇别墅相一致的是，城墙在这里作为高地别墅的挡土墙。

In this sector the walls assume a strong landscape value, notwithstanding the presence of the Muro Torto, a high-speed traffic artery running along the external perimeter of the walls, towards the Villa Borghese. In correspondence with the Villa Medici the walls function as a retaining structure for the villa's hanging.

在弗拉米尼奥广场，交通流向平行于城墙。这就使人民门沦为背景：对于沿着弗拉米尼亚路的古老的执政官道路的轴线上从北方入城的人来说，它是这座城市最具代表性的城门之一。而另一方面，其重要性通过通往波各赛别墅的入口呈现出来，1827年路易吉·卡尼那（Luigi Canina）将其设计为古希腊山门式的纪念性建筑。

At the Piazzale Flaminio, the direction of traffic flow, parallel to the walls, relegates the Porta del Popolo to the background: one of the most representative gates to the city for those arriving from the north, along the axis of the historic Consular Road of the Via Flaminia. Importance is assumed, on the other hand, by the entrance gate to the Villa Borghese, with its monumental Greek Propylea by Luigi Canina (1827).

人民广场 / 弗拉米尼奥广场
Piazza del Popolo / Piazzale Flaminio

人民广场的圣玛丽亚教堂（Santa Maria del Popolo）和水兵营（Acqua Barracks，瓦拉迪耶设计）沿着城墙布局，确定了人民广场的开敞空间与更为混乱而呈现出相当不确定性的弗拉米尼奥广场之间形成的透视关系和过渡区的界面。

The Church of Santa Maria del Popolo and the Acqua Barracks (Valadier) are set alongside the walls and define the perspective view and the threshold of transition between the open space of the Piazza del Popolo and the much more chaotic and substantially unresolved Piazzale Flaminio.

居住着法国学生和艺术家的奥勒良城墙和塔楼
The Aurelian walls and the towers inhabited by french students and artist

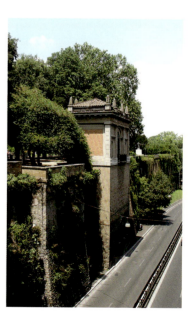

| 第二段　平扎那门至庇亚门段 | Sector 2　Porta Pinciana – Porta Pia |

城墙作为城市的一部分

The walls as part of the city

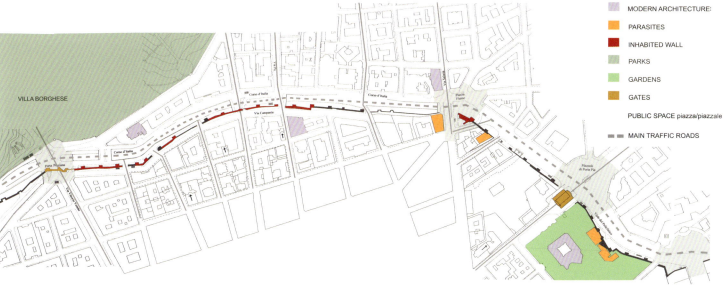

城墙与地下通道

Walls and underpasses

为1960年奥运会修建的地下通道彻底改变了原来城墙和其周边环境的关系。地下通道的挖掘增加了城墙的高度，并且起到了壕沟的作用，尽管历史上从未存在过。

The underpasses created for the 1960 Olympics radically modified the original relationship between the walls and their context. The excavation of the underpasses increased the height of the walls and assumes the value of a moat that, what is more, never existed.

城墙与地下通道　　　　　　　　　　　　　　Walls and Underpasses

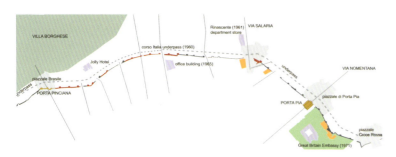

卢多维西邻里是城市唯一以统一的方式发展城墙两边的部分。街道布局呈现出规则的格网，截断了城墙，损害了其连续性，使城墙自身的断面暴露出来。

The Ludovisi neighbourhood is the only part of the city to have developed in a unitary manner on both sides of the walls. The street pattern imposed a regular grid that intercepts the walls, to the detriment of its continuity, and exposes the section of the walls themselves.

奥勒良城墙和现代建筑"复兴百货商店（La Rinascente）"（F. 阿尔比尼，F. 赫尔格，1957—1961 年）

The Aurelian Walls and the modern architecture La Rinascente (F. Albini, F. Helg, 1957–1961)

建筑紧凑的体量，使人想起 19 世纪城市街区的尺度，通过选择面层材料以及粗糙的立面板的波纹状起伏，与城墙产生关联。

The compact volume of the building, which recalls the dimensions of the 19th century city block, relates to the walls through the choice of the cladding materials and the corrugation of the granular facade panels.

第二章 城墙、景观与城市肌理　2 – City Walls, Landscape and Urban Fabric

第三段　卡斯特罗比勒陀里奥至比勒陀里阿诺路（Viale Pretoriano）段　Sector 3　Castro Pretorio – Viale Pretoriano

城墙与公共服务设施　The walls and public services

在奥勒良城墙内部的兵营
The barrack inside the Aurelian Walls

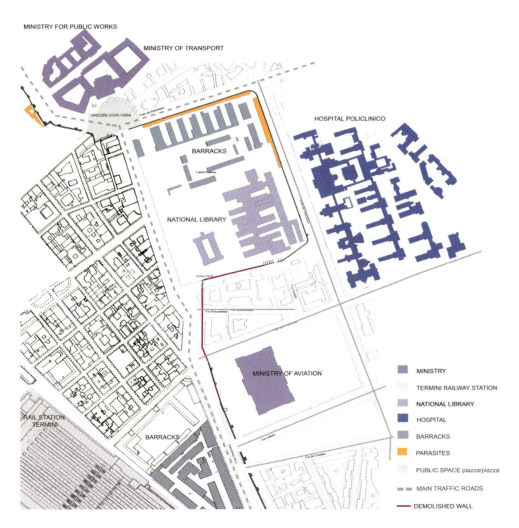

主要的公共服务设施建造在首都罗马城区，这些建筑（交通部、市政工程部、航空部、大学、军事城和医院）自成体系，高度和城墙不相称。
卡斯特罗比勒陀里奥军事城插建在历史上的古罗马兵营（Castro Romano）内。这一段城墙原来沿着周边每隔30 m便有一座塔楼，现塔楼已不存在。

The majority of the public services for Roma Capital were constructed in this urban sector. These structures (Ministry of Transportation, Ministry of Public Works, Ministry of Aviation, the university, the Military City and the hospital) were all configured as highly introverted enclaves, out of scale and indifferent to the presence of the walls.
The Military City of Castro Pretorio is inserted within the historical Castro Romano. This section is missing the defence towers that are located every 30m along the perimeter of the walls.

第四段　比勒陀里阿诺路至拉比卡纳门路段   Sector 4　Viale Pretoriano – Viale di Porta Labicana

城墙与城内外的倒置

The walls and the inversion between interior and exterior

这段城墙创造出对城内外认知的某种倒置。
中央火车站和周边密集的铁轨，就像是城墙之外的技术—基础设施空间。而19世纪末开始建设的圣洛伦佐邻里，在所有方面呈现的效果却有在城墙线以内之感。

This sector creates a sort of inversion in the perception of the relationship between interior–exterior.
The Termini Rail Station, with its swathe of tracks, resembles a technical–infrastructural space that is outside the walls and, vice versa, the neighbourhood of San Lorenzo, whose construction began at the end of the 19th century, appears, to all intents and purposes, to be inside the line of the walls.

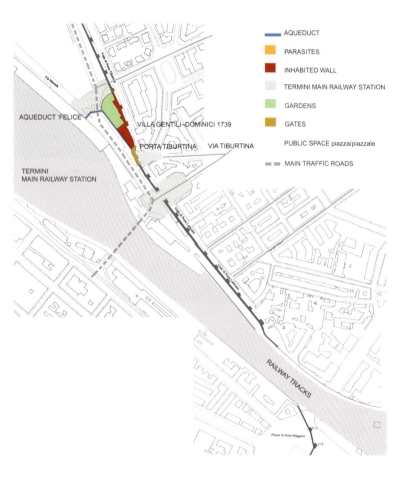

98　　南京城墙与罗马城墙比较　Comparative Study on the City Walls of Nanjing and Rome

第二章　城墙、景观与城市肌理　2 – City Walls, Landscape and Urban Fabric

圣洛伦佐
San Lorenzo

詹蒂利 – 多米尼奇别墅
Villa Gentili-Dominici

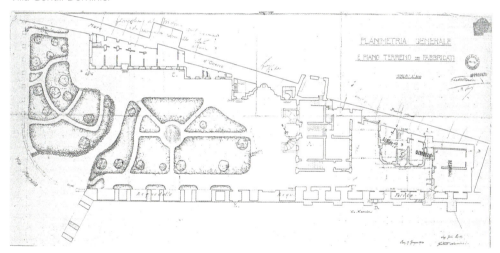

詹蒂利 – 多米尼奇别墅是拉古齐尼（大约1750年）的作品，建在城墙与费利切输水道之间的空隙中。别墅将一座塔楼纳入其中，并将一段输水道改成敞廊。在花园里，水道的出水口紧靠着城墙，重新定义了其形态。

Villa Gentili–Dominici attributed to Raguzzini (c.1750) is set within the interstitial space between the walls and the Felice Aqueduct. The Villa absorbed one of the towers and transformed a segment of the aqueduct into a loggia. In the garden, a nymphaeum was set up against the walls, redefining its shape.

输水道　　　　　　　　　　　　　　　　　　　　　　　　　　The aoueducts

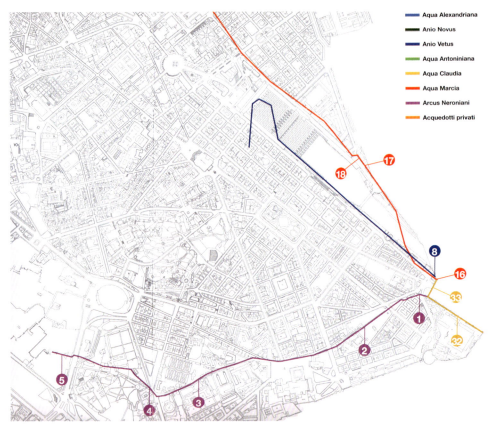

奥勒良城墙内侧的输水道的布局
The layout of the aqueducts inside the Aurelian walls

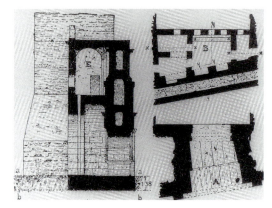

费利切输水道与中央火车站的侧立面
The Felice Aqueduct and the side facade of the Termini Rail Station

第二章 城墙、景观与城市肌理　2 – City Walls, Landscape and Urban Fabric

第五段　马焦雷门至圣乔凡尼门段　　Sector 5　Porta Maggiore – Porta San Giovanni

城墙与纪念性建筑物　　The walls and monumental structures

这段城墙的特点是拥有来自历史上的不同时期的纪念性建筑，在城墙边界内有大片空地。

卡罗·费利塞路（Viale Carlo Felice）的条状空地两端连接了两处主要的纪念建筑：在拉特兰的圣乔凡尼大教堂和耶路撒冷的圣十字拉特兰宫（Palazzi Lateranensi with Santa Croce）。在城墙的对面，沿着城墙的内侧边界，我们看到由合作社建造的大型公寓楼的连续立面。

This sector is characterized by the presence of monumental structures from different periods in history, and vast void spaces located inside the perimeter.
The rectilinear void of the Viale Carlo Felice connects the two main monumental structures: San Giovanni in Laterano and the Palazzi Lateranensi with Santa Croce in Gerusalemme. On the opposite side of the walls, along the internal perimeter, we find the continuous facade of the large apartment blocks constructed by cooperatives.

马焦雷门利用克劳狄输水道的拱券建造
Porta Maggiore was built utilizing the arches of Claudio aqueduct

101

纪念性建筑体系：拉特兰的圣乔凡尼大教堂和拉特兰宫
The system of monumental structures: San Giovanni in Laterano and the Palazzi Lateranensi

沿城墙外围的卡斯特兰塞路是一条高速机动车主干道，利用了东内环路。
The Viale Castrense, on the exterior perimeter of the walls, is a high-speed traffic artery for vehicles using the Tangenziale East inner ring road.

南京城墙与罗马城墙比较　　Comparative Study on the City Walls of Nanjing and Rome

第二章 城墙、景观与城市肌理　2 – City Walls, Landscape and Urban Fabric

第六段　圣乔凡尼门至拉丁纳门段
城墙作为边界

Sector 6　Porta San Giovanni – Porta Latina
The walls as edge

在城墙内侧是阿皮亚古道考古公园——西皮奥尼公园（Parco degli Scipioni），而城墙外侧是现代城市和阿皮奥—拉丁诺邻里。后两者基于道路轴线布局，道路都汇聚在阿皮奥广场和曼特罗尼奥广场。

On the inside of the walls we find the Appia Antica Archaeological Park (Parco degli Scipioni), while on the exterior lies the modern city and the neighborhoods of the Appio Latino. These latter are based on the road axes that converge in the Piazzale Appio and Piazzale Metronio.

103

第七段　拉丁纳门至桑加罗城堡段　　Sctor 7 Porta Latina – Bastione di san Gallo

城墙作为景观要素　　The walls as an element of the landscape

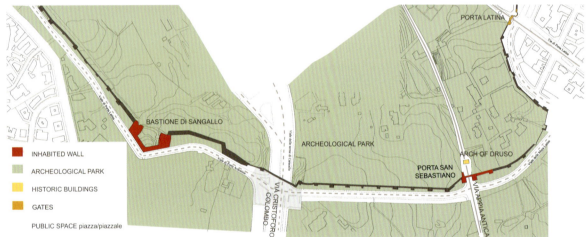

城墙保留了作为防卫工事的最初特征。事实上，这段城墙比其他各处更多地揭示出城墙—城市—领土之间的原始关系。城墙仍然是一个孤立的元素，作为考古学的构筑物，和它周围的空地形成了鲜明的反差，呈现出一种与周边环境分离的形而上学的姿态。

The walls maintain their original character as a defensive structure. In fact, this sector, more than any other, reveals the original relationship between the wall–city–territory. The walls remain an isolated element, an archaeological structure in opposition to the void space around them, existing in a condition of metaphysical alienation from context.

桑加罗城堡，教皇保罗三世时期修建，现在用作艺术工作室　　用作城墙博物馆的圣塞瓦斯蒂安门
The Sangallo Bastion, constructed under the Papacy of Paul III. It is currently used as an arts studio　　The Porta San Sebastiano of the Museo delle Mura

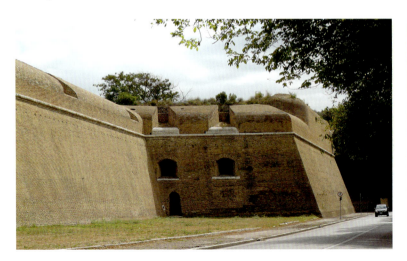

南京城墙与罗马城墙比较　　Comparative Study on the City Walls of Nanjing and Rome

第二章　城墙、景观与城市肌理　2 – City Walls, Landscape and Urban Fabric

第八段　拉丁纳门路至考奇山段 | Sector 8　Via di Porta Latina – Monte dei Cocci

城墙作为形而上学景观的要素　　The walls as an element of the metphysical landscape

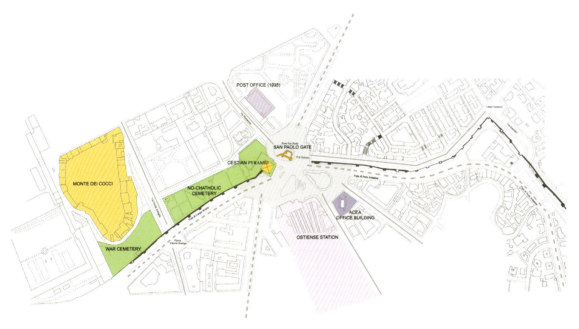

一系列建于不同历史时期的建筑，带有强烈的形式特征，沉浸在以空地主导的大片土地中。体量方面缺少相互联系，使得这一地区呈现出一种形而上学的氛围。城墙吸收了其周界内的切斯提乌斯金字塔，而古老的奥斯提安门由于城墙被切断以便利机动车交通而成为一个孤立的物体，疏离于其原有的环境。

The presence of a series of buildings from different historical periods, with strong formal characteristics and immersed in a vast field dominated by the void and the absence of relations between volumes gives the area a metaphysical aura. The walls have absorbed the Pyramid of Cestius within their perimeter, while the ancient Porta Ostiense, thanks to the cuts made in the walls to facilitate vehicular circulation, has become an isolated object, alienated from its original context.

阿达尔韦托·里伯拉设计的邮局、卡斯·切斯提乌斯金字塔、新教徒墓地，均位于城墙内侧，圣保罗门则成为奥斯提安塞路博物馆所在地。

The Post Office by Adalberto Libera, the Pyramid of Caius Cestius, the Protestant Cemetery, all set alongside the internal perimeter of the walls, and the Porta San Paolo, home of the Museo della Via Ostiense.

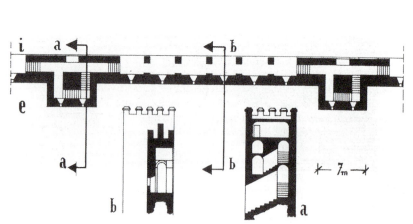

106　　南京城墙与罗马城墙比较　Comparative Study on the City Walls of Nanjing and Rome

第二章 城墙、景观与城市肌理　2 – City Walls, Landscape and Urban Fabric

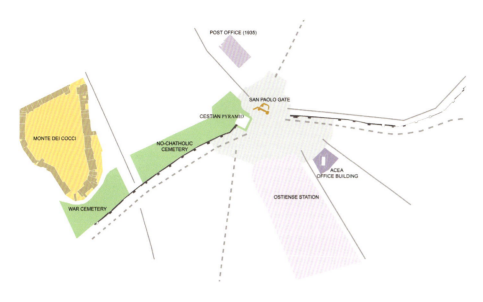

城墙明确界定了新教徒墓地的边界。
The walls define the perimeter of the Protestant Cemetery.

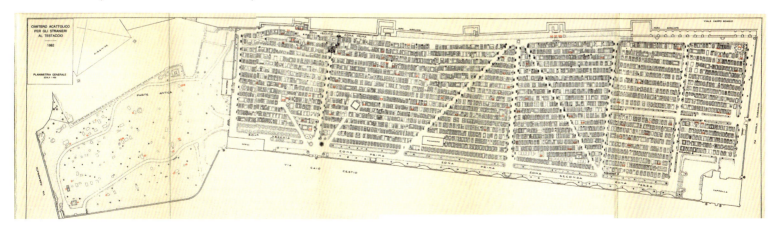

107

第九段 考奇山至台伯河段 | Sector 9 Monte del Cocci – Tevere
城墙和废弃 | The walls and abandonment

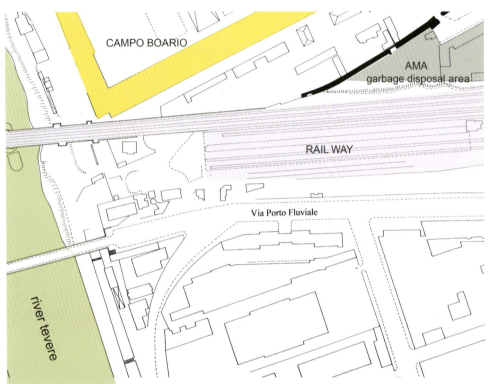

这片曾经的牛市（Campo Boario）地区，其特征是处于衰败的状态。其原因在于遭废弃，以及不恰当地用作市政环卫公司的仓库。

The area of the former Campo Boario is characterized by a state of deterioration, resulting from its abandonment and the improper use of an area as a depot for the municipal sanitation company.

第三章　城墙修复

3 Restoration of City Walls

第一节　南京城墙的保护与修缮
3.1 The Protection and Maintenance of the Nanjing City Wall

杨新华　Yang Xinhua

1. 南京明城墙损毁现象（图1）

膨胀：指城墙表面局部凸起，但城砖尚未脱落，这是城墙墙体外侧城砖与内侧城砖失去拉结的结果，继续发展下去可导致表皮城砖剥落甚至局部坍塌。

开裂：指墙体出现深浅不一、长短不等的裂缝。南京城墙的墙体开裂有纵向开裂和横向开裂两种，纵向开裂指裂缝和城墙走向呈垂直角度，横向开裂指裂缝与城墙走向成水平角度。其中横向裂缝对城墙危害更严重。

剥落：指墙体表面出现城砖松动、脱离墙体的现象，一般出现在膨胀、开裂以后，也有因城墙砖体表皮与墙芯在砌筑中未能相互咬合所致。

坍塌：指城墙表皮连同部分内芯倒塌，有大面积坍塌和局部坍塌两种状况，是城墙破坏的最严重后果。

沉降：沉降是指城墙墙体由于内部出现空洞，强度降低，导致上层城墙砌体下沉，分整体沉降和局部沉降两种。

侧移：又称侧滑，指临近地表的城墙墙体向一侧滑动，致使该段城墙出现整体倾斜、开裂甚至坍塌的现象，多见于包山墙段。

2. 南京明城墙维修原则

从南京明城墙的损毁状况分析，造成城墙破坏和损伤的原因主要是：顶面防水层的破坏、树根伸长与撑展、包山墙内侧山体的压力和推力、人为建设活动的影响等。针对城墙现状和破坏因素，根据《文物保护法》的要求，南京市文物局制定了南京明城墙抢险维修的原则。

真实性原则：城墙的维修应严格遵循不改变城墙原状的要求，保护原有的建筑形制、建筑结构，尽可能采用原有的建筑材料和原有建造工艺。

最小干扰原则：在保护城墙结构基本稳定的前提下，尽可能减少对城墙的扰动，少量修缮。对已毁坏的城墙，修复时要进行考古发掘，找到原始依据，经过文物专家反复论证后方可实施。

修旧如旧原则：对城墙毁坏段的修复坚持"修旧如旧"原则，在有依据的前提下恢复历史本来面貌，同时立碑说明。

1. Damage symptoms (Fig.1)

Bloating: the walls started to become swollen in some areas, though without causing the falling of bricks. The symptom was caused by the disconnection between the interior and exterior bricks. The further development of the symptom may result in the falling of surface bricks, or even cave in.

Cracking: fissures appeared in the walls, though uneven in depth and length. As far as the Nanjing City Wall were concerned, the fissures could either go vertical or go horizontal. Vertical fissures appeared vertically against the running direction of the walls, with horizontal ones at a plane level. Relatively speaking, horizontal fissures caused more damages to the walls.

Peeling off: brick loosening or falling off would occur after bloating and cracking. Falling off may also be caused by the fake connection between the brick and the core of the walls.

Collapse: collapse happens, when surface bricks and some part of the inner core cave in. Collapse, either extensive, or local, is the most serious consequence of the wall damage.

Subsiding: when an inner part of the walls became hollow, bricks at the upper level would go down, due to lacking of the support. Subsiding could happen either as a whole, or as a local phenomenon.

Lateral movement or lateral sliding: the wall near the ground started to make a lateral movement, causing the walls to incline, break, or even cave-in as a whole, mostly seen in the walls built to enclose the mountains.

2. Maintenance and associated principles

Analysis of the reason behind the damaged walls shows that a range of factors, including the damaged water jacket on top, stretching and extension of tree roots, the pressure and push of mountains, and human activities, contributed to the deterioration and decay of the walls. Nanjing Municipal Administration of Cultural Heritage has defined the principles for rescuing and maintaining the city walls, based on the walls'current status, and in line with the by-laws on protecting cultural heritages. They are as follows:

环境协调原则：除了对城墙本体进行抢救性维修外，对与城墙相关的山体和护城河也一并进行整治，恢复城河一体的历史面貌。

原材质原工艺原则：迄今为止，南京城墙抢险性维修均采用回收的明城砖砌筑墙体、雉堞和女墙，由于无法使用原有黏合剂，采用混合砂浆代替，而不采用水泥砂浆。对于条石墙体，选用相同色泽、相同材质的条石为补充材料，以保持原有的风格和风貌。

保存历史信息原则：区别对待城墙出现的局部开裂、剥落等破损现象。如对局部破损、风化处进行挖补，对开裂处局部修复，尽可能避免大面积拆除墙体，以保存古城墙的历史信息。尤其是历代修缮时留下的信息，更要加以保留，以反映完整的建造和修缮历史过程。

Principle of authenticity: the walls shall be maintained and repaired without changing the original profile of the walls, protecting the original form and structures of the old walls, and applying the original building materials and techniques as much as possible.

Principle of minimum disturbance: while keeping the structure of city walls stable, efforts shall be made to minimize the disturbance to the walls. Repair could be made only when necessary. When repairing a broken wall, an archaeological investigation shall be made to look for original evidences. The repair plan shall not be implemented unless it has been reviewed several times by specialists.

Principle of "repaired to what it was": when repairing a broken wall, one has to "repair the wall to what it was". The wall shall be restored to what it looked like in the past, based on the collected evidences. Meanwhile, a stele shall be erected to mark the repair.

Principle of coordinated with the environment: in addition to rescue and repair, the mountains and moats associated with the walls shall be dealt with at the same time, presenting a full historical image of the landscape.

Principle of original materials and techniques: up to date, the old city walls, including the body, battlements, and parapet walls, have been repaired using the original bricks (made in the Ming Dynasty) that were recovered from folks. A special mortar, rather than cement, was applied, as it was impossible to have the original bonding agent. When repairing the walls made of stone slabs, the same color and texture was applied to keep the original touch.

Principle of preserving historical information: walls, when cracked or peeled off, shall be differentiated with the remedies to be applied. For example, to the broken and weathered section, one has to dig out the rotten part before getting it repaired. To a cracked part, simple repair will do the job. Repair has to be made to avoid extensive dismantling of the walls, so as to preserve the historical information in them. The information, especially on the repair efforts in the past, shall be preserved to reflect the historical process of building and repairing the walls.

图1 城墙损坏状态
Fig.1 Damage symptoms

3. 南京明城墙抢险维修实例

南京城墙依山傍水，结构、材质多样，为了最大限度地保护好、维修好南京城墙，针对不同地段、不同材质、不同险情的城墙采用了多种形式的方法进行维修保护。到目前为止，南京城墙本体的维修长度约 21 km，超过现存城墙的 4/5，投入资金超过 2 亿元。维修方式的多样化也构成南京城墙保护的一大特色。

1）遗址保存类

（1）东水关

东水关原为一重要关口，水路防守更为突出。现基本形制大部存在，但顶部破坏严重，且为与北部城墙联系断裂之处。考虑其遗址特性，维修时对三层藏兵洞（拱券）中已毁坏的上层藏兵洞不做修复，仅清理出建筑遗迹，保留遗址状态（图 2）。但考虑东水关是武定门城墙北延的断头，我们对城墙断头做防水处理，依断面的错落而设计登城步道（图 3）。

3. Case studies

The in Nanjing City Wall were built borrowing the contours of mountains and rivers in the vicinity. As a result, the walls were built with diversified structures and materials. To protect and repair the walls, a range of repair plans have been worked out to maintain and protect the walls built with different materials and having different "ailments". Up to date, a section as long as 21 km, or 4/5 of the surviving walls has got repaired, under a budget worth RMB 200 million. The individualized repair plan is a proven practice applied in protecting the old walls.

1）Relics

(1) East Water Pass

The pass was a major defense fortress designed for waterways. Most part of the structure has survived the times, though the top was badly torn up, with a wall section disconnected from the joints in the north. Taking into account the role it had played in the past, the broken upper part of the three-level soldier hiding vaults was left unrepaired. Efforts were made only to clean up the structure of the relics, keeping it mainly as it was(Fig.2). Considering the fact that the pass

图 2 修缮后的东水关
Fig.2 East Water Pass after restoration

图 3 依断面的错落而设计登城步道
Fig.3 Wall-climbing steps built on the uneven section

sits at the terminal of the northern wall extension of Wuding Gate, water-proof treatment was applied to the terminal, and wall-climbing steps were built on the uneven surface of the terminal (Fig. 3).

(2) Qian Lake

This is a wall section that meets with Qian Lake in the east part of Nanjing. In 1991, a heavy summer rain several days in a row triggered up the cave-in of the walls for some 60m long. The cave-in accidentally unveiled another wall inside the collapsed wall, or "wall in the wall". Archaeologists preliminarily concluded that the wall was built before 1372. Specialists at China Institute of Cultural Relics (now Chinese Academy of Cultural Heritages) suggested the remains be protected when preparing a plan to get the collapsed wall repaired. They kept the wall that was built in the early Ming Dynasty inside the collapsed walls, and treated the collapsed walls only with water proof and reinforcement, in an attempt to show the walls built in two different historical times (Fig. 4).

2) **Historical information**

(1) Shence Gate

In the Ming Dynasty, the gate was a northern outlet, and a wall section that was finished the last (Houhu City). This part of wall was built with the bricks made in the Ming Dynasty or in the late Qing Dynasty, occasionally with some rocks. The gate tower was built in a style that was popular in the late Qing Dynasty, which is a far cry from the one built in the Ming Dynasty, in terms of both structure and style. The unevenly laid foundations made the tower start to tilt under a rotten structure. Some people advised to dismantle the tower, and build a new one following the style prevailed in the Ming Dynasty, in an attempt to show the magnificence of the Nanjing Ming City Wall. A range of meetings were convened to listen to specialists' views and advice. The final solution derived from the specialists' analysis was to repair the tower without complete disassembly. Specialists pointed out that the tower was poorly built, which mirrors a historical fact under a given period, and hence it deserves the preservation (Fig.5).

(2) Stone City

This part of the walls is the oldest in Nanjing. As early as in the East Wu Period, SUN Quan built the Stone City borrowing the contours of the mountains as the headquarters of the navy. In the early Ming Dynasty, the walls built in the Six Dynasties were redesigned to enclose the Stone City into Nanjing. The walls were built with both bricks and rocks, attached to the mountain rocks along the Yangtze River. A rock section of the walls showed a ghost image, and

图 4　前湖段修缮后
Fig.4　Qian Lake section after restoration

（2）前湖段城墙

前湖段城墙和南京东部前湖相邻。1991年夏连降大雨，导致该段城墙坍塌60 m余，在清理塌方处城砖时，意外发现在塌方处内侧竟还有一段城墙，呈"墙中墙"的形式。经勘测考证，初步认定为明初洪武五年（1372年）前修的城墙。在做该段城墙维修设计时，中国文物研究所（现中国遗产研究院）专家提出了遗址保护的设想，即保留内侧的明初城墙墙体，对外侧后修的墙体塌方处仅做防水加固处理，以展示两个历史时期的城墙（图4）。

2) **历史信息保留类**

（1）神策门城墙

明南京城的北门，也是南京城墙最后完成的段落（后湖城）。城墙墙体有明代城砖，有清代晚期城砖，甚至还有块石墙体，城楼则为清代晚期府城城楼式样，结构、样式都与明代建筑相去甚远，加上城楼基础不均匀沉降，局部倾斜，造成结构朽烂，已成险房。如何对待这种现象，当时也有人提出是否拆除清代城楼，按明代城楼重建，以展示明南京城的宏伟。我们召开了多次专家会，分析、研究维修对策，最后确定了保留现有城楼进行不落架大修的方案，专家们指出"即使现有的城楼建得不好，但也反映了特定历史时期的历史信息，应该予以保留"（图5）。

图5 维修后的神策门城墙与城楼（左）；维修中的神策门城楼（右）
Fig.5 Shence Gate after restoration (left); Shence Gate under restoration (right)

（2）石头城段城墙

这是南京最古老、最具特色的城墙。早在东吴时期，孙权就在此依山建石头城作为水军大本营；明初修南京城时，将六朝石头城纳入其中，形成砖石混合墙体，并依附当时沿长江的山岩。其中突出的一段岩石由于貌似鬼脸而被称为"鬼脸城"。此段城墙维修，基本保持了原有砖石结合的墙体结构，只在具体险段拆除重砌，对于突出墙体外的山岩，用压力注浆方法加固。其中两处山岩有坍塌的危险，则另树钢架支撑，以示区别。由于这段城墙顶面标高已无法确定，因此顶部除重做防水层外，不修雉堞，仅做残墙处理（图6）。

3）景观展示类

（1）东、西长干巷段城墙

位于南京老城南端中心中华门（明聚宝门）两侧，是南京城墙中最壮观、最坚固的地段。这段城墙外侧为宽阔的外秦淮河，内侧为人文荟萃的内秦淮河，城墙最高处达20 m余，全部为条石砌筑，仅顶面用城砖砌雉堞、女墙、海墁。结合南京市外秦淮河综合整治规划，我们对此段城墙做复原修缮（图7、图8），全线约2 km长城墙的缺口用框架修补，顶面用城砖恢复雉堞、海墁。而修缮后的城墙与外秦淮河、环城绿地形成反映南京古都风貌的最佳景点，受到专家及市民的好评。

was nicknamed as "ghost face wall". The walls were repaired to keep its original structures built with both bricks and rocks. Only the imperiled was dismantled, and rebuilt. Pressure grouting was applied to reinforce the rocks popping out of the walls. Two large mountain rocks that might fall were supported by steel scaffolds. As it was difficult to define the height of wall tops, only the water proof treatment was applied to the top, leaving the battlements as a relic (Fig.6).

3）Landscape

(1) East and west Changganxiang section

The section physically sits on the two sides of Zhonghua Gate (Jubao Gate in the Ming Dynasty) in the far south of the old city proper. It is the most magnificent and sturdy section of the walls in the city. This part of the walls greets with the External Qinhuai River on the outskirts of the city, and with the Internal Qinhuai River that was the cultural cradle of the city as well. The wall may reach some 20m for the highest part. The entire wall section was built will stone slabs. Only the battlements and aprons on the wall top and the parapet walls were built with bricks. Based on a comprehensive plan prepared for managing the

图 6　石头城钢架
Fig.6　The steel scaffolds supporting the mountain rocks

图 8　东西长干巷段整修中
Fig.8　The city wall of east and west Changganxiang section in restoration

图 7　东西长干巷段整修前
Fig.7　The city wall of east and west Changganxiang section before restoration

（2）狮子山小桃园一线城墙

位于南京西城墙北段，于长江及长江西岸可一览，构成南京城北大江风貌区的重要景观之一。这段城墙全部为包山墙，内侧自北而南为狮子山、红土山、八字山、丁山等一系列山岗。在维修这段城墙时，我们按照城墙原貌进行恢复，疏浚护城河，结合城墙外侧的地形地貌和自然景观建成了以城墙为主体的一系列公园：狮子山公园、绣球公园、小桃园公园等（图9）。

External Qinhuai River, we had the walls repaired to keep its original style(Fig. 7, Fig.8). A frame approach was applied to repair the missing parts in the walls that may add up to 2km long, and bricks were employed to restore the battlements and aprons on the wall top. The restored walls, the External Qinhuai River, and the greenery belt circling the town constitute a most popular landscape showing the beauty of an ancient capital.

图9 小桃园段城墙维修前（左）和维修后（右）
Fig.9 The city wall of Xiaotaoyuan section before (left) and after (right) restoration

（3）九华山至玄武门段城墙

位于南京玄武湖南及西侧，又东及钟山风景区边缘。我们也是按照原样恢复城墙（图10）。维修后的这段城墙成为南京山水城林最佳观景点，吸引了国内外许多政要和专家学者以及广大市民登城观赏，产生了良好的社会影响，对体现南京的山水城市起到重要的作用。

(2) Mount Shizi–Xiaotaoyuan section

It is the northern part of the west walls, overlooking the Yangtze River and its west bank. As a major landscape showing the river scenes in the northern part of the city, the section was dominated by the walls built to enclose a range of mountains running from the north to the south, including Shizi, Hongtu, Bazi, and Ding. This part of the walls was restored to its original style. The moats were also dredged up. A string of public parks were built to combine the terrains and natural landscapes on the outskirts of the walls, including Shizishan Park, Xiuqiu Park, and Xiaotaoyuan Park (Fig.9).

(3) Mount Jiuhua–Xuanwu Gate

This part of the walls stretches to Xuanwu Lake in the south and west, and to the rim of Zhongshan Scenery Park in the east. The wall was restored to its original style (Fig.10). making it a most popular scenic attraction for the combined beauty of mountains, rivers, and city walls. Visitors could climb up the walls, viewing the beautiful landscape of Nanjing. It plays an important role in making Nanjing a city sitting in the mountains and rivers.

图10 九华山段城墙
Fig.10 The city wall of Mount Jiuhua section

4）原状保存类

（1）新民门

是南京城墙从狮子山转向金川门的重要地标性建筑，为民国时期修建，有近现代建筑的特色。现门两侧的城墙都已被拆除，门本身为近现代形式，砖混结构。近年来，有不少人提出此门非明代原物，建议拆除，我们认为，新民门虽然是民国时期所开，结构、外观也非明代风格，但这毕竟是南京一个历史时期的代表，同时它还是明城墙走向的一个重要标志，应予以保留。于是，我们对其未做大的修缮，仅进行排险和局部小修。

（2）汉西门瓮城

汉西门位于南京西城墙南段。因为历史原因，瓮城内部的城墙已被拆除，在维修时，我们保留了两座城门和原有城墙，不恢复已拆除的城墙，改成汉中门遗址公园，原汁原味地展示已经留下历史遗憾的瓮城，并成为南京城西的古典标志性建筑（图11）。

5）现代工艺加固类

（1）中山门

中山门位于原朝阳门位置，清代朝阳门毁，民国时期为运送孙中山先生灵柩于1929年在明朝阳门基础上重建。由于中山门顶部城楼未建，加之抗日战争时又受到日军炮火轰击而坍塌，汪伪时期仅对其进行了简单修缮，导致这座城门存在严重险情。

4) Original sites

(1) Xinmin Gate

The gate is a major landmark showing the transit of the walls from Mount Shizi to Jinchuan Gate. Built in the Republican times, the gate was designed with the touch of modern architecture. The walls on the two sides of the gate have been dismantled. The gate itself was built with brick and concrete in a modern style. In recent years, some people advised to remove the gate, as it was not originally built in the Ming Dynasty. Author believes that the gate represents a historical period, though it was built in the Republican times, without the structure and outlook a typical Ming-era gate would have. Furthermore, it shows the course of the walls built in the Ming Dynasty. In this context, it deserves the conservation. Limited repair has been made to the gate.

(2) Hanxi Gate Fortress

Hanxi Gate sits in the southern part of the west walls. The defensive walls inside the fortified outpost had been dismantled due to some historical reasons. When repairing, we kept two gates and original walls. The dismantled walls were not restored. A Hanzhong Gate Relic Park was built on the remains, keeping the fortified outpost intact to reflect the sorrow left by history. It becomes an ancient landmark structure in the west part of the city (Fig. 11).

5) Protection using modern techniques

(1) Zhongshan Gate

The gate stands on the original site of Chaoyang Gate which was destroyed in the Qing Dynasty. Folks built the gate on the remains of Chaoyang Gate in 1929 to convey the coffin of Dr. Sun Yat-sen. The gate was originally built without castle. It was shelled to collapse during the Anti-Japanese War. It got some simple repairs under the rule of WANG Jingwei. The gate became seriously in danger when a highway tunnel was built in the vicinity at the end of 1990s. Elapsed time made the gate tilt outwards, and subside with deformed side rooms, which endangered the traffic in the east part of the town, and the safety of the structure itself as well. In 2003, a maintenance plan was made to have it repaired under the following principles: uninstall and reinforce the gates, under

图11　汉西门瓮城
Fig.11　Hanxi Gate Fortress

1990年代末,修公路隧道又加剧了中山门墙体外倾、沉降,耳室变形,直接威胁到南京城东市民的交通和文物安全。2003年,我们在制订中山门维修方案时,在保证城门墙体、拱券安全的前提下,制订了卸载、加固城门的方案,即卸除城门拱券顶部上千吨回填土,代之以混凝土框架,对拱券裂缝压力注浆,对局部墙体重砌。这样做,既解决了中山门的险情,也使文物的外观未受影响,以至许多市民看后竟不相信已经修缮过(图12)。

(2)九华山至解放门城墙

位于南京城墙北部、玄武湖南侧。1950年代为方便开路及取砖建房形成多处缺口。针对此段城墙上六、七处因为拆城取砖形成的大缺口,我们采取了内部设混凝土框架,外贴城砖的方法,既解决了没有足够的城砖回填的现状,又利用内部空间为这段城墙提供了展览、服务、休息的空闲,形成了临湖、九华、台城等几个展厅。这种方法在2000年召开的"中国古城墙保护研讨会"上得到与会专家学者的肯定。以后在集庆门和东、西长干巷城墙修复施工中也有采用(图13)。

4. 南京明城墙城砖回收的进程与成果

1998年3月,《南京日报》以整版篇幅刊登文章"南京明城墙距离世界遗产还有多远",拉开了新一轮对南京城墙的保护和维修序幕。同时,南京的城市建设其时也进入了大发展阶段,更加注重人居环境的打造和城市特色的表达,因此当时的一个

the prerequisite that the walls and arches are kept safe. As a result, several thousand tons of earth was removed from top of the arches, and a concrete frame was refilled in. Pressure grouting was employed to fill up the fissures in the arches. Some part of the walls was rebuilt. The effort saved the endangered Zhongshan Gate. The restored gate was so untouched of its original outlook that some citizens didn't believe the gate had been repaired (Fig. 12).

(2) Mount Jiuhua– Jiefang Gate

The section is physically located in the north of the walls, and the south of Xuanwu Lake. Numerous holes and gaps could be seen as the result of opening new roads and building new structures using old bricks in the 1950s. Concrete frames were employed to fill in 7 large gaps caused by brick dismantling. The exterior part of the concrete refilling was bounded with bricks. The methodology was proved a desirable solution to the shortage of original bricks for refill, while making the interior part of the walls a place for exhibition, service, and rest. A number of show rooms, including Lin Lake, Jiuhua, and Taicheng, were set up. The methodology was thought highly at a seminar convened in 2000 to discuss the protection of old city walls in China. The technique was reemployed later in repairing the walls along Jiqing Gate, and E. & W. Changganxiang(Fig. 13).

图12 修缮后的中山门
Fig.12 Zhongshan Gate after restoration

图 13 集庆门整修前（上）与整修后（下）对比
Fig.13 Jiqing Gate before(up) and after(down) restoration

举措是建设南京明城墙风光带。与此相配合的是政府加大了对南京明城墙的维修以及周边环境的整治力度，用于城墙保护的投资在逐年增加，回收散失城砖用于维修城墙的任务也在不断增加。

另一方面，20 世纪末南京老城改造全面展开，原用城砖砌筑的建筑物、构筑物被拆除时，大量散失的城砖被重新发现，这为回收散失城砖提供了契机。在大批历史上用城砖砌筑的建（构）筑物被拆除时，广大市民积极提供线索，施工单位主动配合支持，使得大量散失城砖得到了最大限度地回收。近几年每年的城砖

4. Recovering old bricks

A paper named "How far will the Nanjing Ming City Wall have to go before becoming a world heritage?" was published in 1998 in Nanjing Daily, which heralded a new round of protection and maintenance of the old city walls. Meanwhile, Nanjing has entered a stage enjoying the booming development, paying more attention to improving people's living environment, and highlighting the unique features of the city. An action was staged at the time to build a landscape belt centered on the city walls. To make

回收数量都在30万块以上，政府用于城砖回收搬运的费用平均每年也达到30万元左右。

南京明城墙的每一块城砖上都有铭文，这是极其丰富的文化信息和十分珍贵的历史资料。铭文不仅为研究中国明代官营建筑制造机构和制度、建造水平和工艺、城砖产地的分布、中国汉字在明初的简化与异化、中国民间书法、篆刻艺术、中国姓氏文化在明初的演变以及明初实行的责任制等，提供了第一手翔实的资料，而且铭文和城墙一体构成南京明初独特的历史价值，有许多内容还填补了史书记载的不足。

从实际效果看，南京由于采取了特殊而有效的政策，回收散失的城墙砖，既可用于城墙修复，又可成为历史、文化、经济和政治研究的活化石。长期以来，城砖回收和有效利用已经成为南京城墙保护工作的重要内容之一。

the attempt feasible for implementation, municipal authorities enhanced the maintenance of the walls and associated environment, with increased annual budget allocated for protecting the walls. At the same time, efforts have been enhanced to recover the lost old bricks, in an attempt to use them to repair the broken walls.

On the other hand, a campaign to renovate the old city was unfolded at the end of the last century. Hundreds and thousands of lost old bricks were found and recovered when dismantling the structures built with the old city walls' bricks. Thanks to citizens' tips and the understanding of construction units at the scene, most of the lost old bricks have been recovered. In recent years, municipal authorities would recover at least 300,000 old bricks each year. The money paid to ship the recovered old bricks would cost RMB 300,000 a year on average.

Each brick employed to build the Nanjing Ming City Wall has an inscription. The inscription provides a range of first-hand historical information, including the name of official building organizations, architectural regimes applied, technology and techniques employed, distribution of brick producing sites, simplification and diversification of Chinese characters, folks' calligraphy and seal engraving, the evolution of people's names in the early Ming Dynasty, and the responsibility system applied in the early Ming Dynasty. Meanwhile, the inscription and the city walls may work together to tell the unique historical value of Nanjing in the early Ming Dynasty, and fill up the deficiency of historical records.

Thanks to the special and effective policies adopted by municipal authorities, the lost old bricks have been recovered in a steady manner, and employed to repair the broken walls, making the old bricks a living fossil telling the history, culture, economy, and politics of Nanjing at the time. Recovery of old bricks and associated effective utilization has become a long term task in protecting the Nanjing City Wall.

第二节　19世纪至今奥勒良城墙的修复过程

3.2 The Restoration of the Aurelian Walls from 19th Century until Today

罗萨纳·曼齐尼　Rossana Mancini

在19世纪的前10年，曾有过一场历史与人文的文化争论。当时，奥勒良城墙的修复方式成为争论的焦点。争论的一方由安东尼奥·尼拜（Antonio Nibby）为代表，以建筑学的视角进行表达；而另一方的观点基于朱塞佩·瓦拉迪耶（Giuseppe Valadier）的著作，注重修复的差别。这两位都对古城墙充满兴趣。安东尼奥·尼拜，对有关城墙的文字资料进行了彻底的整理，完成了第一部系统、全面地研究这座历史遗迹的著作（Le mura di Roma, 1820），朱塞佩·瓦拉迪耶则以个人身份参与到奥勒良城墙的修复工程中。

在一份1806年的档案中，记载了一个由建筑师自己提出的城墙修复计划，13年后计划重新修改，预算为5 884斯库多（注：意大利在16—19世纪流行的货币）。修复计划的内容主要有全面清理城墙上的杂草植被，将缺失的护墙重新整合起来，修建在很多情形中都需要的、作为"公共步道"使用的双重环路，从而再现古老城市记忆中的历史遗迹。对尼拜的一个主要批评是，应对当时的托尔托城墙采取必要措施。托尔托城墙是一段建于奥古斯都（Augustus）时期的城墙，在平西欧山（Pincio）山脚下合并到了奥勒良环路。瓦拉迪耶设计了大型拱券用来卸荷，拱券围绕着山脚的斜坡，由方形的tuff凝灰岩块砌成，柱子上点缀着砖块。对于花园上方的拱券与栏杆，则用砖砌筑，至于整个建筑的墙体，他们计划采用抹灰墙面。

1830年，新的修复工程之初，这个阶段本应当关注于这段城墙，尼拜却对瓦拉迪耶的计划提出反对，认为此计划太具有侵略性。他强调了古城墙具有重要的意义，记载了古代的修建技术，因此，应当尽可能地保留城墙的原始状态。

瓦拉迪耶在1839年去世，1848年，皮乌斯九世（Pius IX）指派了他所嘱意的新的修缮建筑师。在这位建筑师去世的前一年，按照格列高利十六世（Gregorio XVI）的意愿，古城墙失去了两座城门，拉比卡纳门和普雷内斯蒂纳门，毁弃这两座城门是为了"增强"克劳狄和新阿尼奥（Anio Novus）输水道的展示效果。如今只能从17世纪和18世纪遗留下来的画作中看到当时的场景了。在遗迹的两侧，他们保留了"Travertine"石灰石的砌块，刻有普雷内斯蒂纳城门的重要献词，献词的内容与霍诺里乌斯（Honorius）王朝的成就相关。

在皮乌斯九世的调停下，城墙的修复工程于1847年正式从教廷（Apostolic Chamber）转到罗马市政府的管辖下。在第一位负责的建筑师路易吉·波莱蒂

In the first decades of the nineteenth century, the Aurelian walls of Rome was in the middle of a controversial dispute between the historical and humanistic culture, in this case, represented by Antonio Nibby, and that expressed by the architectural thoughts and also by the works of Giuseppe Valadier, who was more attentive to keeping the first and the second time in of renewal. Both characters were taking much interest to the ancient walls, Nibby, during a thorough text on the walls, completed the first comprehensive, systematic study of the monument (A. Nibby, Le mura di Roma, Roma 1820), Valadier as personally involved in the restoration of the Aurelian walls.

In a document from 1806 there is a restoration project from the architect himself modified thirteen years later, with plans of spending 5,884 scudi. The proposed interventions are mainly' in the general cleaning of the walls of the weed vegetation, the reintegration of the missing curtain and of the implementation called for in many occasions of a double ring road to be used as a "public walkway", which would make the monument visible in memory of the ancient city. The main criticism about Nibby was the necessary work needed done on the so-called Muro Torto, a stretch of the Augustus age structure incorporated into the Aurelian circuit at the foot of the Pincio. Valadier designed large arches for discharging that surround the slopes of the hill, made of squared blocks of tuff, interspersed with bricks in the pillars. For the arches and the parapet above the garden they made use of bricks, for the walls of the whole structure they planned to use plastered walls.

In 1830, at the beginning of a new work phase, that would have interested this stretch, Nibby protested to Valadier's project, considering it too invasive, he underlined the importance of the ancient walls and documented the antique construction techniques, and therefore to conserve as much as possible in its original state.

Valadier died in 1839 and a new restorer was introduced in 1848, as wanted by Pius IX. The year before the architect's death, the ancient walls lost two of its gates (wanted by Gregorio XVI), the Labicana and the Prenestina, sacrificed to "enhance" the exhibition of the aqueducts, Acqua Claudia and

（Luigi Poletti）（1792—1869年）去世后，由建筑师维吉尼奥·维斯皮那尼（Virginio Vespignani）（1808—1882年）长期负责城墙修复工作。他对庇亚门和萨拉利亚门尤其感兴趣，并与另一位建筑师卡洛·卢多维科·维斯康蒂（Carlo Ludovico Visconti）合作，拆除了弗拉米尼亚门两侧的塔楼。

他主持的修复工程的重点落在对护墙和塔楼的修复上，有时对单薄的墙体整段重建，剩余部分则仅仅重修墙帷，保留了奥勒良或霍诺里乌斯城墙的核心部分的原貌。对于这部分工作，建筑师使用了一种易于识别的、黄色贴面砖，这些砖是在梵蒂冈的砖窑里烧制的。它们被非常整齐地铺设，常常使用"劈头"设备，这是唯一可行的复制三角形罗马砖的方式，从而确保外侧墙体与城墙内核之间的适当的稳定性。所使用的砂浆是由石灰、火山灰、沙土混合而成，通常具有很高的品质。连接处的结构使用一层薄灰，以保护下部的砂浆铺砌层。

特别有趣的是，那些较少暴露在自然环境中的砖石，也会出现硬壳面。维修时用紫色粉刷表面，这很可能十分适于营造古旧的外观。这显示出由维斯皮那尼重建的塔楼与墙面之间存在不协调。1870年，罗马成为新的意大利首都，城市进入了快速变化时期，市镇快速扩张，新建了许多居住邻里。1870年10月31日，陆军部责成委员会起草一份新建城市防御工事系统的计划以保卫首都，其后果是古代城墙废弃了。

在建成之后，历经1500多年的风雨，古城墙终于完全失去其功能。

古城墙的废弃以及缺乏对城墙价值的认识，其结果导致城墙的许多部分从周边毗邻的地区开始被拆除，这种投机倒卖也牵扯到了原波考帕尼·卢多维西（Boncompagni Ludovisi）别墅的地块。实际上，新的土地划分产生了严重的人口压力，特别是在城市北部靠近坎帕尼亚路的地区。这样在1896年，他们开始考虑有必要拆除部分位于边界的城墙，以提高地区的流动性，最终拆除法案得到通过。

同年11月26日，拆除城墙的行动首先从阿布鲁佐路（Via Abruzzi）沿线开始，其他处城墙的拆除也紧随其后。最终约有70 m长的城墙被全部拆除。

1921年萨拉利亚门被拆除，目的是使得道路更为通畅。由于1870年罗马沦陷时城墙遭到破坏，这座古老的城门曾经在1873年由维斯皮那尼进行过重建。随着奥勒良城墙的所有权归市政府所有，1900年颁布了法令，启动了一系列由市政府部门实施的长期干预计划。直至今日，这个干预计划仍在遗址管理部门和古罗马考古遗址的挖掘等方面延续着。

1914年到1915年之间，紧邻萨拉利亚门西侧的部分城墙和圣萨巴（San Saba）地区的部分城墙得到修复。这些修缮工程都是些小修小补，只需要投入极少的资金。修复使用的是"Tor di Quinto"红砖，幸运的是，这使得重建的部分能够被

Anio Novus. Today remains only the drawings of the sights from the seventeenth and eighteenth century. At the sides of the monument they had conserved blocks of travertine with carvings of the important dedication of the Prenestina gate, which connected the realisation of the emperor Honorius.

Under the conditions of Pius IX, the restoration of the walls was officially passed on in 1847 from the Apostolic Chamber, to the City of Rome. It was Virginio Vespignani (1808–1882) who then took care of the ancient walls for a long period after the death of the architect Luigi Poletti (1792–1869). He had a particular interest in porta Pia and porta Salaria and also worked with Carlo Ludovico Visconti demolishing the side towers of porta Flaminia.

His work is valued for the restoration of curtains and towers, sometimes reconstructed for the entire thickness of the walls, others only in hangings, preserving the original core of Aurelian or Honorius. For this work the architect used a well recognised, yellow paste type of brick, which comes from the Vatican kilns. These bricks were laid in a very regular way, always using the "head cutting" apparatus, the only capable way of reproducing the triangular Roman brick to insure proper stability between the outer walls and the inner core of the walls. The mortar used was a mixture of lime, pozzolana and sand, and was generally of high quality. The structure of the joints was made with a very thin dough to protect the bedding of mortar below.

Something interestingly particular, that can be seen from the portion of masonry less exposed to the elements, is the presence of a sail surface, purple colour brushed on the masonry restoration, most probably applied to give an antique look. This shows how the current dissonance between the towers and curtain walls, rebuilt by Vespignani, and the ancient walls was less obvious. In 1870, when Rome became the capital of the new Italian state, there was a period of rapid transformation in the city, where the town expanded rapidly with new neighborhoods. Already on 31 October 1870, the Ministry of War charged a committee to draft a plan for the new system of fortifications that was supposed to defend the capital with the consequent abandonment of the ancient walls.

After more than fifteen hundred years after their construction they were completely deprived of its function.

The result of this abandonment and lack of recognition of their value was the demolition of numerous sections of the walls, starting from the adjacent area, the speculation that regarded to what had been Boncompagni Ludovisi's Villa. The new subdivisions, in fact, generated a strong

识别出来。各种重建项目在 1926 年开始。1928 年至 1935 年期间，保护古城墙的任务交给了建筑师安东尼奥·马利亚·戈利尼（Antonio Maria Colini）。1933 年他着手修复马焦雷门及其周边环境。这项干预首要的是复兴古时城墙形制，让曾经被掩埋的部分重见天日，提供更佳的观赏视角，以及重新设计周边环境。

阿西那里亚门周边的发掘干预工作可追溯到 1951 年。这是保存得比较好的城门之一，位于拉特兰附近。目前的外观主要成型于霍诺里乌斯时期的干预修复，这次修复使它从简易的便门改造为真正意义上的城门。发掘工作结束后，修复工作随之展开，由古利埃尔莫·盖蒂（Guglielmo Gatti）负责，卢考斯·科扎（Lucos Cozza）协助工作。当时，他们用新的"travertine"石灰石砌块建起霍诺里乌斯式拱门，以代替在这座城门最后一次封门时被移走的构件。构件是 1574 年皮乌斯四世下令移走的，当时正在修建圣乔凡尼门（图 1）。

1965 年至 1966 年，开展了大规模的修复运动，修复的主要目标是 1962 到 1963 年因寒冬造成的严重损坏。皮耶路易吉·罗密欧（Pieruigi Romeo）为修复工

demographic pressure on the Northern part of the city, in correspondence to Via Campania, so that in 1896, they began to discuss the need to demolish some parts of the boundary walls to improve mobility in the area, therefore they gave permission to start the "cuts".

On 26 November the demolishing of the walls started along Via Abruzzi, the others followed nearly immediately, with an outcome of almost 70m of walls demolished.

1921 saw the demolition of porta Salaria, eliminated to smooth the roads. The antique door had been rebuilt by Vespignani in 1873 because of the damage it received in the fall of Rome in 1870. With the Aurelian walls owned by the city, a law in 1900, gave the launch to a long series of interventions on the monument by the city administration which continues today through the monuments Service and excavations of the city on the archaeological sites of Rome.

Between 1914 and 1915, the section immediately west of porta Salaria and some parts of the walls at San Saba were restored. They were small repairs carried out with little money and making use of "red bricks of Tor di Quinto" which fortunately made the rebuilt parts recognisable. Various restorations started in 1926. Between 1928 and 1935 the task of preserving the ancient city walls was given to Antonio Maria Colini, who in 1933 began the restoration of porta Maggiore and its surroundings. The intervention was primarily at the revival of the ancient levels, to bring to light parts of the monument that had been buried and to propose a better view, and to redesign the adjacent area.

The intervention of digging around porta Asinaria dates back to 1951. This being one of the more conserved gates. Located in the ground near Lateran, its present appearance is mainly due to the intervention by Honorius, which transformed it from a simple postern into a real urban gate. After completing the excavation, the restoration is performed, under direction of Guglielmo Gatti, assisted by Lucos Cozza. That time they built the Honorius fornix with new blocks of travertine, to replace the stolen ones at the time of the final closure of the door; this all took place by orders from Pius IV in 1574, when porta San Giovanni was built (Fig.1).

图 1　阿西那里亚门——考古发掘（1951 年）之后的霍诺里乌斯重建的券顶（A. M. Colini）

Fig.1　Porta Asinaria– Rebuilding of the Honorius fornix (A.M. Colini) after the archaeological excavations (1951)

程提供技术指导，卢考斯·科扎为考古方面的顾问。这次干预修复工程涉及的城墙有：平扎那门附近的一段沿着拉比卡纳门的现有道路的城墙，曼特罗尼亚门附近的一小段以及拉丁纳门与跨越克里斯托弗·哥伦布路（Via Cristoforo Colombo）的城墙拱门之间相当长的一段，还有从这一点到台伯河岸的其他几段。

那一时期的修复工程主要是重建之前由于倒塌而造成不连续的城墙，因此必须通过结构加固和重建，使墙体更为稳定和安全，从而可以抵御雨雪天气的侵袭。这些干预工程重点关注城墙中为机动车和行人穿越的拱门，主要考虑安全问题。

在必要的地方加建了顶棚，采用的是钢梁以及与倒塌的塔楼和步道同时期的砖。表层部分使用石材和水泥砂浆加固，对已损坏的部分使用钢链维修，用相同的材料进行锚固和楔牢。

在所有的修复工程中，对墙体表面的处理均使用"tuff"凝灰岩，并用石料和水泥砂浆砌成带坡的排水沟，表面抹石灰后再浇沥青。在有大量积水的地方，他们就要准备"清理"，方法是用"travertine"石灰石或火石作为基底层砌块，上面用罗马瓦（coppi，类似筒瓦的盖瓦）做排水沟，这些砌块粗凿成方形，放置在城墙的外侧。

工程结束时，他们做了一层涂层，掩盖了重建城墙的位置。在将近一个世纪之后，维斯皮那尼提出的用上色的方式协调新旧两部分的方法再次得到应用（图2）。

阿皮亚门与克里斯托弗·哥伦布路之间的通道对公众开放的时间可以追溯到

Between 1965 and 1966 an extensive restoration campaign was carried out, primarily designed to repair the severe damage caused by a terrible winter 1962–1963, under the technical guidance of Pieruigi Romeo and the archaeological guidance of Lucos Cozza. The interventions involved a stretch of the walls near porta Pinciana, the walls along the existing avenue of porta Labicana, a small stretch near porta Metronia and a very large stretch between porta Latina and the arches of the walls made for crossing Via Cristoforo Colombo as well as a few other walls from that point until the Tiber banks.

The restorations done in that period were mainly reconstructions on walls that had collapsed years before which gave discontinuity and so had to make them more stable and secure by structuring and repairing the walls as to prevent water weathering. These interventions focused mainly vehicular and pedestrian crossing arches of the walls for security reasons.

Roofs were built where necessary, with steel beams and bricks in correspondence to the time of the collapsed towers and walkways. The consolidation work on the superficial parts was built of masonry with mortar cement, and the mending of broken parts were made by steel chains, anchored and wedged with the same material.

The arrangement of the surface of the walls, for all the

图2　1965年至1966年间进行的一次大规模修复运动 (P. Romeo)
Fig.2　Extensive restoration campaign between 1965 and 1966 (P. Romeo)

图2-a　曼特罗尼亚门：内侧墙体的重建
Fig.2-a　Porta Metronia: rebuilding of the inner walls

图2-b　平扎那门西侧的第三座塔楼：斜穿孔，以便插入铁件，随后以水泥浇筑
Fig.2-b　Third tower west of porta Pinciana: oblique ration to insert iron bars cemented afterwards

图2-c　拉丁纳门和阿皮亚门之间的城墙顶部修复
Fig.2-c　Rebuilding of the top of the wall between Porta Latina and Porta Appia

1970 年。

在为文化遗产而准备的拨款到位之后，借助"千禧 2000"计划（Jubilee of 2000）（周年庆典行动计划，1996 年第 651 号法案），开展了新一轮更广泛的修复运动。此项计划的部分资金连同来自埃斯奎利诺城市再生计划（URES–Urban Regeneration Esquiline Schemes）的资金一起，主要用于对卡斯特兰塞圆形剧场和圣乔凡尼门之间的一段城墙的修复工作，此段城墙的塔楼和防护墙已明显倾斜。西斯廷（Sistine）规划主要是在这个片区的城墙的内侧建立一条林荫大道。1594 年克雷芒八世（Clemente Ⅷ）重提此案，直到 1744 年本笃十四世（Benedict XIV）时期，这个计划才真正得到实施。他建造了有六排树木的林荫大道，树种有榆树和桑树。当时的地面标高已经与现在的卡罗·费利塞路差不多了，这远高于奥勒良城墙建造时的地面标高。1818 年到 1823 年间，朱塞佩·瓦拉迪耶也组织过解决方案，约一个世纪后（1926 年），负责花园景观设计的拉斐尔·德·维科（Raffaele de Vico）试图减少位于城墙背后的罗马市政府的服务设施工棚造成的视觉影响。

由于土壤加诸强大的压力，这段城墙的整体结构都出现了倾斜，1893 年至 1902 年间的暴雨导致城墙两次灾难性的倒塌，总体损失至少有 60 m。在 1999 年 4 月 29 日到 12 月 4 日之间，罗马农业与环境部实施措施修复了城墙背面城内的沉降区，将这一片土地的标高填至最初修建时的高度（图 3）。工棚最终被拆除了，这是市政府

restoration, was built in tuff, building stone and mortar cement for the containment of the slopes, applied after lime settings and poured on asphalt. Where there was storm water, they prepared "clear outs" made of Roman tiles (coppi) on bed-bound blocks of travertine stone or flint roughly squared and placed on the outer part of the walls.

At the end of the work they made a coating to disguise where the walls had been rebuilt. After almost a century, the attention voiced by Vespignani came back, to tune chromatically the new with the old (Fig. 2).

The public opening of the passageway between porta Appia and Via Cristoforo Colombo dates back to 1970.

A new and extensive campaign of restoration was carried out following the appropriations intended for the cultural heritage, on occasion of the Jubilee of 2000 (Plan of Action for the anniversary, Act 651 of 1996). Some of these funds, together with those from Urban Regeneration Esquiline Schemes, were used for the part of the walls between the amphitheatre Castrense and porta San Giovanni, of which its towers and curtains had an apparent loss of verticality. On the domestic front of the walls in this area, the Sistine plan was to build a tree lined avenue. The project resumed in 1594 by Clemente VIII, was implemented not until 1744 by Benedict XIV, who created a lined avenue with six rows of trees, made of elms and mulberries. Already at that time, the level of the ground was almost the same as the current Via Carlo Felice, which was much higher than when the Aurelian walls was constructed. Giuseppe Valadier also organised the arrangements, between 1818 and 1823, and a century later (1926), Raffaele de Vico, who took care of the garden landscaping, tried to mitigate the visual impact of the service sheds situated in the municipality of Rome, which had been placed behind the walls.

图 3 对卡斯特兰塞圆形剧场到圣乔凡尼门之间的城墙背后的城市古老的洼地进行修复

Fig.3 Restoration of the ancient depression that existed in the city behind the walls between anfiteatro Castrense and porta San Giovanni

自己于 20 世纪初紧靠城墙建造的设施，它损害了城墙的稳定，并影响了这一长段防御工事的展示。同一时期利用千禧 2000 项目的资金得到修复的有奥斯提安塞门、阿皮亚门、弗拉米尼亚门，包括跨越克里斯托弗·哥伦布路和奥斯提安塞门的拱券之间的城墙，以及牛市大街沿路的城墙。

这样的修复在不同的城墙段展开。新的砖护墙采用了"底框法"（sottosquadro），这种方法使得干预痕迹清晰可见。古利埃尔莫·德·安吉利斯·奥萨特（Guglielmo de Angelis d' Ossat）认为，新的修复不应与原有的墙体在同一个层面（图 4），而是应当略微后退"做底"，而原有墙体则成为修补部分的"框"。

在千禧年之后不久，城墙又遭遇了一次灾难性事件。2001 年 4 月，一次强暴风雨过后，位于阿皮亚门与跨克里斯托弗·哥伦布路的拱券之间的部分护墙坍塌（从城门数第 7 和第 8 座塔楼之间）。这是一段砖砌护墙，由英诺森十世（Innocent X）（1644—1655 年）下令重建，坍塌后散落的石块上面的盾形纹样和落成纪念铭文确定了其重建时间（图 5）。坍塌的原因在于古代墙体与 17 世纪的石材衬砌之间缺乏连接，而城墙的顶部根本没有任何保护措施，真是雪上加霜。而暴雨的雨水从原始的墙体与石材衬砌之间的缝隙里渗入，使得两者完全分离，导致城墙坍塌。内窥镜的分析表明，凡是砖护墙不是原构之处，均已经与奥勒良城墙的核心部分分离开来。

Because of the strong pressure exerted by the soil, there was a loss of verticality of the whole structure in that stretch, and two disastrous collapses that occurred during heavy rains between 1893 and 1902, and which caused an overall loss of at least 60m of walls. The operation carried out by the Department of Agriculture and Environment of Rome, between 29 April and 4 December 1999, has restored the depression that existed in the city behind the walls, bringing the share of land back to its existing level at the time of the construction (Fig.3). The sheds were finally eliminated, which the municipality itself set against the walls since the beginning of the twentieth century and damaged the static conditions of the city walls, not showing the long section of fortification. During those same years there had been subject of restoration, using the funds of the Jubilee 2000, the gates Ostiense, Appia, Flaminia, including the parts of the walls between the arches crossing Via Cristoforo Colombo and porta Ostiense and along Campo Boario street.

These restorations were done in different stretches, the new brick curtains were done with the "sottosquadro" technique, a method which makes the intervention visibly clear. The theory of Guglielmo de Angelis d'Ossat was that the new work must not be done in the same level of the original one (Fig. 4) but in a inner level (sottosquadro).

Not long after the Jubilee year the walls were concerned by a disastrous event. April 2001, after a violent storm, a part of the curtain walls collapsed between porta Appia and the arches crossing Via Cristoforo Colombo (between the seventh and the eighth tower starting from the gate). It was a brick curtain, rebuilt under instructions of Innocent X (1644–1655), as the coat of arms and below the dedicatory inscription, along with the fallen masonry; they were there to testify with absolute certainty (Fig. 5). The collapse was caused by the lack of binding between the ancient walls and the seventeenth century stone lining, which got worse by the fact that in that stretch there is no protection covering the top of the walls. This allowed the storm water to enter in the gaps between the original walls and the stone lining causing a complete separation and the fall of the walls. The endoscopic analysis shows that where the brick curtain isn't original, it has come apart from the Aurelian core.

图 4　使用"底框"方式修复的护墙
Fig.4　Restoration on the curtain using "sottosquadro" technique

图 5 英诺森十世时期重修的护墙（摄于倒塌前）
Fig.5 Curtain was rebuilt by Innocent X (photo made before the collapse)

修复工程的资金总额达 1 000 万欧元，除了用于从阿皮亚门到阿尔代阿提诺堡垒之间的坍塌的城墙部分，也用于其他部分的修复工作。修复工作包括 15 m^2 的新的石材衬砌，以取代缺失的部分（图 6）。在一次修复工作时，在碎石之下发现了盾形纹样和铭文，现已移至阿皮亚门内的城墙博物馆保存。

对坍塌的城墙的修复工作，尽可能保留原始墙体，在外层砖砌部分遵循原有式样。在修复中，其余的护墙并未使用"底框"技术，原因是该技术过度改变了墙帷，使之与先前的修复差别太大，仅仅留下了小巧的铭文，说明修复日期。这些铭文通常可以在城墙底部找到，在这些部位，因为年久失修或者潮湿导致部分护墙缺失，替换材料是必需的（图 7）。出于安全考虑，在塔楼内部安装了加固环，在霍诺里乌斯长廊的顶部加装了金属链（图 8）。

修复工作从阿尔代阿提诺堡垒开始。安东尼奥·桑加罗受命于保罗三世法尔内塞（Paul III Farnese）的加固城墙的计划，目的在于提高城市的整体防御系统，使之进一步更新，从而更好地应对新的攻城技术。

桑加罗的总体方案是从保存在乌菲兹美术馆（Uffizi）的手稿中发现的。这个方案在整个城墙中规划了 18 座新建的堡垒，它们与另外 5 座一同保护着周边地区。这是一个工程浩大的干预计划，但是几乎仅仅在阿尔代阿提诺堡垒附近的城墙段

There was a sum of ten million euro for the restoration; to be used in other areas as well as where the walls had collapsed, from porta Appia to Bastione Ardeatino. The work consisted of 15m^2 of new stone lining, to replace what was lost (Fig 6). The coat of arms and the inscription were found under the rubble after an attempt of restoration and kept in a museum of the walls inside Porta Appia.

The work on the part of the walls where it collapsed was done by conserving the original walls as much as possible and by keeping an original final look on the outer bricks. The rest of the courtains concerning the restoration wasn't used by the "sottosquadro" technique, which had excessively changed the walls hangings from the previous work done, but leaving small inscriptions stating the date of the restoration. These indications are usually found at the bottom of the walls, where some replacements were necessary due to the deterioration and the loss of some curtains caused by humidity (Fig. 7). For safety they put reinforcement rings in the towers and metal chains over the Honorian gallery (Fig. 8).

The restoration started from Bastione Ardeatino. Antonio da Sangallo's project to strengthen the walls, commanded by Paul III Farnese, had the purpose of improving the whole defensive system of the city,

图 6　重建 2001 年坍塌的圣乔凡尼门城墙的护墙
Fig.6　Rebuilding of the curtain collapsed in 2001 San Giovanni

图 7　护墙坍塌之后对墙体底部的修复
Fig.7　Restorations on the lower part of the wall after the collapse of the curtain

第三章 城墙修复 3 – Restoration of City Walls

图8 塔楼和霍诺里乌斯长廊中的加固环和金属链
Fig.8 Reinforcement rings and metal chains in the towers and in the Honorius gallery

得以实施。这个计划被认为是自前一个世纪以来所有加固城墙的理论中最完美的一个。

他们在大块的墙面上使用除草剂，以保护墙面。其处理方法就是在砖块上和石材的顶部罩上一层生物杀灭剂产品，之后再进行检查与修复工作。为保护城墙的顶部，也为了使得护墙能够抵御暴雨雨水的侵蚀，他们采用了一种称为"碎陶"（cocciopesto）的技术。"碎陶"常用于修复工程，甚至在维特鲁威的专著中也对其性能给予高度评价。它由石灰、沙或火山灰和大量捣碎的质地均匀的碎礤瓦颗粒组成。火山灰（一种来自火山喷发的原料，具有很高的水硬性）和碎砖块的特性，使得墙体具有很好的防水性能。

对破损的砖块采用微型黏合剂，用于填补较为明显的缝隙、连接件的一般清理、石块上的破损部位和小洞的密封。一处尤其精确的干预是关于保罗三世法尔内塞的徽章纹样，在1539—1540年间插入在主城墙的角部，由雕塑大师洛伦佐·菲奥伦蒂诺（Lorenzo Fiorentino）完成。这件尺度巨大的作品雕刻在富于纹理和聚合颗粒的"travertine"石灰石上，通过石材中的铸铁托架将这个砖石砌体支撑起来，嵌入上部结构中。

and to update it so it would work better against the new siege techniques.
Sangallo's general project was discovered through drawings they conserved at the Uffizi; it regarded the whole walls with plans of eighteen new ramparts plus another five to defend the surroundings. A plan of a vast intervention, but which almost only took place in correspondence to the Bastione Ardeatino, was considered to be the most perfect out of all the theories in making the walls stronger since the previous century.
They used weed killer on the big walls to protect it, this treatment is done with biocide products of vestments in bricks and on the top of the area in stone, and it is then looked over and restored. To protect the top of the walls and to keep the curtains waterproof from the flow of storm water they used "cocciopesto". "Cocciopesto" is often used in restoration and has praised characteristics even in Vitruvio's treatise. It's made with lime, sand or pozzolana and quite large but homogeneous crushed brick. The characteristics of pozzolana (a charge of volcanic origin by high hydraulic properties) and of the crushed bricks allow there to be a good resistance to the water.

岩石表皮的剥落使得这块雕刻作品损失了部分纹样，比如教皇三重冠的前部，两个小皇冠和其他一些装饰性的花纹。

使用生物杀灭剂去除生物层之后，较小的构件可以通过环氧树脂黏合在一起，而一些较重的石材构件需要用玻璃纤维钉完成连接。

在2004年到2006年间，对阿西那里亚门进行了修复。他们必须修复两座塔楼的破损部分，但是主要的工作量在于石材表面的清理和重新整合。在方案中规划了一条残疾车专用通道，可以通往左侧塔楼的二层。

目前，城墙环路沿线还有许多施工场地，包括马焦雷门和卡斯特兰塞路之间的一块修复现场，在这里，他们清除了所有的大型杂草和植物，杂草和植物已经严重损坏了部分城墙。采取这些干预措施是因为缺少对城墙环路内侧的日常维护，如今只能作修补。美第奇别墅和马尔凯路（Via Marche）之间的城墙段也有一块施工工地，范围贯穿城内与城外，就在平扎那门的维修之后。奥勒良城墙与其他古罗马遗迹一起正受到新的地铁线建设施工的影响。尤其是新的格局将会影响拉特兰路（Via dei Laterani）和曼特罗尼亚门之间的一段城墙。所以这一段城墙和许多其他处于类似情形的遗迹正一起受到密切的观察与持续的监测，以尽可能消除或避免由震动产生的问题，有关部门正在计划在地铁隧道层的上部喷射隔离层（灌浆）。在新的地铁线施工结束正式通车后，将对所涉及的所有城墙段进行必要的修复。

Also the micro-bindings from the damaged bricks were used, filling the more obvious gaps, the general cleaning of the joints and the sealing of the broken parts and holes in the stone. A particular accurate intervention concerned the coat of arms of Paul III Farnese, inserted on the corner of the main walls between 1539 and 1540 by the sculptor Master Lorenzo Fiorentino. The work of great dimensions was carved on a travertine rich of concretions and veins, made of stone elements that embed the supported brick masonry in the upper part by iron brackets.
The exfoliation caused the total loss of some of its parts, such as the front part of the triple crown, the two crowns and some other decorative elements.
After having eliminated the biological coating for means of the biocide products, the smaller parts were consolidated with epoxy resins, whereas for the bonding of the heavier stone elements it was necessary to use pins of fibreglass.
Between 2004 and 2006 there was restoration work done on Porta Asinaria. They had to mend the broken parts of the two towers, but the main job was the cleaning and the reintegration of the masonry surfaces. In the project there is a path for physical disabled cars planned which provides access to the first floor of the tower on the left.
Currently there are some work yards along the walls circuit, including one between porta Maggiore and viale Castrense in which they are eliminating all the large weeds and plants that have severely damaged parts of the walls. These interventions are due to a lack of ordinary maintenance on the inside of the walls circuit, which only now is in the course of repair. There is also work being done on the stretch between Villa Medici and Via Marche, on the inside and the outside, just after porta Pinciana. The Aurelian Walls, together with other Roman monuments is being affected by work yards that are constructing the new underground line. In particular the new layout could interfere with the stretch between Via dei Laterani and porta Metronia. This is the reason that this stretch of the walls, like many other monuments in similar situations, are under close observations and continuously monitored to eliminate, or to avoid as much as possible, the problems that could arise from the vibrations, they are planning to inject layers of insulation into the soil (grouting) above the level of the tube tunnel. After the realization and the activation of the new line, the whole section which it concerns will be provided the restoration required.

第三节 奥勒良城墙修建和维修
3.3 The Construction and Restoration of the Aurelian Walls

贾亭立　Ja Tingli

1. 背景

今天，在罗马仍然可以看到的最早城墙是塞维安城墙（Servian wall），它建于公元前 6 世纪中叶，是当时的罗马共和国第六位国王塞尔维乌斯·图利乌斯下令修建的，故被命名为塞维安城墙。城墙大部分土筑（agger），还有部分使用凝灰岩（cappellaccio）——罗马当地的一种粒状"tuff"凝灰岩石块砌筑。公元前 4 世纪，为了抵御高卢人入侵，塞维安城墙被重新建造。这时，随着采石技术的进步，更加密实的凝灰岩"lithoid tuff"被开采出来，最后以"travertine"石灰岩替代凝灰岩筑城。城墙采用干法砌筑，即在砌筑时不用石灰浆等黏结材料，直接将大块的条石（高约 59cm）按"一顺一丁"砌在一起（图 1、图 2）。这道城墙在公元前 353 年、公元前 217 年、公元前 212 年和公元前 87 年分别被维修过。

1. Background

In the middle of the 6th century BC, Servius Tullius (578BC–535BC), the sixth king of ancient Rome, made the Servian walls (Italian: Mura Serviane) which is believed as the earliest extant city wall of Rome. Most of the walls were Agger (Latin word, meaning a defensive ramp of earth bearing the wall along the inside). Large blocks of Cappellaccio (a type of local granular grey tuff) were used. In the 4th century BC, the walls were rebuilt in response to the invasion of the Gauls. The improvement of quarrying methods leaded to stronger tuff – lithoid tuff. At last, the wall construction used travertine in stead of tuff. The blocks were laid without the use of mortar, and this technique is called the dry-stone technique. Large square blocks (opus quadratum) were piled one on top of the other, in multiple rows(Fig.1, Fig.2). The walls were repaired in 353BC, 217BC, 212BC, and 87BC.

图 1　塞维安城墙剖面（引自：罗马城墙博物馆）
Fig.1　Servialn wall, section (from: Museum of the City Walls of Rome)

图 2　古代城墙修建示意图（引自：罗马城墙博物馆）
Fig.2　City wall construction in ancient times (from: Museum of the City Walls of Rome)

　　到奥古斯都时期，奥古斯都给这个多灾多难的城市带来和平，城墙的防御功能明显下降。直到 3 世纪，城墙再也没有修缮过，而是和城市的扩张连在一起。很多城墙段不可避免地被括入了不同性质、功能的建筑（首先是皇家建筑，其次是公共建筑或者是私人建筑）。在很多情况下，城门券洞的上方有输水道经过，因此它的修缮往往和输水道的修缮相关联。一个更显著的现象则是，城门作为"进入城市心脏的重要道路入口节点"，被当作"纪念性的拱门"来修缮。同样，宏伟的城墙防护体系"最终沦为装点城市的元素"。到奥勒良皇帝统治时期，来自北欧的蛮族入侵（270—271 年），加之罗马帝国内部的东部巴尔米拉（Palmyra）王国叛乱，使沿城市边界建造一道强大的防御工事成为当务之急。

2. 奥勒良城墙修建、重建、维修的历史（3—18 世纪）

1）奥勒良城墙的建造（271—403 年）

　　奥勒良城墙并不是一开始建成就是今天看到的样子，它的建造分为三个时期：第一时期，271—275 年，城墙最初被建造；第二时期，大约在 311 年，城墙被局部加高；最后是 401—402 年，城墙被彻底改造，最终形成了我们今天所见的情形。

（1）第一时期——最初的建造（271—275 年）

　　271 年，奥勒良皇帝下令修建城墙，新的城墙把城市扩大的范围包括在其中，城

Since Augustus brought the peace to the turbulent city, the defensive function of the Servian Walls declines significantly. The wall was never restored and began to blend with the expanding city until the 3rd century. Several sections of the walls were employed into various kinds of buildings, first those imperial architecture then the public or private buildings. The restoration of the gates were often related the restoration of the Aqueducts, which usually go through the gates above the vault. But a remarkable phenomenon is that the gates, "as the accesses to the heart of the city," were restored and transformed in order to build "real monumental arches". Meanwhile, the great fortifications "were then degraded to the elements of city decoration". From 270 to 271, during the reign of the emperor Aurelian, it's very urgent to build a stronger fortification due to the invasion from northern Europe and the revolt of Palmyra in the east part of Roman Empire.

2. The construction, reconstruction and restoration of the Aurelian Walls 3–18 century

1) The construction of the Aurelian Walls (271–403)

The Aurelian Walls (Italian: Mura Aureliane) were different from the current appearance when they were initially constructed. There are three construction periods: the first period is from 271 to 275; the second

墙的走向根据地形、经济和战略因素确定。比如，高地被包括在城墙内，可以更有效地抵抗敌人的进攻，同时，具有防御作用的河流也被利用起来。在经济因素方面，城墙要尽可能地占用皇家土地，尽量减少因征用私人或公共土地带来的支出。

这一时期的奥勒良城墙全长 18.837 km，高 6.5 m，厚 3.5 m。基础部分用"travertine"石灰石砌筑，基础以上墙体，表层用面砖，内部则是夹杂着碎石、碎砖的混凝土核心（图 3）。城墙顶部有防卫用的走道，外侧是起防护作用的"垛口墙"，约有 1 m 多高。每隔 30 m 有一座方形的塔楼从墙上突出，它高于走道，在走道的标高处设有一个开有 4 个拱券窗的房间，被用来设置作战的武器，塔楼的顶部是由"垛口墙"围合的平台（图 4）。

在与城市道路相交处，城墙上设有城门，城门一般以道路的名字来命名。这一时期的城墙上建有 17 座城门，按照样式可以将它们分为三类（表 1）：第一类城门由两个拱券门洞构成，门洞两旁是半圆形塔楼；第二类城门只有一个拱券门洞，门洞两侧是半圆形塔楼；第三类城门只是在城墙相邻的两座方形塔楼之间开一个拱券门洞。

城墙的建造速度非常快，仅用了短短的五年时间。城墙经过的地区，许多已有建

is around 311 when the walls were heightened; from 401 to 402 is the third period during which the walls were reconstructed and subsequently shaped the final form.

(1) The first period – initial construction (271 – 275)

The wall construction started in 271 by order of Emperor Aurelian. The walls enclosed the extended range of the city and also was attributed to the topography, the military and the economy aspects. The walls enclosed the hills and the rivers which facilitate defense. Taking account of economy aspects, the costs for expropriation of the private or public land were reduced by employing the royal land as much as possible.

The walls built in this period ran for 18 837m, 6.5m height and 3.5m thick. The base was constructed by stones (travertine), the main part upon the base were brick-faced concrete (mixed with broken pieces of stones and bricks) (Fig.3). On the top of the wall there was a passage, on the outside of which stood the parapet about 1m height with crenellations. Rectangular towers protruded from the wall every 30m. The tower was higher than the passage, at the same level of which there was a room with four arch windows inside the tower. The room was equipped with weapons. A terrace with battlements is built on the top of tower (Fig.4).

The gates were established where the walls intersected the roads of the city. Thus the gates were usually named after the roads. Seventeen gates of the walls could lie in three categories according to the patterns (Table 1). The first type consisted of two archways and two semicircular towers on each side; the second type had one archway and two semicircular towers; the third type had one archway between two square towers.

The construction was so fast that it was finished in five years. Most of the buildings on the way of the walls were demolished, and then the materials from these buildings were reused in the walls. Other buildings were incorporated into the structure as a part of the walls. There were economy and military advantages: on the one hand, the material and time for construction were saved; on the other hand, it prevented the enemies to take these buildings as

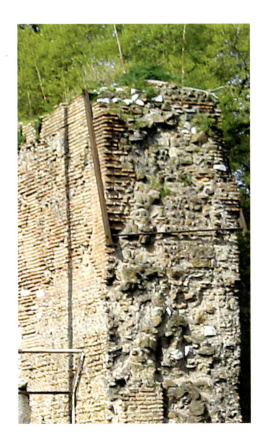

图 3　城墙横断面（左）以及石基础（右）
Fig.3　The section of the wall (left) and the stone base (right)

图 4-a 奥勒良时期城墙塔楼平面（引自：《古典时代切利欧山的历史和地理》）
Fig.4-a The towers of the Aurelian period, plan (from: Storia e topografia del Celio nell'antichita)

图 4-b 奥勒良时期城墙塔楼示意图（引自：罗马城墙博物馆）
Fig.4-b A tower of the Aurelian period (from: Museum of the City Walls of Rome)

表 1 城门的分类

城门类型		图示	城门名称
第一类	城门为双券洞，两旁有两座半圆形塔楼		弗拉米尼亚门
			阿皮亚门
			奥斯提安塞门
			波图恩塞门
第二类	城门为单券洞，两旁有两座半圆形塔楼		萨拉利亚门
			诺曼塔纳门
			拉丁纳门
第三类	城门为城墙相邻的两座方形塔楼之间开一个券洞		平扎那门
			克劳萨门
			阿西那里亚门
			曼特罗尼亚门
			阿尔代阿提那门
			奥里利亚门
			赛第米亚那门
			科奈利亚门

注：图片来自于罗马城墙博物馆

Table 1 Classification of gates in the Aurelian period

Types of the Gate	Illustrations	Gates
The first type	two archways and two semicircular towers on each side	Porta Flaminia
		Porta Appia
		Porta Ostiense
		Porta Portuense
The second type	one archway and two semicircular towers on each side	Porta Salaria
		Porta Nomentana
		Porta Latina
The third type	one archway between two square towers	Porta Pinciana
		Porta Clausa
		Porta Asinaria
		Porta Metronia
		Porta Ardeatina
		Porta Aurelia
		Porta Settimiana
		Porta Corneria

Note: Pictures are from Museum of the City Walls of Rome

筑被拆除，拆下来的材料被重新利用到城墙上。不过，一些已有建筑由于战略和经济的原因没有被拆除，直接成为城墙的一部分。这大大节省了材料和建造时间，也防止敌人占领这些建筑后作为据点包围城市。其中较有代表的五座建筑如下（图5）：

古罗马禁卫军兵营：建于1世纪初，属提比略（Tiberius）时期（图5-a）。

马勒查(Marcia)，蒂普拉(Tepula)和尤莉娅(Iulia)输水道：建于公元前5年，属奥古斯都时期（图5-b）。

克劳狄输水道：建于1世纪，属克劳狄乌斯（Claudius）时期（图5-c）。

卡斯特兰塞圆形剧场：建于3世纪初，早于城墙50年（图5-d）。

盖乌斯·切斯提乌斯（Gaius Cestius）金字塔：建于公元前12年，是坟墓（图5-e）。

（2）第二时期——局部加高（约311年）

在第一期城墙建成使用了仅40年之后，面对敌人更加先进的武器和专业化的装备，奥勒良城墙显示出它的弱点，需要有更高更坚固的防御性能。马克森提乌斯皇帝（Maxentius）时期（278—312年）对其进行了加高，不过，并没有对整座城墙增高加固，只是对城墙的部分区段加高了3 m。这些加高的部分很有特点，它们的表面不是全部由砖砌筑，而是用砖与小块的石灰石隔行砌筑，形成横向线性的肌理（图6）。

fortifications. Five typical instances are as follows (Fig.5):

Castra Praetoria: Constructed as the barracks of ancient Rome in early 1st century; by Emperor Tiberius (Fig.5-a).

Acqua Marcia, Tepula and Iulia: The aqueducts of ancient Rome built in 5BC, by Emperor Augustus (Fig.5-b).

Acqua Claudia: The aqueduct built in 1st century; by Emperor Claudius (Fig.5-c).

Amphitheatrum Catrense: Fifty years before the construction of the Aurelian Walls (Fig.5-d).

Pyramid of Cestius: The bomb of Gaius Cestius constructed in 12BC (Fig.5-e).

(2) The second period – heightening (around 311)

Just 40 years after the initial construction, Emperor Maxentius (278–312) increased the height of the Aurelian Walls since they were not strong enough facing the improved equipments and techniques of siege. Nevertheless, only one part of the walls, rather than the entire circuit, was heightened about 3 meters. The sections constructed in this period can still be recognized through the special techniques: horizontal linear bricks and small pieces of tuff (Fig.6).

5-a

5-b

5-c

5-d

5-e

图5　城墙连接不同的建筑
Fig. 5　Different buildings connected by city walls
图5-a　古罗马禁卫军兵营
Fig. 5-a　Castra Praetoria
图5-b　马勒查、蒂普拉和尤莉娅输水道
Fig. 5-b　Acqua Marcia, Tepula and Iulia
图5-c　克劳狄输水道
Fig. 5-c　Acqua Claudia
图5-d　卡斯特兰塞圆形剧场
Fig. 5-d　Amphitheatrum Catrense
图5-e　切斯提乌斯金字塔
Fig. 5-e　Pyramid of Cestius

图 6　马克森提乌斯时期的加高工程（左）（引自：罗马城墙博物馆）
Fig. 6　The heightening part of the Aurelian Walls, by emperor Maxentius (left)(from: Museum of the City Walls of Rome)

图 7　第一阶段城墙的垛口痕迹（中）（引自：罗马城墙博物馆）
Fig. 7　The trace of the battlements of the first phase (middle)(from: Museum of the City Walls of Rome)

图 8　封闭廊道
Fig. 8　The passage

（3）第三时期——彻底改造（401—403 年）

在霍诺里乌斯和阿尔卡狄乌斯时期，面对野蛮人（西哥特人）的进一步入侵，出于战略原因并应对武器和攻城战术的进步，城墙于 401 到 403 年被彻底改建。改建包括以下内容：

① 墙体高度增加一倍：达到 15 m 左右，塔楼被加高到 23 m 左右（图 7）。

② 增设封闭廊道：配合墙体的增高，在原来城墙顶部走道的基础上，设一层有拱顶的廊道，这条廊道的内侧以大的拱门形式敞开，向外则在增高的墙面上开设箭孔。这条封闭廊道的顶部依然是外侧砌有"垛口墙"的开敞式走道。战争中，弓箭手在廊道里放箭，大型的武器则放置在上面敞开的平台上（图 8）。

③ 塔楼加层：随着城墙的增高，塔楼在原有的基础上增加了一层，上层的房间开有 8 个拱券窗，并将下层房间原有的大多数拱券窗封闭，或改造成小箭孔。塔楼顶部是四坡屋顶，并有石质的檐口（图 9）。

④ 增设厕所：厕所悬挑伸出城墙的外侧表面，由一块"travertine"石灰石板支撑。从塔楼的顶层房间走出到城墙顶的走道上，便可以抵达厕所（图 10）。

⑤ 加固城门：为了使城门更加坚固，这次改建中城门的变化也非常大。在主要城门的外表面加砌了白色的"travertine"石灰石（图 11），并将原有的两个门洞的城门改建为一个门洞，或是直接封闭其中的一个门洞。同时，加高了两侧半圆形的塔

(3) The third period – reconstruction (401–403)
During the reign of Honorius (384–423) and Arcadius (377/378–408), the walls were reconstructed from 401 to 403 due to the further improvement of siege techniques. The reconstruction was also attributed to the military considerations when the Visigoths invaded. The reconstruction included:

① Heightening: The walls were doubled in height, to 15m, with the towers up to 23m high (Fig.7).

② Enclosed passages with vaults were added on the top of the walls. There were large arches open to the inside of the wall and small embrasures on the outside of the wall. During the war, the archers were inside the sentry passage and the heavy weapons were placed on the top of passage(Fig. 8).

③ One more floor was added on the top of the tower. The new room usually had eight arch windows. While, the arch windows of the old room below were plugged up or changed into small embrasures. The tower had a pyramidal roof with stone cornices(Fig.9).

④ Adding latrines: The latrine protruded on the outer surface of the wall, supported by a travertine slab. People could reach the latrine from the upper passage(Fig.10).

⑤ White travertine blocks were added onto the outer surface of the gate for reinforcement (Fig.11). Some double-arched gates were rebuilt to one-arched gates. Some ones only used one archway and

楼。此外，为了更加安全，有的城门还在内侧建一个小院，并增设了第二道（城）门，类似中国古代城池中的"瓮城"（图12）。

经过这一时期的建设，奥勒良城墙更加坚固，成为一座拥有383个塔楼，7 020个垛口，5个边门，116个厕所和2 066个塔楼外部大窗的防御性工事。

blocked the other. Besides, the semicircular towers on both sides were heightened. Furthermore, one additional courtyard was added to the inner side of the gate as a postern gate for greater security (Fig.12). Aurelian Walls became firmer and formed a fortification consisting of 383 towers, 7,020 battlements, 5 side gates, 116 toilets and 2,066 outer

图 9-a 塔楼（引自：罗马城墙博物馆）
Fig. 9-a The towers of the Aurelian Walls (from: Museum of the City Walls of Rome)

图 9-b 塔楼
Fig. 9-b The tower of the Aurelian Walls

图 10 厕所
Fig. 10 The latrine

图 11-a 表面为白色"travertine"石灰石的拉丁纳门
Fig. 11-a Porta Latina with white travertine blocks

图 11-b 表面为白色"travertine"石灰石的平扎那门
Fig. 11-b Porta Pinciana with white travertine blocks

图 12 内侧被加上了一道门的阿西那里亚门
Fig. 12 Porta Asinaria with a postern gate inside

2) 干预（5—14 世纪）

中世纪早期，410 年至 5 世纪末，罗马又遭到蛮族的入侵，城墙多段被破坏，狄奥多里克（Theodoric）皇帝主持对其进行维修。在公元 6 世纪的哥特战争（535—552 年）中，有许多重要的事件都发生在奥勒良城墙周围。这一时期对城墙的维修，主要由东罗马帝国查士丁尼皇帝时期的贝利萨里奥将军负责。这一时期的维修没有考虑所用材料的种类、形状和砌筑方式，许多材料显然是取自其他旧建筑物，从而形成了非常明显的特点，即城墙表面的砖砌体中夹杂着外形不规则的法华、"travertine"石灰石、大理石、白榴凝灰岩等小块石材，使原本整齐的砖行不再平整，呈上下起伏的波浪状（图 13）。

3) 修复（15—18 世纪）

到了 15—18 世纪，由于材料老化、人为和自然因素的破坏，城墙需要不断地维修加固，更换残损的材料。另外，由于城市的发展，城墙上也进行了一些建设活动。从镶嵌在城墙上的不同的教皇徽章可以看出，这一时期的修复及建设工程主要是教皇

windows after this Period of consturction.

2) Intervention (5-14 century)

From 410 to the end of the 5th century, Rome was again under the invasion of barbarians. Many parts of the walls were damaged. So Emperor Theodoric made an order to maintain the walls. During the Gothic war (535–552) there were many events around the Aurelian Walls. In this period the restorations were carried out by General Belisario during the reign of Emperor Justinian. The construction mixed diverse materials (some were from other buildings) and masonries. As a result, the work of this period can still be easily recognized today: there are small pieces of tuff, travertine, marble and peperino in the wall, in irregular composition (Fig.13).

3) Restorations (15-18 century)

It was necessary to repair and reinforce the walls due to the aging of the materials and the demolishment by nature and people. Beside, new constructions needed to be carried out for the city development. The restoration and constructions were mainly under the order of the Pope, which could be implied by the Papal insignias on the walls (Fig.14).

图 13　砖构中夹杂着不规则的小块石材，"tuff"凝灰岩、"travertine"石灰石、大理石、白榴凝灰岩
Fig. 13　Mixed uses of small pieces of tuff, travertine, marble and peperino in the wall

图 14　城墙上教皇的徽章
Fig. 14　The Papal insignias on the walls

下令进行的（图14）。

城墙的变化主要体现在两个方面。首先，由于城市道路的变化，城门随之改变（图15）。增开了两座城门，分别是庇亚门（教皇皮乌斯四世时期，1559—1565年，图15-c）和圣乔凡尼门（1574年，教皇格列高利十三世时期，图15-d）。由于两座新城门的建成，位于它们旁边的诺曼塔纳门（图15-a）和阿西那里亚门（图15-b）就被封闭废弃了。还对四座城门进行了重建，它们是弗拉米尼亚门（图15-e）、波图恩塞门（图15-f）、奥里利亚门和赛第米亚那门。新建及重建的城门具有明显的

The walls changed in two ways (Fig.15). First, the evolvement of the transport system reshaped the gates. Two new gates, Porta Pia (Pius IV, Fig.15-c) and Porta San Giovanni (Pope Gregorius the XIII, Fig.15-d) were added to the walls. As a result, Porta Nomentana (Fig.15-a) and Porta Asinaria (Fig.15-b) were abandoned for they were too close to the new ones. Second, four gates including Porta Flaminia (Fig.15-e), Porta Portuense (Fig.15-f), Porta Aurelia and Porta Settimiana were reconstructed. Both the new gates and reconstructed ones reflected

15-a

15-b

15-c

15-d

15-e

15-f

图15　城门
Fig.15　City wall gates
图15-a　诺曼塔纳门
Fig.15-a　Porta Nomentana
图15-b　阿西那里亚门
Fig.15-b　Porta Asinaria
图15-c　庇亚门
Fig.15-c　Porta Pia
图15-d　圣乔凡尼门
Fig.15-d　Porta San Giovanni
图15-e　弗拉米尼亚门
Fig.15-e　Porta Flaminia
图15-f　波图塞恩门
Fig.15-f　Porta Portuense

图 16　小安东尼奥·桑加罗设计的堡垒，教皇保罗三世时期

Fig.16　The rampart designed by Antonio da Sangallo the Younger during the period of Pope Paul III

文艺复兴时期的建筑风格。

其次，在教皇保罗三世时期，1534—1549 年，小安东尼奥·桑加罗（1484—1546 年）设计了一段长约 200 多米的堡垒。为了建造堡垒，他拆除了一段奥勒良城墙，这也成为唯一一段被完全重建的奥勒良城墙。新建的堡垒和这一时期建造的其他堡垒（主要由小桑加罗设计）一样，具有陡峻的斜面，上部有一条白色的镶边石，并且有许多为火炮而设的大窗（图 16）。

Renaissance style.

Besides, Antonio da Sangallo the Younger (1484–1546) designed a rampart more than 200m long during the period of Pope Paul III, from 1534 to1549. He pulled down a segment of the Aurelian Walls for building the new rampart. It is regarded as the only part of the Aurelian Walls which was totally rebuilt. This rampart featured steep slopes, white kerbstones encircling the upper part of the rampart, and a number

3. 当代城墙修缮的研究

19世纪以来，奥勒良城墙不再作为防卫设施。由于城市的发展建设，部分城墙被拆除，道路的扩宽使大部分城门两侧增开门洞。这一时期也对城墙进行了大量的重建工作，基本上只是简单地拆除损毁的部分，用新材料重新砌筑。20世纪后半叶，随着文物保护意识的提高，如何对城墙进行保护和修缮成为越来越受关注的问题。

1）修复原则

一系列关于文物保护的国际宪章，为文物保护及修复制定了许多一般性的原则。但是，针对城墙这一特殊的文物建筑，结合近几十年来罗马城墙维修工程的经验教训，可以总结出以下一些特定的原则。

（1）充分评估

城墙不只是一道防御工事，更是一座城市，甚至是一个国家的象征。并且在城墙周边曾发生过很多重大历史事件，城墙是这些事件的见证，所以要充分认识并尊重城墙的多重价值，特别是在城墙失去了防御作用的今天，不能将其视作城市发展的障碍。

（2）选择和创新

虽然从整体上看城墙是一座巨大的砖石建筑，但这并不意味着只用一种方法就可以对城墙的各个部分进行维修。城墙上不同区段所用的材料、砌筑方式等都不尽相同，建造年代、维修经历等也不会相同，这就需要在维修时针对不同的对象、具体的问题进行分析和多种方法比较，从而进行合适的选择。并且在可能的情况下，创造更科学更先进的技术方法。

（3）避免修复的"均一性"

城墙是一类很特殊的文物，它的历史很长，并且经过了历代不断的维修和重建，它为我们提供了许多有用信息，包括在不同时期所使用的不同的材料和采取的结构构造。我们今天的维修不能把这些信息抹掉。

（4）修缮的目标

最大限度地保护原有材料，正像上一点提到的，鉴于城墙的特殊性，对它的原有材料无法作出一个明确统一的规定，要根据情况具体分析。

2）城墙损坏的现状

为了采用更有效的维修方法，首先需要深入分析城墙上使用的砖、石、灰浆等材料，了解它们的物理、化学特征，并能准确地查找出损坏的原因。

（1）表层

城墙大致由三层构成，中间是混凝土核心，两侧表层是砖砌体，表层的砖砌体只是简单地水平插入混凝土核心中，因此表层砌体的脱落成为一个严重的问题（图17）。

of wide windows for firing, just as other fortifications from that time (most of them were designed by Antonio da Sangallo the Younger) (Fig.16).

3. Research on contemporary restoration

The city walls lost the defense function since 19th century. Some parts of the walls were pulled down for urban development. It's common that new gateways were added on both sides of the gates as the roads grew wider. Reconstruction projects were carried out, for instance, pulling down demolished parts and replacing them with new materials. It became a crucial issue about how to conserve and restore the walls since more and more attentions were paid to the relic conservation.

1) Principles of restoration

A few of general rules has been stated by a series of international charters for the conservation of relics, however, the walls need more specific rules as a very special heritage. Several decades of restoration of the walls revealed some principles:

(1) Sufficient evaluation

The walls are not only fortifications but also representations of the city or even the whole country. The walls are witnesses to a number of historic events which just happened around the walls. Thus, it is of great importance to understand and respect the multiple values of the walls, though they may be regarded as the obstacles to urban development after they lost the defense function.

(2) Alternatives and innovations

The walls can be considered as a huge architecture composed by blocks, however, it doesn't mean that there should be a uniform methods for restorations on all kinds conditions. There are a great diversity of materials, the masonries, the ages and the history of the restorations. Thus, the appropriate methods heavily depend on the particular situations of the project. Alternatives and innovations rely on the systematic analysis of the problems.

(3) Holding the differences

The walls are special relics with a long history of reconstructions and restoration. So they hold diverse information about material, tectonics and structures from different times. It is essential for the restoration to hold and show the information about the "differences".

(4) The goal

Generally, the goal of the restoration is to preserve the original materials and information as much as possible. As mentioned above, we need special

表层砖块脱落的主要原因是受自然界和城墙材料性能老化的影响，包括来自外界及内部毛细作用下的含水、热胀冷缩作用、混凝土材料碳化等。多种因素的共同作用使城墙表层砖块与混凝土内核的连接变得不再稳定。此外，由于面砖的缺失松动，使得植物开始在砖与混凝土之间生长，这就加速了墙体表面砖块的脱落，形成恶性循环。

（2）灰浆

灰浆的损坏主要表现在材料的老化、松散、粉化，从而导致脱落（图18）。

原因有内、外两种因素。外因主要是大气作用，如风、雨等。此外，水的毛细上升和渗透作用，以及植物生长吸取灰浆中的矿物盐，都加剧了灰浆老化脱落。

内因主要是灰浆材料自身的稳定性、黏性以及材料配比、水的纯度和加工技术的不同。比如，中世纪早期的灰浆内含有火山灰的成分，呈紫红色，它的性能很好，抗自然侵蚀能力较强，到目前都很坚固。而12—13世纪的灰浆中没有了火山灰的成分，呈白色或灰白色，很容易松散粉化。

（3）基础石和砖

砖石的损坏主要表现在材料的剥落和侵蚀（图19）。

石块主要用于城墙的基础部分，直接与土壤接触，主要损坏的原因是受水的侵害，道理比较简单。

原因也分为内因和外因，内因主要是来自材料本身，不同时期用不同的烧制方法、不同的材料配比，都可能使砖的性能不同，或引发材料自身的缺陷。外因主要是风、雨、日照等来自大自然的作用。

（4）土丘引发的损害

这是一种比较独特的情况。城墙部分区段的内侧是私人或公共花园，紧靠城墙存有土丘，与外侧地坪的高差很大，使墙体承受着很大的土压力，这对城墙安全构成很

approaches in special situations, for there is not a definitive methodology suitable for all cases.

2) Actual state of damages

Efficient restoration requires the systematic analysis of the materials of the walls such as bricks, stones and mortars. The physical and chemical traits of the materials are essential. The sources of the damages to the walls are also very important.

(1) The surface

The walls are composed of three layers. In the middle is the concrete, both sides of which are covered with bricks. The bricks are inserted to the concrete core and sometimes drop down from the core(Fig.17) . It's a vital problem.

The main sources for this problem are the capillary actions which bring the moisture from the air into the surface of the wall. All kinds of infiltration and the aging of the material make the connections between the brick surface and the concrete core unstable. Furthermore, these week connections allow the growth of various plants, which makes the connections weaker and subsequently forms a loop of damage.

(2) The mortar

The mortar can become loose and be crushed into powders when the material becomes old. It finally makes the mortar drop down (Fig.18).

There are both external and internal factors for the damage to the mortar. One of the external factors is from the atmosphere, for example, the influences of wind and rain. Capillary actions and infiltration are fatal to the mortar. Besides, the roots of the plants on the wall absorb the salt from the mortar, which also makes damages.

Internal factors are the mortar's stability and the viscosity related to its ingredients, the quality of the

图17　面层脱落
Fig.17　The bricks on the surface dropped down from the concrete core

图18　灰浆脱落
Fig.18　Shedding of the mortar

图19　石材的侵蚀
Fig.19　The erosion of the stones

大威胁。主要有两段城墙是这种情况，一段是从圆形剧场到圣乔凡尼门，另一段从拉丁纳门到奥斯提安塞门。墙体受损的表象主要是砖块表层的大面积脱落，墙体和塔楼的倾斜、裂缝甚至坍塌（图20）。

造成这种破坏的原因之一是土丘土壤中含水量较高，特别是下过雨之后，水分不能及时排走，渗入城墙墙体之中，只能通过城墙外侧表面蒸发，这一过程促使墙体表层砖块的松动脱落。同时产生的盐析作用也加速了这一破坏。

此外，土压力的增大是造成城墙倾斜和裂缝的主要原因。大雨使土丘中土壤的含

water and the manufacture techniques. For instance, the mortars from early middle ages in mauve color are strong for they contain a sort of volcanic ash called pozzolana. In contrast, the mortars from 12th to 13th century in white or gray color are much more vulnerable without pozzolana.

(3) Foot stones and bricks

The foot stones and the bricks can be eroded and drop down from the wall (Fig.19).

The capillarity is a main reason for the damage to the foot stones, for they contacts with the earth directly as the base of the walls.

The damages to the bricks result from many factors. Internal factors include the firing techniques, the ingredients of the clay and the defects of the material. External factors involve the influences from atmosphere such as wind and rain.

(4) Embankments against the earth

There is a special circumstance that some private or public gardens are located inside of the walls and the earth is heaped up to the inner surface of the embankments (walls). As a result, the embankments get a lot of pressure from the earth due to the different levels of the earth on the two sides of the embankments. There are two typical instances. One is the segment from the amphitheatre to Porta San Giovanni and another is from Porta Latina to Porta Ostiense. There were several types of damages: the bricks dropped down, walls and towers inclined, some parts cracked and even collapsed (Fig.20).

One main reason for these damages is that the earth contains a lot of water after rain and the water is not able to come out of the embankments quickly. As a result, the inner side of the embankments contains too much water. While, the water in the outer side of the embankment vaporizes easily. The different moisture levels on the two sides can destroy the whole structure and make the bricks on the outer surface drop down. Besides, salting-out effect is also harmful.

Earth pressure lead to the incline of the embankments, for the pressure increases when there is more

图20　圣乔凡尼城门附近的城墙
Fig.20 The embankment near Porta San Giovanni

水量增大，从而大大增加了对城墙的压力。在1893和1902年间，由于大雨，圆形剧场至圣乔凡尼门间的一段城墙出现过两次坍塌，长度约60m。另外，导致土压力的增大还有人为因素，由于不断的建设，城墙内侧花园中的堆土越来越高，使城墙承受的土压力也会越来越大。

3）修缮方法的建议

19—20世纪对奥勒良城墙进行了大量的重建工作，城墙顶部的面砖几乎全部进行了重砌，但这些工程没能保存城墙的历史信息，破坏了大量的原始面砖并影响到城墙的文物价值。为此，针对不同的修缮工程提出以下几点建议。

（1）表层砖砌体的修复

表层砖块的脱落至今还是不断出现的老问题，目前唯一能做的就是继续更换。

确保文物的真实性是任何修缮的根本前提，科学的保护要求修复师寻找可用的方法保护原材料，以求用最佳的技术措施达到令人满意的结果。20世纪的面砖修复主要存在以下问题：①使用根本不同于原有材料的材料进行修复，如把城墙底部的石材换成砖，过分地改变了城墙的本来面貌。②过度模仿原始的样式，即便有说明标示牌，从外观上也很难分辨出哪部分是原始的，哪部分是修复的。

为了确保修复的可识别性，古利埃尔莫·德·安吉利斯·奥萨特提出了两种方法：①"底框法"，即修复部分的表面略微错后，不与原始部分处于同一平面（图21）。②共面法，使用的修复材料要与原始材料有所区别，如使用颜色略不相同的砖，或改

water in the earth after rain. A segment about 60m long from the amphitheatre to Porta San Giovanni collapsed twice after rain during 1893 and 1902. Besides, people sometime make this situation worse. For instance, the earth was heaped up higher and higher for the garden works and subsequently the pressure from the earth became stronger.

3) Proposals for restoration

Most of the bricks on the top of walls were restored in several reconstruction projects during 19th and 20th century. However, a lot of historical information didn't survive through these projects. Many original bricks were lost or destroyed and the value of the walls as a relic decreased. While, there are some proposals for the restoration of different parts of the walls.

(1) Restoration of bricks

The bricks drop from the surface of the walls time after time. Replacing them constantly is a common solution to this problem.

Restoration should emphasize the authenticity of the relic. It needs appropriate methods with the right techniques according to the particular situations. During the 20th century, some problems emerged in a number of restoration projects. First, some approaches altered the material of the walls completely, for example, replacing the travertine blocks on the bottom with bricks. On the contrary, some others eliminated the differences between the original parts and the new ones. As a result, people couldn't recognize the two parts any more even with illustrations.

To make the restoration recognizable, Guglielmo De Angelis d' Ossat had addressed two methods. First, shift the renovated surface to the inner side slightly. Thus, the new surface and the original face are not on the same plane (Fig.21). The Second method is called "sottosquadro": use distinguishable materials such as bricks in another color or employ different masonry (e.g. with different mortar thickness) (Fig.22). The appropriate methods always heavily depend on the particular circumstances. Several restorations in the

图21 "底框法"
Fig.21 Shift the renovated surface to the inner side slightly

变材料的砌筑手法，如扩大灰缝（图22）。要根据不同工程的具体情况做出更合适的选择。20世纪末进行的表层砖块修补，就结合采用了上面的两种方法，在底框法的基础上应用颜色不同但色调相近的砖，既保存了修补的形状，又考虑了色调的一致。

（2）石材的修复

石材的修复工作主要有表面清洁、加固。清洁时要注意不要抹去石材表面人为或时间留下的痕迹，比如，在砌筑时加工工具在石材表面留下的痕迹（图23）。

（3）灰浆的修复

对灰浆的修复是最需要慎重的，因为很容易消除掉隐存于不同时期灰浆中的信息。比如奥勒良时期修建的城墙垛口和霍诺里乌斯时期加高的部分原本有非常明显的区别，但经过多次维修后，这一区别就不那么明显了。为此，对灰浆的修复要求是：①保护城墙修建不连续性的痕迹。②尽可能加固现存的原有灰浆。③修复用的灰浆的颗粒物含量和化学成分要与原灰浆可区别，但不能改变城墙的外观。④新灰浆的强度要低于原始灰浆，以避免老灰浆的老化快于新灰浆。

（4）植物清除

城墙上的植物虽然增加了城墙的美观，但却对城墙产生损害，需要严格清除、控制有害植物。植物清除的工作要基于对植物种类的深入认识，对于那些有害于城墙保护的植物要坚决清除，而与城墙保护不矛盾的植物可以保留下来，借以增加城墙的美感。同时要注意清除植物的目的，是仅限于城墙表面的初步清洗，还是在某一区域大

end of the 20th century employed shifting method with the bricks in slightly different color. These approaches kept the original appearance of the walls and made the new parts distinguishable in the same time.

(2) Restoration of stones

The restoration of stones usually includes cleaning and reinforcement. It should be prevented that the cleaning work removes the diverse trails made by nature or people, for example, the trails left by the tools during manufacture (Fig.23).

(3) Restoration of mortar

Restoration of mortar needs a lot of considerations, for the information in the mortar from different times are very vulnerable. For instance, the crenellations built during Aurelian period were very different from the heightened parts from Honorious period in terms of mortar, however, it became very difficult to distinguish them after a few of restorations. There are several principles for mortar restoration. First, reserve the trails which indicate different constructions during different times. Second, reinforce the survived mortar as much as possible. Third, the ingredients and the mixtures of the mortar for restoration should be different from that of the old one, however, the appearance of the walls should not be changed a lot. At last, it should be noticed that the corrosion of the old mortar will be accelerated if the new mortar is stronger than the old one.

(4) Weeding

Sometimes plants are dangerous to walls though they could be considered as the decorations of the walls. It's essential to know the plants. Some of them should be eliminated for they do harm to the walls. While, some others could be left on the walls for they are innocuous and decorate the walls(Fig.24). Nevertheless, there are different purposes for removing plants. Some projects only remove the plants on the surface of the wall; some others make thorough clearing which covers large areas.

(5) Restoration of the embankment against the earth

There are a few of methods for restorations of

图22　共面法（左）
Fig.22　An instance of "sottosquadro" method (left)

图23　石材上的痕迹（右）
Fig.23　The trails left by nature or people (right)

面积地清除有害植物，要根据不同的目的采取不同的方法（图24）。

（5）针对土丘所引起的问题的修复

主要可采取以下措施：①加固城墙墙体，如采用拉杆拉结，增加墙体的整体性（图25）。②修建挡土墙，在城墙内侧距城墙几步距离处修建一道挡土墙，使城墙承受的土压力保持原来的状况。③建立有效的排水系统，使雨水能迅速排走，从而控制土壤和城墙墙体过分吸水。

embankment according to the sources of the damage. First, reinforce the embankment (e.g. employing cables or steel bars, Fig.25). Second, build additional embankments offsetting (inside) from the original embankment to reduce the press from the earth. Third, construct effective irrigation system to prevent the earth and the embankments to get too much water.

图24　城墙上生长的植物
Fig.24　Plants growing on the walls

图25　城墙墙体本身的加固
Fig.25　The reinforcement of the wall

参考书目

1. 曼奇尼R. 罗莎娜罗马奥勒良城墙——城墙历代建设图集. 罗马：Edizioni Quasar di Severino Tognon s. r. l 出版社，2001
2. 科茨-斯蒂芬R. 马焦雷城门历史遗迹与景观. 罗马：<L'ERMA> di Bretschneider 出版社，2004
3. http://www.geocities.com
4. 罗马城墙博物馆展出资料

Reference

1. Mancini R. LE Mura Aureliane di Roma——atlante di un palinsesto murario. Roma: Edizioni Quasar di Severino Tognon s. r. l, 2001
2. Coates-Stephens R. Porta Maggiore Monument and Landscape. Roma: <L'ERMA> di Bretschneider, 2004
3. http: // www.geocities.com
4. Museum of the City Walls of Rome

第四章 城墙规划

4 Planning for City Walls

第一节　明城墙保护总体规划
4.1　The Conservation Master Plan for the Nanjing Ming City Wall

陈薇　Chen Wei

南京明城墙由于线型长和曲折，又跨山越河，同时和日益发展的现代城市连为一体，所以情形十分复杂，对其开展保护规划，其难点：一在研究——对保护对象正确认识，二在创新——对保护方法探索实践。

1. 南京明城墙概况与价值理解

南京明城墙1988年1月被国务院公布为第三批全国重点文物保护单位，属于古建筑及历史纪念建筑物，包括城墙和外郭两部分。南京明城墙保护总体规划于2007—2008年受南京市政府委托，由东南大学建筑学院和建筑设计研究院担纲完成。2009年8月国家文物局经过专家鉴定正式通过并进行批复，自此，南京明城墙保护总体规划作为文物保护的行业性专业规划，正式纳入南京城市总体规划中。

南京明城墙实为依托明代以前历代城墙而建，又拓展和重新建置而成，开创了中国古代城墙史的新篇章；南京明城墙又因地制宜地利用山形走势和官方管理组织监造，是自然和人工完美结合的大型工程典范。

对于南京明城墙进行保护规划，认识基础是价值理解与评估，总结如下：

1) 历史价值

（1）历史悠久，文化深厚，利用孙吴石头城、六朝建康城和南唐金陵城址，又明代拓展建造，是南京悠久历史文化的象征和见证。

（2）规模宏大，是我国以至世界上保留至今最长的城垣，是人类共同的一项文化遗产。

（3）南京城墙是中国历史上唯一建造在长江以南的统一国家的都城城墙，它综合反映了明初的科技、文化、军事等水平。

（4）南京城墙自建成以来，有众多重大的历史事件与之有关，成为中国封建晚期至近现代中国历史的缩影。

（5）南京城墙城砖上的大量铭文内容，所折射出的明初社会制度和经济状况及管理水平，是一座活的明初资料库，充分体现了南京城墙的历史文化和社会价值。

The Nanjing Ming City Wall makes a sophisticated case for its long and zigzagged wall lines, for its skillful ride over mountains and rivers, and for its increased integration with today's urban life. Conservation planning, therefore, has to be supported by a study to deepen the understanding of the targets to be protected, and by innovations designed to tap up new and effective ways to accomplish the protection.

1. Nanjing Ming City Wall: basic facts and values

On January 1988, the Nanjing Ming City Wall has been endorsed by the State Council to be a major cultural heritage protected at the national level. The wall system is made up of city walls and defensive walls, and has been rated as an ancient and historical structure. Southeast University School of Architecture and Institute of Architectural Design were assigned by the Nanjing Municipal Government to jointly prepare the Nanjing Ming City Wall Conservation Master Plan in 2007–2008. The Conservation Master plan was reviewed by experts, and endorsed on August 2009 by State Administration of Cultural Heritages. Consequentially, the plan has become part of the master planning of Nanjing Municipality, and the wall system is eventually placed under the protection of professional hands.

The Nanjing Ming City Wall was rebuilt or expanded on the wall foundations started in the preceding dynasties. It opens a new page in the history of ancient city walls. The wall makes a perfect combination of Mother Nature and human efforts, and tops other ancient city walls survived the times, as it was built borrowing the contours of natural terrains and under the supervision and control of imperial officials.

Understanding the value of Nanjing Ming City Wall and associated assessment creates a ground for conserving the ancient wall system on a well planned basis.

1) Historical values

(1) The wall is of a long history and profound cultural roots. The Stone City built in the times of Sun and Wu, the Jiankang City founded in the Six Dynasty Period, and the Jinling City created in the South Tang Dynasty are the evidence confirming the long history and deep cultural roots of Nanjing.

2）艺术价值

（1）踞山带江，依山傍水，气势磅礴，是江南山水城市建设的典型代表。

（2）灵活的总体布局，一方面顺应自然地形，另一方面与城市功能分区紧密结合，为古代都城建设的杰作之一。

3）科学价值

（1）因地制宜的设计思想和建造手法具有独创性。

（2）严密的施工组织与严格的质量监督机制，充分显示了我国古代大规模工程建设组织的能力与科学方法，为研究中国古代工官制度及工程设计与施工的组织提供了宝贵资料。

（3）南京城墙与护城河作为军事防御体系，布局独具匠心，是研究中国古代军事科学的重要实物依据。

（4）南京城墙和外郭充分利用天然山势和材料进行建造，形成城墙高度和长度的世界之最。

4）社会价值

（1）南京城墙体现了我国古代高超的建筑技术与先进的规划思想，综合反映了明初的科技、文化、经济发展水平。对于南京城墙在"保护为主、抢救第一、合理利用、加强管理"的指导方针下加以研究与保护，有助于促进人们对中华民族文化历史与传统的了解，增强民族凝聚力。

（2）南京城墙作为全国重点文物保护单位，是南京历史文化名城的重要组成部分，保护好南京城墙，将对南京历史文化名城保护产生积极的推动作用。

（3）南京城墙是深厚历史文化积淀的象征，它所凝聚的古人创造性智慧和才能在人类文化遗产中具有独特的地位，目前国家文物局将南京城墙纳入申请世界文化遗产的候选名录，保护好南京城墙，使城墙体系的历史城市对世界的贡献产生重要影响。

（4）南京城墙还是南京的重要旅游资源，保护城墙对提升南京历史文化名城的品质和形象，促进南京旅游业的可持续发展，具有重要的现实意义。

（5）南京外郭和现代南京都市发展有互动和契合关系，保护好外郭将推动南京的都市化发展，并将历史场所和现代生活融为一体。

(2) The huge size of the wall makes it the longest surviving city wall not only in the context of China, but also in the context of the world. It is a cultural heritage shared by humans.
(3) The wall is the only capital city wall built by the central government under a unified plan, bordering the southern part of the Yangtze River. It is an embodiment of scientific, technical, cultural, and military levels reached in the early Ming Dynasty.
(4) The wall has survived many important historical events, and is a reflection of Chinese history from the late feudal times to today.
(5) Rich inscriptions on the ancient bricks employed to build the walls mirrored the social regimes, economic conditions, and management levels in the early Ming Dynasty. They are literally a living database for the early Ming Dynasty, showing the historical, cultural, and social values of the city wall.

2) Artistic values
(1) The magnificent wall system was built riding mountains and bordering rivers, a typical architectural style commonly seen in the "mountain–river" cities in South China.
(2) The wall was built in a flexible manner, borrowing the contours of natural terrains on the one hand, and playing a role in dividing the functions of the city on the other. It is an outstanding example of ancient structures in a capital city.

3) Scientific values
(1) Unique design and construction plan, taking advantage of the strength and convenience offered by natural terrains.
(2) Strict organizational and quality control mechanisms for building the structures, demonstrating people's skills and scientific methods applied in building a large structure in ancient China, and providing valuable evidences for studying the government-run structure building system, engineering design, and construction activities at that time.
(3) The walls and associated moats were built as a defense system in a unique manner, providing an important evidence for studying the military sciences applied in ancient China.
(4) Both the city wall and defensive wall were built taking full advantage of the natural hilly terrains and materials, which makes it the largest and longest city wall in the world.

4) Social values
(1) The wall makes an embodiment of advanced building technologies and planning techniques applied in ancient China, and is a combined reflection of the scientific, technical, cultural, and economic development levels reached at the time. Under the

2. 南京明城墙体系的特点与保护范围及建设控制地带区划

南京明城墙不是简单的墙体，目前保存较好的明城墙是明初建设的南京四重城的一部分，自内而外筑有宫城、皇城、城墙、外郭，同时每重墙外侧依地形建有护城河，形成非常坚固的防御体系，这是南京明城墙的特点之一。

除了宫城和皇城按照中国古代传统的规制建造外，南京城墙（包括城墙和外郭）因天材，就地利，蜿蜒曲折，腾山跨水，山水环境与城墙相依相伴，如玄武湖乃南京城墙北墙外的最大和最开阔的护城水面，鸡笼山（今鸡鸣山）和覆舟山（今九华山）则为北墙的天然基石，这种城墙体系和山水环境融为一体的建城理念与手法运用，是南京明城墙的特点之二。

此外，外郭的建设实质使偏于明南京一隅的宫城成为明代大帝国南京的中心，是对中国传统礼制宫城居中的创造性表达和做法，而外郭的走势和界面也和今天大南京的发展唇齿相依；另一方面，城墙和外郭所在的地理环境基本一致，即由北而东山峦起伏，丘陵跌宕，而自南而西引水入江，水系充沛。这种历史关系和历史环境，是南京明城墙的特点之三。

那么，我们在对保护对象明城墙划定保护范围时，如何兼顾这些南京明城墙特殊的体系特点，就是一项需要细分缕析的研究和注重实际的工作。

1）区划策略

根据文物保护的安全性要求，结合城墙体系的整体性要求，重视历史环境和地理条件，考虑实际管理操作的可行性，结合相关规定，调整上位《南京明城墙风光带规划》的相关要求，形成南京城墙的保护范围和建设控制地带，并制定相应的管理条例。

2）保护范围区划

城墙保护范围分为两部分

（1）城墙安全线（本体保护范围）

原则上墙体内侧从内墙皮向内延伸15 m，外侧从外墙皮向外延伸墙体高度的1.5倍且不小于15 m。对于城门处，除满足安全原则外，结合道路进行具体划定（图1）。

guideline of "protection and rescue comes first, rational utilization, and enhanced management", the study and protection of the wall is made to improve people's understanding of Chinese culture, history, and tradition, enhancing the national coercion.

(2) Nanjing City Wall is a major cultural heritage protected at the national level, and is an important component of Nanjing as a renowned historical and cultural city. The rational protection of the wall makes part of the activities protecting Nanjing as a renowned historical and cultural city.

(3) Nanjing City Wall is a symbol showing Nanjing's historical and cultural roots. It enjoys a unique position among the cultural heritages left by forefathers, thanks to the creative wisdom and capability displayed by folks in ancient times. Chinese State Administration of Cultural Heritages has made Nanjing City Wall a candidate for the World Cultural Heritage. In this context, protecting the wall in a systematic manner will render an important contribution to protecting the historical cities with a city wall system.

(4) The wall is also an important tourist attraction for the city. In this context, protecting the wall is desirable for raising the quality and image of Nanjing as a renowned historical and cultural city, and for promoting the sustainable development of tourism in the city.

(5) The defensive wall is of an interactive and coupling tie with the development of the urban area. Protecting the wall facilitates the development of Nanjing as a cosmopolitan city, allowing historical sites being part of modern life.

2. Uniqueness of the Nanjing Ming City Wall and the associated protection scope and construction activities control

The Nanjing Ming City Wall is, strictly speaking, not a wall built in its literal sense. The surviving wall people see today is part of the four enclosures of walls built in the early Ming Dynasty (palace city, imperial city, city wall, and defensive wall). Each enclosure of walls was protected by a moat that was built borrowing the contours of local terrains, which made the wall an extremely solid and strong defense system, a special feature enjoyed by the Nanjing Ming City Wall.

Apart from the palace city and imperial city that had been built in line with the loyal traditions prevailed at the time, the city walls, including both city wall and defensive wall, were built using the natural materials available in the locality, and borrowing the contours of natural terrains. The wall stretched out in a zigzagged manner, riding mountains and traversing waters.

The mountain and river landscape makes a matching company to the walls. For example, Xuanwu Lake is the largest and widest water surface bordering the northern section of the walls. Both Mount Jilong (today's Mount Jiming) and Mount Fuzhou (today's Mount Jiuhua) became the natural foundation for building the northern walls. The combination of city walls and mountain-river landscape makes another feature enjoyed by the Nanjing Ming City Wall.

In addition, the design of defensive walls makes the palace city sitting in the corner of Ming Nanjing the center of the Ming Empire. It is a creative expression of the central position of the imperial palace. Interestingly, the riding course and interface of defensive walls went hand in hand with the development of Nanjing as a cosmopolitan city. On the other hand, the geographic environment where the city wall and defensive wall sat were fairly matched one another. They were built borrowing the contours of mountains from the north to the east, and diverting water from the south and west into the rivers. The historical ties and environmental elements embedded in the walls makes another feature possessed by the walls.

While protecting the walls, especially defining the area where the walls shall be protected, one has to study the details of protection activities, making them in line with the aforesaid special features.

1) Zoning strategy

Apparently, the requirements defined by the Nanjing Ming City Wall Landscape Planning needs to be readjusted over time to define the part of the city walls to be protected and the area where construction activities have to be restricted. Meanwhile, regulations shall be prepared for the purpose, based on the safety requirements for protecting cultural heritages and the integrity of the wall system, paying more attention to the historical elements of environment and geographic conditions, and evaluating the feasibility of management and operation.

2) Define the wall sections to be protected

Two-part protection strategy

(1) Define the safe line for the walls, protecting the physical part of the wall

In principle, an area 15m stretching out from the internal part of the walls, and an area 15m stretching out from the external part of the walls, with a height 1.5 times the height of external part of the walls, shall be defined as the safe line. Apart from meeting the safety requirements, the section of the walls to be protected in the vicinity of city gates shall be defined in line with ambient road conditions (Fig.1).

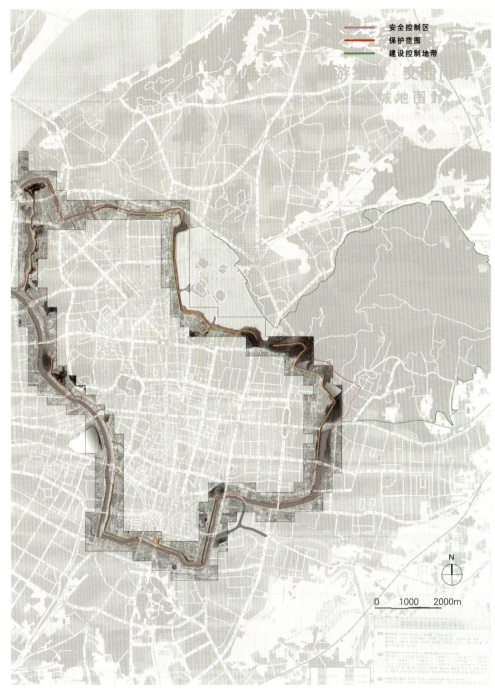

图 1　南京城墙保护区划图
Fig.1　Define the wall sections to be protected

（2）城墙保护范围

原则上城墙（包括现存城墙、城墙遗迹、城墙遗址）外侧从本体保护范围向外延伸直至护城河外15 m，包括城墙与护城河之间地带（图2）。

城墙外侧为紫金山麓的地段，依据地形划定保护范围。

城墙外侧为玄武湖的地段，保护范围划至玄武湖西岸与南岸。

城墙内侧如为包山墙，有划至山体坡脚外放15 m和山脊两种；如非包山墙，则安全线即保护范围。

城墙遗址段内侧保护范围依据历史资料及遗址段两端城墙（现存城墙与城墙遗迹）的保护范围进行划定。

（3）外郭保护范围

墙体本体两侧各30～50 m，遇有山体将山体部分包入保护范围。

3）保护范围管理要求

原则上保护范围内不得进行任何建设，根据实际情况，规定有基本原则和具体规定。

（1）保证从城墙外侧的保护范围内能够无阻碍地观测到城墙上部的至少1/3墙面。据此，城墙外侧保护范围内的配套建筑屋顶（或构筑物）高度应小于或等于5 m。

（2）城墙遗迹段保护范围内建筑屋顶高度不应超过该段城墙的平均高度。

（3）城墙内侧保护范围内原则上不允许进行建设，以使得城墙的原有环境的原真性和城墙的真实轮廓得以体现。

(2) Define the scope of protection.
In principle, an area 15m stretching out from the moat of the walls (the surviving walls, wall relics, and wall remains), including the area between the walls and the moat, shall be defined as the area to be protected(Fig.2).
The section bordering Zijin Mountains to be protected shall be defined in line with local terrains. The section on the rims of Xuanwu Lake shall be protected, including the west and south banks.
In the context of the walls built to enclose mountains, the protection area shall either be 15m stretching out from the foot of the mountains, or from the ridges. The walls other than the walls built to enclose mountains shall be protected with the safe line as the area under protection.
The internal part of wall remains shall be protected based on available historical data and the protection scope defined for the surviving walls on two ends.
(3) Define the sections of defensive walls to be protected
The area 30m or 50m stretching out from the physical part of the wall, both internally and externally, shall be placed under protection. The mountainous part shall be included when it is part of the walls.
 3) Management
In principle, no construction activities shall be allowed within the protection area. Detailed codes are defined in line with real situations as follows:
(1) One shall be able to see, without obstruction, at least one thirds of the upper part of the walls from the protection area outside of the walls. In this context, the structures built in the protection area outside of the walls shall not exceed 5m in height;
(2) The structures built in the protection area of wall remains shall not exceed the averaged height of the walls within the section;
(3) In principle, no construction activities shall be allowed within the protection area inside the walls, allowing the fullest possible expression of the original environment of the walls and their outlines.

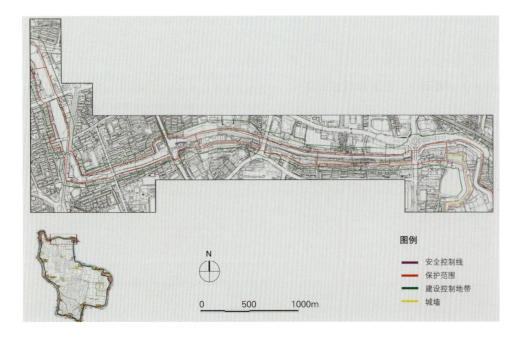

图2 神策门西至狮子山东大门
Fig.2 Define the protected wall section from the west of Shence Gate to the east Gate of Mount Shizi

4）建设控制地带区划

（1）界划依据：相关历史环境、人文环境、城市空间环境的完整性。

（2）区划范围：原则上城墙内侧由城墙保护范围向内延伸 35 m，当环境保护范围内为山体时，建设控制地带划至坡脚或山脊；外侧由环境保护范围向外延伸 50 m，遇及水体时将整个水体划入，遇及山体时划至山脊或坡脚。具体范围结合地形及城市肌理，详见图 1。

外郭仅区划保护范围，不划定建设控制地带。

5）建设控制地带的高度控制

高度控制结合南京城墙与城市环境的具体情况，原则上保证南京城墙的整体轮廓线及与历史环境的整体关系，尊重城墙所在与相关城市环境的互为遗存关系。在此总体原则基础上，依城墙的东、西、南、北各方向根据具体情况制定高度控制的细化要求（图 3）。

（1）东段：保证在护城河东岸沿线观看城墙时能把握城墙的线性延伸感。

（2）东北段：保证在台城、太平门段城墙上能较为全面地观看到钟山的山形走势，至少可观测到山体自然风貌高度应在山体整体高度的 1/2 以上（图 4）。

（3）西段：保证在此段（三山门、西水关以南段）秦淮河游览时，从水道中线观测城墙，其背景和轮廓不被城墙内侧的高层建筑或构筑物破坏，同时城墙外的树木不应对城墙形成过多遮挡。

（4）西北段：保证在护城河西岸沿线观看城墙时能把握城墙的线性延伸感；保证在长江航道内能观看到狮子山及阅江楼的形势，要求可观测到的山体高度应达到狮子山整体高度的 2/3 以上（图 5）。

（5）南段：南段城墙可登临，应重点表现南京老城南的城市肌理与形态。高度控制要求在《南京老城控制性详细规划（秦淮区片）》的基础上，结合本规划高度控制的基本原则执行。

4) Define the area for limited construction activities
(1) The area for limited construction activities shall be defined in line with the integrity of historical, humanitarian, and urban environment;
(2) The area for limited construction activities inside the walls shall be, in principle, a 35m further stretch-out from the protection area. When mountains sitting in the protection area, the area for limited construction activities shall be stretched to the foot or the ridge of the mountains. Outside of the walls, the area for limited construction activities shall be stretched out for 50m. When a water body is part of the protection area, the entire water body shall be included. When mountains sitting in the protection area, the area for limited construction activities shall be stretched out to the foot or the ridge of the mountains. Additionally, the area for limited construction activities shall be defined in line with the local terrains and urban systems (see details in the zoning map).

5) Height control in the limited construction area
Height control shall be made based on the actual settings of the walls and urban environment. In principle, efforts shall be made to ensure the integrity of the outlines of the city walls and its ties with historical environment. The heritage ties between the walls and related urban environment shall be taken into account in the first place. Height control shall be specified in four directions (east, west, south, and north), based on the local situation and in line with the aforesaid principles(Fig.3).

(1) East section: People shall be able to see the stretching contours of the walls when viewing them from the east bank of the moat.
(2) Northeast section: People shall be allowed to view a relatively complete riding course of Mount Zhong, or at least half of the averaged height of the mountains, from Taicheng and Taiping Gate sections (Fig.4).
(3) West section: People shall have the opportunity to view the walls from the middle course of the waterway when cruising over the Qinhuai River (south of Sanshan Gate and West Water Pass). The background and contours of the walls shall not be blocked by high rise buildings or structures. Meanwhile, the trees grown outside the walls shall not impose excessive shades over the walls.
(4) Northwest section: People shall be able to

see the stretching walls when viewing it from the west bank of the moat, and to view Mount Shizi and River Viewing Pavilion from the water routes of the Yangtze River, or at least two thirds of the averaged height of Mount Shizi(Fig.5).

(5) Southern section: People shall be allowed to climb up the wall in the section, enjoying the view of old southern city proper. Height control shall be defined in line with the height control requirements defined by the Old City Proper Control Plan (Qinhuai area).

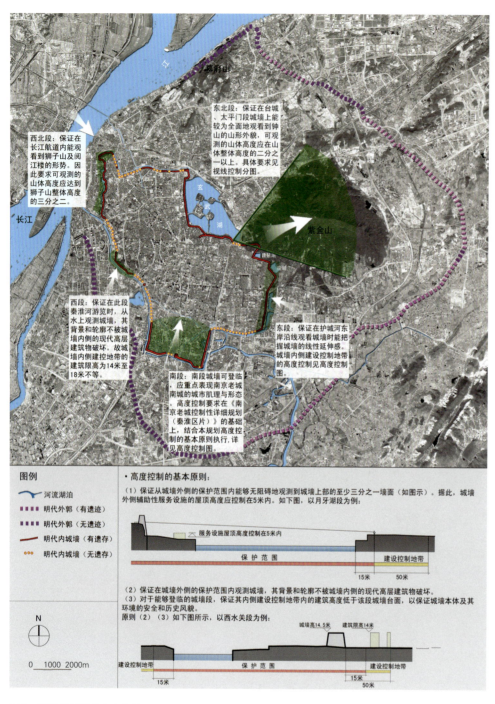

图3 建设控制地带高度控制
Fig.3 Height control in the limited construction

第四章 城墙规划　4 – Planning for City Walls

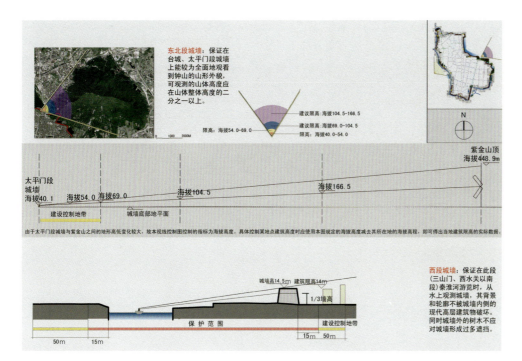

图 4　东北段和西段建设控制高度
Fig.4　Height control in the limited construction (the northeast and the west sections)

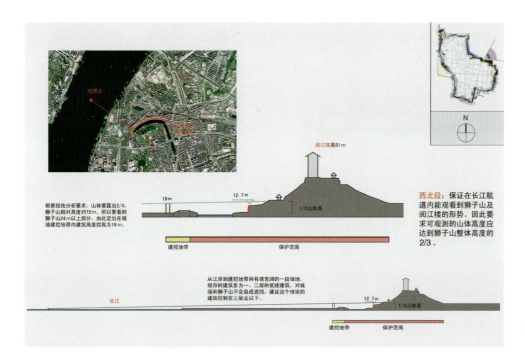

图 5　西北段视线控制分析图
Fig.5　Height control in the limited construction (the northwest section)

6）关于建立南京城墙与外郭视觉通廊的建议

考虑南京城墙与外郭的形制关系对于认识南京历史文化名城的重要意义，以及在南京特殊历史环境与地理环境中它们的相互关联度，在保护规划中，提出在东南西北四个方向上建立南京城墙与外郭或环境形成视觉通廊的建议（图6），即东：中山门（明朝阳门）—邵家山；南：中华门（明聚宝门）—雨花台；西：狮子山阅江楼—浦口公园；北：神策门—幕府山，其之间加强控制，形成视觉通廊，或注重绿化形成绿色廊道。

3. 南京明城墙本体的分类、分段、分节点、分地点与相关保护措施

1）首先根据城墙现存状况进行分类，有针对性地提出保护措施

（1）城墙墙体：加强日常保养，清扫城墙顶面，保证城墙本体的防、排水系统

6) **Proposal on creating a visual city wall corridor**

Considering the important role played by the wall system (including the defensive wall) in making Nanjing a renowned historical and cultural city, and taking into account the fact that the special historical environment where the walls are located is closely associated with local geographic environment, it is proposed to establish a visual city wall corridor, connecting the walls (including the defensive wall) in four directions (east, south, west, and north) (Fig.6). In the east: Zhongshan Gate (or Chaoyang Gate in the Ming Dynasty)–Mount Shaojia; in the south: Zhonghua Gate (or Jubao Gate in the Ming Dynasty)–Yuhuatai; in the west: River Viewing Pavilion on Mount Shizi–Pukou Park; and in the north: Shence Gate–Mount Mufu. Efforts shall be made to enhance the accessibility between them, making them into a visual corridor, or a green corridor.

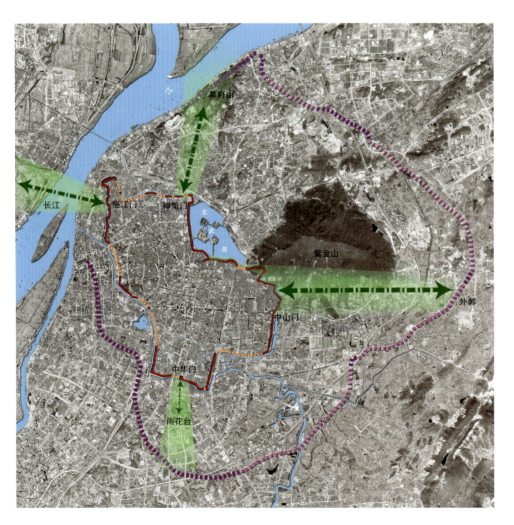

图6 南京城墙与山水环境视廊控制
Fig.6 Visual corridors between the Nanjing Ming City Wall and the Shanshui environment

畅通，保持城墙两侧空旷、开阔，控制墙体的干湿度，及时清除墙体顶面和侧面的杂树、杂草。对于出现损伤的地段，针对不同的病害，查明原因采取相应的防护加固、现状修整的保护措施，局部损伤严重的地段采取重点修复，消除安全隐患。

（2）包山墙：加强城墙顶面防、排水处理；引导控制山体排水，消除隐患。

（3）城墙遗迹：加强日常维护与管理，杜绝人为破坏。对土芯夯土层进行加固，有计划地进行绿化，保护城墙遗迹不再受到蚕食，保持土芯水土。

（4）城墙遗址：为确保南京明城墙轮廓线的完整性，对地面墙体无存的一些地段，清理出城墙遗址地面，采用栽种树林、竖立保护标志碑等措施进行保护。

2）其次依据城墙不同段的具体现状评估，提出相关保护措施（图 7、表 1 ~ 表 3）

3. Categorization of the city wall's protection and associated measures

1) Categorization based on current status and associated protection measures

(1) Physical part of the wall: the physical part of the wall, including body and top, shall be maintained and cleaned up on a regular basis, ensuring the smooth operation of the draining system. The wall shall be kept unblocked for ventilation on both sides, allowing an adequate humidity for the physical part of the wall. Trees and weeds grown out on the top and sides of the walls shall be removed in a timely manner. The damaged sections, and the sections infected by pests, shall be repaired or disinfected. The sites showing serous damages shall get fixed promptly, eliminating the hidden risks.

(2) Walls built to enclose mountains: improve water proof treatment, ensuring the smooth operation of the drainage system, especially on the mountain side, and eliminating the hidden risks.

(3) Wall relics: enhance daily maintenance and management, fencing off man-made damages. Reinforce the earth layer, growing greeneries in a planned manner, preventing the nibbling-off of the relics, and keeping soil from erosion.

(4) Wall remains: the surface of the remains without physical walls shall be cleared to grow trees, erecting protection signs and keeping the integrity of the wall outlines.

2) Wall protection measures based on the status assessment (Fig.7, Table 1~Table 3)

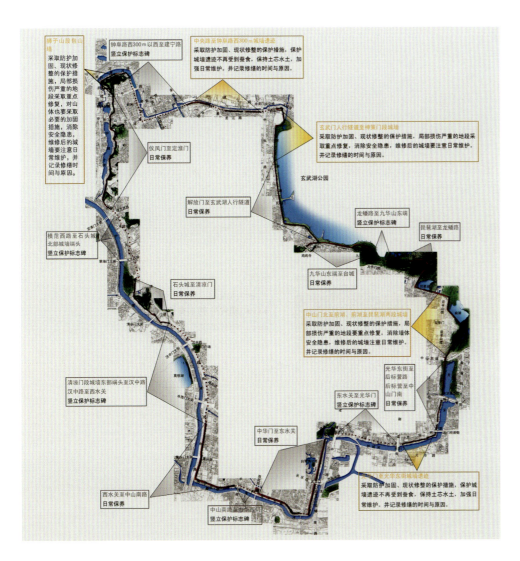

图 7 城墙保护措施分段图
Fig.7 Different sections of the wall's protection measures

表 1　城墙分段处置方式表

序号	城墙段		现状	病害类别	存在问题	保护措施
1	中华门—东水关		城墙长度 3 017 m，维修后较完好长度 2 825 m，损坏长度 192 m	墙面损伤；顶面防、排水系统损毁	—	日常保养
2	东水关—月牙湖老墙南端	东水关至光华门	地面已无痕迹	—	—	竖立保护标志碑
		光华门至光华东街	尚存城墙遗迹	缺乏维护与管理，人为破坏严重，存在较大隐患	缺乏维护与管理，人为破坏严重，存在较大隐患	采取防护加固、现状修整的保护措施，保护城墙遗迹不再受到蚕食，保持土芯水土，并要加强日常维护，并记录修缮的时间与原因
3	月牙湖（含中山门）—太平门	光华东街至后标营路	城墙遗迹长度 680 m，以新砖维修，部分修复至地面以上 5 m	墙面损伤；顶面防、排水系统损毁	—	日常保养
		后标营至中山门南	城墙长度约 800 m，墙体基本保存完好	墙面损伤	—	日常保养
		中山门北至前湖	城墙长约 798 m，保存较完好	墙面损伤局部墙体裂损	年久失修，结构稳定性较差，存在较大安全隐患	采取防护加固、现状修整的保护措施，局部损伤严重的地段采取重点修复，消除安全隐患，维修后的城墙要注意日常维护，并记录修缮的时间与原因
		前湖至琵琶湖	墙体基本保存，局部损坏较严重	墙面损伤；墙体裂损；局部坍塌		采取防护加固、现状修整的保护措施，局部损伤严重的地段采取重点修复，消除安全隐患，维修后的城墙要注意日常维护，并记录修缮的时间与原因
		琵琶湖至龙蟠路	墙体基本保存完好	墙面损伤	—	日常保养
4	太平门—台城	龙蟠路至九华山东端	地面已无痕迹	—	—	竖立保护标志碑
		九华山东端至台城	城墙总长度 1 660 m 左右，经近年维修保存较好	维修后暂无明显病害		日常保养
5	解放门—神策门	解放门至玄武湖人行隧道	城墙总长度约 2 500 m，经近年维修保存较好	维修后暂无明显病害		日常保养
		玄武湖人行隧道至神侧门	城墙总长度约 1 570 m，城墙局部损坏较严重	墙面损伤；局部墙体裂损；顶面防、排水系统损毁	年久失修，结构稳定性较差，存在较大安全隐患	采取防护加固、现状修整的保护措施，局部损伤严重的地段采取重点修复，消除安全隐患，维修后的城墙要注意日常维护，并记录修缮的时间与原因
6	神策门西—狮子山东大门（含中央门遗迹段）	中央路至钟阜路西 300 m	现状仅剩下内部小城墙砖以及矮墙、墙基	城墙遗迹被蚕食	缺乏维护与管理，人为破坏严重，存在较大隐患	采取防护加固、现状修整的保护措施，局部损伤严重的地段采取重点修复，消除安全隐患，维修后的城墙要注意日常维护，并记录修缮的时间与原因
		钟阜路西 300 m 以西至建宁路	地面已无存留	—	—	竖立保护标志碑

续表

序号	城墙段		现状	病害类别	存在问题	保护措施
7	狮子山—定淮门	狮子山东大门至仪凤门	城墙长度约962 m，目前局部城墙受损坍塌	顶面防、排水系统损毁；墙面损伤，局部坍塌	年久失修，结构稳定性较差，存在较大安全隐患	采取防护加固、现状修整的保护措施，局部损伤严重的地段采取重点修复，对山体也要采取必要的加固措施，消除安全隐患，维修后的城墙要注意日常维护，并记录修缮的时间与原因
		仪凤门至定淮门	城墙长度约3 000 m，经近年维修保存较好	墙面损伤	—	日常保养
8	定淮门南—汉西门北侧（含石头城）	模范西路至石头城北部城墙端头	无地面遗存			竖立保护标志碑
		石头城北部端头至清凉门段城墙东部端头	城墙长度约1 669 m	墙面损伤	—	日常保养
		清凉门段城墙东部端头至汉中路	已无地面遗存	—	—	竖立保护标志碑
9	汉西门北—中华门西	汉中路至西水关	已无地面遗存	—	—	竖立保护标志碑
		西水关至中山南路	城墙长约1 658 m，经近年维修保存较好	墙面损伤	—	日常保养

表2　城墙墙体植被整治措施表

现象	不良影响	城墙段	整治方式
墙体与墙顶藤本植物或草本植物	根系可能钻进明城墙的砖缝里，继而破坏原本已经脆弱的城砖；部分藤本植物的生长客观上会使明城墙的墙壁渗水，而为蚊蝇的生长提供了温床。典型种类：爬山虎	雨花门—东水关 后标营路—台城 玄武湖隧道入口—神策门 狮子山—定淮门 石头城	根据实际情况调查各段爬藤植物对城墙的影响，有破坏的要清除；其余要控制其生长
墙体顶部生长木本植物	多数乔木根系发达，具有强大的破坏力，长在城墙上的乔木能破坏夯土墙基和墙体。典型树种：青桐、梧桐、槐树	后标营路—中山门 前湖—太平门	清理城墙上的树木

Table 1 Treatment by section

No	Section		Status	Damage	Problem	Protection measures
1	Zhonghua Gate– East Water Pass		3,017m long before repair, 2,825m after repair, 192m for the damaged	Wall surface, top drainage system	—	Daily maintenance
2	East-Water Pass–s. End of Yueya Lake old wall	East Water Pass–Guanghua Gate	No wall traces on the ground	—	—	Erect protection signs
		Guanghua Gate–Guanghua E.	Wall relics	Poor maintenance and management, serious man-made damages, noticeable hidden risks	Poor maintenance and management, serious man-made damages, noticeable hidden risks	Repair and reinforce the walls, preventing further nibbling off and soil erosion; strengthen daily maintenance, and keep a repair journal
3	Yueya Lake (incl.Zhongshan Gate)–Taiping Gate	Guanghua E.–Houbiaoying Rd.	The relics is 680m long, repaired with new bricks, partially restored to a height of 5m	Damaged wall surface and top drainage system	—	Daily maintenance
		Houbiaoying–Shangshan Gate S.	800m long, relatively well kept	Damaged wall surface	—	Daily maintenance
		Zhongshan Gate N.–Qian Lake	798m long, relatively well kept	Damaged wall surface with some fissures	Lacking of maintenance for a long time, poor stability, noticeable hidden risks	Repair and reinforce the walls, focusing on seriously damaged sites, eliminating hidden risks, and strengthening daily maintenance; keep a repair journal
		Qian Lake–Pipa Lake	Surviving walls with serious local damage	Damaged wall surface, fissures on wall body, and local cave-in		Repair and reinforce the walls, focusing on seriously damaged sites, eliminating hidden risks, and strengthening daily maintenance; keep a repair journal
		Pipa Lake–Longpan Rd.	relatively well kept wall body	Damaged wall surface	—	Daily maintenance
4	Taiping Gate–Taicheng	Longpan Rd.–Mount Jiuhua E.	No wall traces on the ground	—	—	Erect protection signs
		Mount Jiuhua E.–Taicheng	1,660m long, well preserved thanks to the maintenance and repair in recent years	No noticeable damage after repair	—	Daily maintenance
5	Jiefang Gate–Shence Gate	Jiefang Gate–Xuanwu Lake Passenger Tunnel	2,500 m long, well preserved thanks to the maintenance and repair in recent years	No noticeable damage after repair	—	Daily maintenance
		Xuanwu Lake Passenger Tunnel–Shence Gate	1,570m long, with serious local damage	Damaged wall surface, local fissures on wall body, and damaged top drainage system	Lacking of maintenance for a long time, poor stability, noticeable hidden risks	Repair and reinforce the walls, focusing on seriously damaged sites, eliminating hidden risks, and strengthening daily maintenance; keep a repair journal
6	Shence Gate W.–Shizishan Gate E.(incl. Zhongyang Gate remains)	Zhongyang Rd.–Zhongfu Rd. 300m W.	The relics of inner walls, parapet, and foundations	The relics is being nibbled away	Poor maintenance and management, serious man-made damages, large hidden risks	Repair and reinforce the walls, focusing on seriously damaged sites, eliminating hidden risks, and strengthening daily maintenance; keep a repair journal
		Zhongfu Rd. 300m W.–Jianning Rd.	No wall traces on the ground	—	—	Erect protection signs

Continued Table

No	Section		Status	Damage	Problem	Protection measures
7	Mount Shizi–Dinghuai Gate	Shizishan Gate E.–Yifeng Gate	962m long, damaged local sites and cave-in	Damaged top drainage system, wall surface, and local cave-in	Unrepaied for a long time, poor structural stability, noticeable hidden risks	Repair and reinforce the walls, focusing on seriously damaged sites, eliminating hidden risks, strengthening daily maintenance, and reinforcing the mountain side; pay more attention to daily maintenance; and keep a repair journal
		Yifeng Gate–Dinghuai Gate	3,000 m long, well preserved thanks to the maintenance and repair in recent years	Damaged wall surface	—	Daily maintenance
8	Dinghuai Gate S.–Hanxi Gate N.(incl. Stone City)	Mofan Rd. W.–Stone City N.	No wall traces on the ground	—	—	Erect protection signs
		Stone City N.–Qingliang Gate E.	1,669m long	Damaged wall surface	—	Daily maintenance
		Qingliang Gate E.–Hanzhong Rd.	No wall traces on the ground	—	—	Erect protection signs
9	Hanxi Gate N.—Zhonghua Gate W.	Hanzhong Rd.–West Water Pass	No wall traces on the ground	—	—	Erect protection signs
		West Water Pass–Zhongshan Rd.W.	1,658 m long, well preserved thanks to the maintenance and repair in recent years	Damaged wall surface	—	Daily maintenance

Table 2 Wall vegetation protection measures

Status	Adverse effects	Wall section	Treatment
Vine and herb plants grown on wall surface and top	Roots penetration into the walls may further weaken the weathered bricks; some vine plants may cause water dripping across the walls, desirable for fly and mosquito breeding. Typical type: Parthenocissus trcuspidata	Yuhua Gate – East Water Pass, Houbiaoying Rd.–Taicheng, Xuanhu Lake tunnel entrance–Shence Gate, Mount Shizi–Dinghuai Gate, and Stone City	Based on the results of investigation, the vine plants that have caused damages to the walls were removed, and measures were taken to control the growth of other plants
Woody plants grown on the wall tops	Developed roots can break up the earth foundation and wall body. Typical species: phoenix tree, and locust tree	Houbiaoying Rd. –Zhongshan Gate Qian Lake — Taiping Gate	Woody plants grown on the wall tops were removed

表3 城门处置方式表

序号	城门	保护措施
1	聚宝门（中华门）	日常保养。其上现有的临时性展示建筑，应在构件老化前拆除，防止其对城墙本体造成损害
2	神策门（和平门）	日常保养
3	仪凤门（兴中门）	日常保养。树立标牌，说明其修缮的时间与原因
4	清凉门（清江门）	日常保养
5	石城门（汉西门）	日常保养
附	东水关	日常保养
6	丰润门（民国后改称玄武门）	树立标牌，说明其设置的时间与原因
7	挹江门	日常保养。树立标牌，说明其设置的时间与原因
8	中山门	日常保养。树立标牌，说明其设置的时间与原因
9	新民门	日常保养
10	武定门	日常保养。树立标牌，说明其修建的时间与原因
11	解放门	日常保养。树立标牌，说明其设置的时间与原因，以区别于城墙本体之原状
12	解放门小门	日常保养
13	集庆门（集庆通道）	日常保养。树立标牌，说明其设置的时间与原因，以区别于城墙本体之原状
14	富贵山小门	封堵门洞，恢复城墙原状
15	后半山园小区小门	综合治理小门附近的环境，取缔紧贴城墙脚摆设的摊贩，保证城墙本体安全。树立标牌，说明其设置的时间与原因，以区别于城墙本体之原状
16	伏龟楼北小门	封堵门洞，恢复城墙原状
17	热电厂南小门	暂不封堵小门。对热电厂实施搬迁，消除对城墙本体潜在的安全威胁。树立标牌，说明其设置的时间与原因，以区别于城墙本体之原状
18	玄武湖人行隧道	日常保养。树立标牌，说明其设置、变迁的历史，以区别于城墙本体原状
19	中华东门、中华西门	日常保养。树立标牌，说明其设置、变迁的历史，以区别于城墙本体原状
20	华严岗门	日常保养。树立标牌，说明其与城墙本体的区别

Table3 Gates protection

No.	Gate	Protection measures
1	Jubao Gate（Zhonghua Gate）	Daily maintenance. There is an interim commercial structure on top, which shall be removed before getting decayed, preventing it causing damages to the wall
2	Shence Gate (Heping Gate)	Daily maintenance
3	Yifeng Gate（Xingzhong Gate）	Daily maintenance. Signs have been erected to show the time and part of repair
4	Qingliang Gate(Qingjiang Gate)	Daily maintenance
5	Shicheng Gate（Hanxi Gate）	Daily maintenance
Appendix	East Water Pass	Daily maintenance
6	Fengrun Gate（Xuanwu Gate after the Republican time）	Signs have been erected to show the time and part of repair
7	Yijiang Gate	Daily maintenance. Signs have been erected to show the time and part of repair
8	Zhongshan Gate	Daily maintenance. Signs have been erected to show the time and part of repair
9	Xinmin Gate	Daily maintenance
10	Wuding Gate	Daily maintenance. Signs have been erected to show the time and part of repair
11	Jiefang Gate	Daily maintenance. Signs have been erected to show the time and part of repair, indicating the difference from the original wall
12	Jiefang Side Gate	Daily maintenance
13	Jiqing Gate (Jiqing Passage)	Daily maintenance. Signs have been erected to show the time and part of repair, indicating the difference from the original wall
14	Fuguishan Side Gate	The gate was sealed off to restore the original wall
15	Houbanshan residential area side gate	Protection activities have been along with the residential area control efforts. Illegal vendors along the foot of the walls were removed, ensuring the safety of the walls. Signs were erected to show the time and part of repair, indicating the difference from the original wall
16	Fugui Tower N. Side Gate	The gate was sealed off to restore the original wall
17	Redianchang S. Side Gate	The gate was not sealed off for the time being. The thermal power plant was moved away, eradicating the hidden risks to the wall. Signs have been erected to show the time and part of repair, indicating the difference from the original wall
18	Xuanwu Lake passenger tunnel	Daily maintenance. Signs have been erected to show the history of the gate and associated evolutions, indicating the difference from the original wall
19	Zhonghua Gate E., Zhonghua Gate W.	Daily maintenance. Signs have been erected to show the history of the gate and associated evolutions, indicating the difference from the original wall
20	Huayangang Gate	Daily maintenance. Signs have been erected to show the differences from the original wall

3）涵闸、涵洞保护措施

城墙在进行维修、考古或其他建设时，遇到有涵闸、涵洞处，要注意涵闸、涵洞的保护与展示。

4）外郭保护措施

（1）对于现在还遗留城墙土芯遗迹的地段，要注意土芯的水土保持。

（2）对于已作为路基通车的部分，逐步调整为只通小车。加强对墙体的日常维护和监控。

（3）对地面墙体无存的一些地段，在考古确定后树立保护标志碑。

4. 南京明城墙关联的文化遗产与展示利用规划

对南京明城墙保护的目的，还在于对其价值进行展示，对其功能进行利用，其中也包括对南京明城墙关联的文化遗产进行整体的串联和表达，因为南京明城墙包含的南京老城范围和外郭围合的城市范围存有丰富的文化遗产，特别是明代存留的相关内容和一些无形的文化遗产如民俗，缺少整合展示。为此，提出如下展示利用规划思考和内容：

1）将本体保护、考古寻踪与南京风俗、历史资源相结合的展示利用，形成四季主题游（图8）

（1）春去百病登南城：游线为：中华门—东水关—内秦淮—西水关。将展示中国最大的瓮城中华门的雄姿，在城头上纳阳走春，品味城砖上的历史信息，考察东水关的遗址遗迹，从秦淮河观看南京城墙，体验西水关的历史遗迹和历史场所与现代生活的交融。

（2）秋寻宫迹绕东界：游线为：光华门（正阳门）—明故宫—前湖、琵琶湖—太平门—台城。将结合南京的城门遗址、历史轴线、宫城遗址、自然资源、城墙峻险，展现南京在历史上作为都城的遗迹和特别风光，也是观览南京山水城林的最佳游线。

（3）冬踏曲瓮觅北垣：游线为：神策门—拟建城墙博物馆—黑龙江路遗迹—新民门—狮子山东门。将结合城门、城墙博物馆、考古遗迹、近代城门遗物、断续的城河，在考察和寻觅中认识体验南京不同地形和不同时期建造的城墙路线，黑龙江路等处将结合现状绿化和遗址展示，倡导以绿化补足和加强标识来突出原有城墙走向的做法。

（4）夏泛河舟观石城：游线为水路：串联起西水关—清凉山石头城—三汊河—宝船遗址。主要通过外秦淮河作为护城河的水上游，考察南京明城墙的墙河一体的防

4. Exhibition and utilization of the wall related cultural heritages

The protection of Nanjing Ming City Wall is meant to exhibit its values, and to utilize its functions, including the combined expression of the wall related cultural heritages as a whole. The city wall built in the Ming Dynasty has covered rich cultural heritages from the old city proper to the defensive wall. Unfortunately, some heritages associated with the walls, and some intangible cultural heritages, such as folk's custom, have not yet been integrated properly. In this context, the following thinking lines are proposed for the future exhibition and utilization of wall related cultural heritages:

1) Combine the wall protection/archaeological investigation with the exhibition of folk's custom and historical resources in the city, creating themed four-season tourist routes(Fig.8)

(1) Spring southern wall section tour, Tourist routes: Zhonghua Gate–East Water Pass–Inner Qinhuai–West Water Pass. People can enjoy the magnificence of Zhonghua Gate, the largest fortified outpost in the country, taking a walk on the top of the wall, breathing energized Spring breeze, viewing the historical information inscribed on ancient bricks, feeling the remains of East Water Pass, watching the City Wall from the Qinhuai River, visiting the historical relics of West Water Pass, and experiencing the combination of historical sites and modern life.

(2) Autumn east section tour, Tourist routes: Guanghua Gate (Zhengyang Gate)–Ming Imperial Palace –Qian Lake and Pipa Lake–Taiping Gate–Taicheng. Visitors will see the relics of ancient Nanjing as a capital city and its unique landscape, through

3) Culvert gates and tunnel protection

When repairing the walls, making archaeological investigations, or engaging in other construction activities, doers are asked to protect the culvert gates or tunnels that they may encounter based on the culvert gate and tunnel maps.

4) Defensive wall protection

(1) More attention is asked to pay to soil erosions at the sections having ancient earthy cores.

(2) Strengthen the daily maintenance and monitoring of the wall sections that have been employed to be the foundation of roads. Rules shall be worked out to gradually narrow down the type of automobiles allowed to pass through the roads to sedan car only.

(3) Protection signs shall be erected at the remains without physical walls, after the archaeological confirmation.

御系统，认识南京城墙和历史环境的整体性，体会南京明城墙在对孙吴石头城利用上的独到之处，以及宝船遗址在特殊地理条件下的特别创造和遗产价值。

2）将城墙遗产、文化遗产、山水资源相结合的明代特别游（图9）

（1）具体路线：燕子矶—土城头（外郭）—明孝陵—明故宫（遗址）—东水关—大报恩寺遗址公园（建设中）—中华门—（沿水路）石头城—宝船遗址公园—天妃宫—静海寺—狮子山阅江楼。

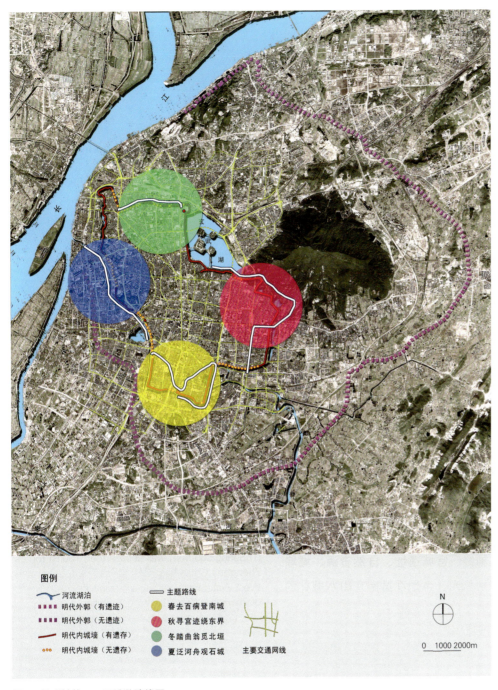

图8　景观结构——四季游路线图
Fig.8 Landscape structure— four-season tourist routes

visiting the gates relics, historical axis line, palace relics, natural resources, and steep walls. It makes the best tourist attraction for viewing the mountains, waters, and forests in a single trip.
(3) Winter northern section tour, Tourist routes: Shence Gate–City Wall Museum (to be built)–Heilongjiang Rd. relics–Xinmin Gate–Shizishan East Gate. Visitors will see the city walls built on different terrains and in different historical periods, through visiting the gates, museum, archaeological relics, contemporary gate relics, and moat relics. Heilongjiang Rd section shows people the combination of greeneries and relics, a fine example to keep the continuity of the broken walls using greeneries.
(4) Summer boat tour visiting the Stone City, Tourist routes: West Water Pass–Mount Qingliang and Stone City–Sancha River– Precious Boat Relics. Visitors will be led to view the ancient defense system made up of both walls and rivers, understanding the integrity of the walls and historical environment, experiencing the unique way of utilizing the Stone City in building the city wall, and knowing the special values of the Precious Boat Relics, by cruising across the External Qinhuai River, a moat in ancient times.

（2）具体内容：概括形成歌谣："燕子飞来石矶，穿行土城绿廊，拜祭明朝先祖，寻觅当年殿堂，出城观塔报恩，一路来到瓮城，泛舟西行北上，遥见造船作塘，怀想天妃郑和，登山狮子阅江"。

3) 将城墙和外郭作为南京明城墙一体结构关系的双环游

目前南京城墙沿线结合《南京明城墙风光带规划》和长期的整治，已形成较好的城墙和秦淮河一体的风光带，为市民提供了休闲愉悦的场所，也为游客提供了解读南京独特品质的游线。

另一方面，2010年南京市政府委托东南大学建筑学院和城市规划设计研究院承担

2) Ming Dynasty tour including city walls, cultural heritages, and natural landscape(Fig.9)
(1) Routes: Yanziji–Tuchengtou (defensive walls)–Ming Xiaoling Mausoleum–Ming Imperil Palace Relics–East Water Pass–Dabaoen Temple Relics park (under construction)–Zhonghua Gate–(via waterway) Stone City–Precious Boat Relics Park–Tianfei Palace–Jinghai Temple–River Viewing Pavilion on Mount Shizi.
(2) Contents: When swallows hit Shiji, the Tucheng area will become a green corridor. One worships his or her forefathers in the Ming Dynasty, visiting old palaces and pavilions. People return their thanks at Dabaoen Temple, and visit the fortified outposts on the way. Then they will have a boat trip heading north, viewing the old precious boat in the distance, and memorizing beauties and heroes in the history, before climbing up Mount Shizi to get a panoramic view of the river.

3) Dual-wall tour (city wall and defensive wall)
A nice landscape made up of city walls and the Qinhuai River has taken shape, thanks to the implementation of the Nanjing Ming City Wall Landscape Plan, and to the long term control efforts made to the city walls. The landscape makes nice entertainment sites available for citizens, creating a tourist route for people to taste the unique quality of Nanjing.

图9 明代文化遗址串联游
Fig.9 Ming cultural heritages tourist route

南京外郭沿线综合规划，将外郭走向存留的 43 km 的土城头保护与展示利用规划纳入南京新的城市规划体系中，也将形成历史场所和现代生活叠合的南京外环休闲、绿化、观览的游线（图10）。

对于城墙和外郭这双环线，我们在规划时还注重它们原先在城市形制和结构上的关联，如从神策门经中央北路与外郭上元门的连接，从中山门经中山门大街与外郭麒麟门的连接等，既是对保护规划时视觉通廊的进一步发展和实现，也是对南京明城墙体系保护、展示与利用的进一步表达。

In 2010, the Nanjing Municipal Government assigned Southeast University School of Architecture and Institute of Architectural Design to make a comprehensive plan for streamlining the landscapes along the defensive walls. Researchers made the exhibition and utilization of the 43km surviving defensive walls part of the new urban planning system, which will eventually result in a recreational, greenery, and tourist route combining historical sites and modern life(Fig.10).

To achieve the goals, a dual-wall tour is designed to reveal the ties between the original urban system/structure and the walls. For example, Shence Gate is made accessible to Shangyuan Gate in the defensive walls via Zhongyang Road N., and Zhongshan Gate to Qiling Gate in the defensive walls via Zhongshanmen Ave.. It not only makes a visual corridor for conservation planning, but is also an enhanced expression of protection, exhibition, and utilization of the wall system.

1 金川门桥头公园
2 上元门公园
3 幕府山公园
4 燕子矶—观音门风景区
5 产业遗产景观走廊
6 尧化门公园
7 聚宝山公园
8 龟山外郭遗址公园
9 外郭本体景观展廊
10 萧宏墓园
11 跑马场度假旅游中心
12 麒麟关高地公园
13 六朝石刻主题公园—初宁陵
14 生态艺术长廊
15 中央公园
16 农耕文化地景公园
17 上方门水上公园

图 10　南京明外郭沿线地区规划设计图
Fig.10　Planning and design for the defensive walls

参考书目

东南大学建筑设计研究院. 全国重点文物保护单位南京明城墙保护总体规划，2008

Reference

Architectural Design and Research Institute of Southeast University. The Conservation Master Plan for the Nanjing Ming City Wall (National Cultural Heritage), 2008

第二节　城墙系统与罗马的新城市总体规划
4.2　The Walls System and the New General Urban Plan in Rome

保拉·法利尼　Paola Falini

这是一项非常重要的专项规划。它首次提出将城墙视作具有重要考古价值的人工构筑物，需要运用特殊手段加以保护与保留，还将城墙看作城市的主要结构，在强化整个城市系统中扮演着决定性的角色。

这项新的规划还有一个任务，并在新的罗马城市总体规划中第一次得到强调，即将历史环境的调研列入这项新的策略。

调研内容，首先包括区域层级特性尺度下历史城市肌理的重要性，其次包括强调大尺度城市结构和景观背景下的战略规划领域，它们将成为重新解读逐渐清晰的历史关系中的同一城市系统的主要支撑（图1、图2）。

意大利城市历史文化古城保护协会（ANCSA）在1990年代初向罗马市政府提交的一些议案中就已经强调过类似的规划思想。这些思想为重新定位历史中心的概念予以机会，以适于既存的城市和历史的领域，而且关注于将现有城市与其各种特定运作系统（博物馆城、旅游城市、政治中心）相关联，尤其关注于简化这种关系中的复杂流程。值得注意的是，罗马不同于其他欧洲大城市，它几乎完整保留了城墙，全长接近19 km，分别建于不同的时期和不同的地形条件下，并且从未获得过统一的特性。即使是在国家统一、城墙最终失去了防卫功能后，这些城墙也没有被作为整体进行全盘考虑。事实上，在其生长中，城市扩张为形态和功能方面各具特色的片区，这已经超越了城墙自身，进一步导致了城墙的四分五裂。

从一开始，这种思考就已经为研究确定了方向，强调了服从整体战略的必要性，以总体规划的形式来表达，分为不同的行动层面：

第一个层面是由全部城墙区域的整体项目组成（图3），它被视作真正的、新的公共建设工程，即整合成线性公园（图4）。在这个新的实体中，所有的公共空间将通过文化和旅游两种方式得到强化。对整个城墙环线进行整修和重新连接，修复被破坏的连续性将会对此有所助益。

第二个层面由明确的城市项目组成，与那些为了城墙的再开发而需要本地化运作的区域相关，它们也可成为更广泛的城市转型的驱动力，例如梵蒂冈城墙（Vatican Wall）、波尔泰赛（Portese）城门、桑尼奥（Sannio）大街和卡斯特罗比勒陀里奥区域。

This proposal has been a very important one, as it is the first time that Walls are known not only for the great value as archaeological artifact, subject to specific measures of protection and preservation, but also for their being an urban primary structure that can play a decisive role in enhancing the entire urban system.

The new proposal is connected as well to the role, underlined for the first time in the new General Urban Plan, that the survey of the historical environment has in this new strategy.

That is in first, the importance of the historical urban fabric as dimension of the stratified quality in the territory, and secondly, the strategic planning fields (including the walls) as emphasis of urban structures and landscapes of large dimension, able to become a new backbone for the reinterpretation of the same city systems in its historical relationship with the emerging configurations (Fig.1, Fig.2).

A similar approach was already underlined in the proposals that ANCSA association brought to the Municipality of Rome in the early 1990s. Those ideas regarded not only the opportunity of a final overcoming of the concept of historical center in favor of the one of the existing city and historical territory, but also to articulate the existing city in its various specific operating systems (the museum city, the tourist city, the politic city) with particular attention to the need of simplify the complex circuits of its relationships. Is important to underline that Rome, unlike most large European cities, has preserved almost all of its walls circle. A circuit of almost 19 km, which was built in different topographical conditions and at different times, and that has never obtained an unitary nature. Even after the unification of the country, when the walls finally lost its defensive function, they have never been subject to any overall consideration. In its growth the city has in fact expanded in morphologically and functionally distinct parts, which have exceeded the walls themselves, further contributing to their segmentation.

Since the beginning, this kind of consideration has orientated the study, and emphasized the need to follow an overall strategy, expressed in the form of General Plan, with different levels of action:

– The first level consists of an unitary project for the entire Walls area (Fig.3), considered as a real new

第四章 城墙规划　4 – Planning for City Walls

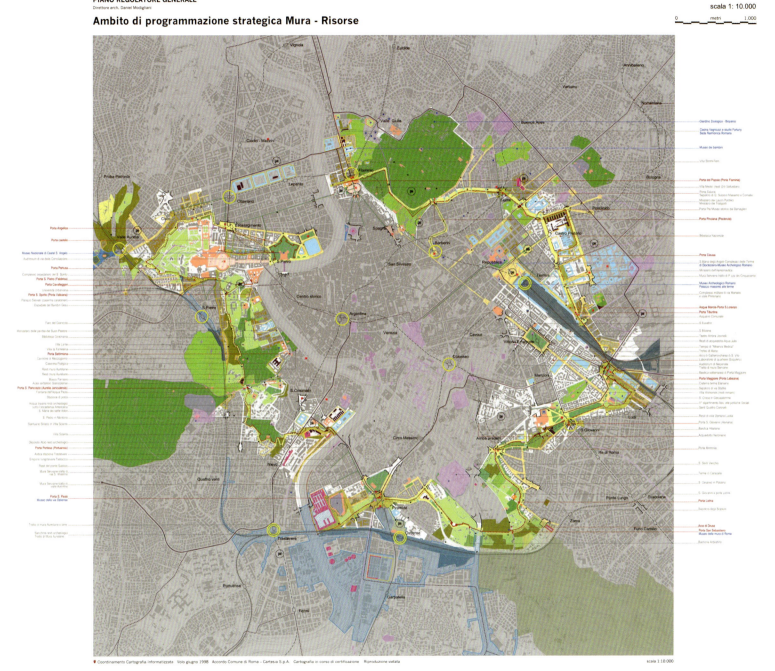

图1　罗马城墙区域战略规划——资源
Fig.1　Rome City Wall strategic planning–Resources

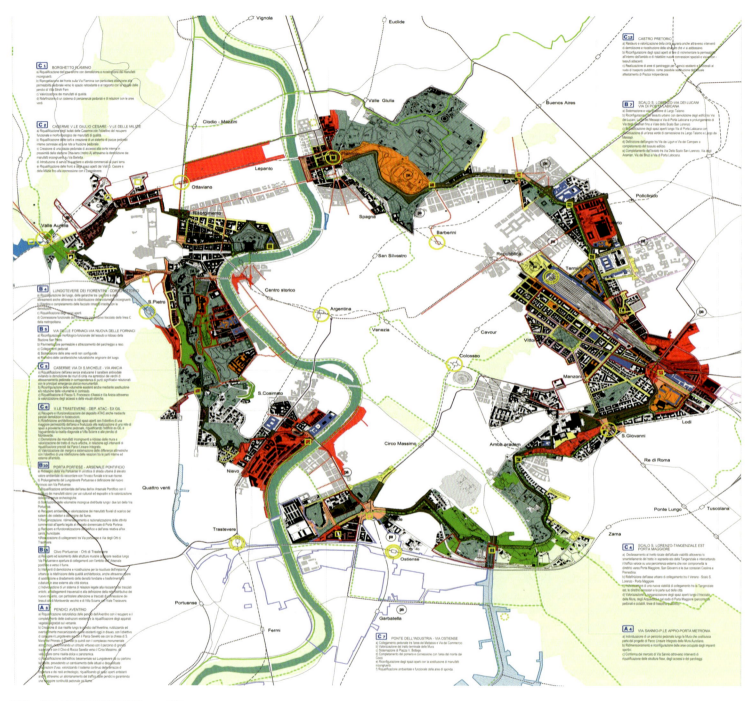

图2 罗马城墙区域战略规划——目标
Fig.2 Rome City Wall strategic planning–Objectives

第四章 城墙规划　4 – Planning for City Walls

图3　城墙区域需要规划整治的项目
Fig.3　Planning projects for the entire walls area

　　第三个层面是复杂的城市项目之一，它将对那些城墙问题与周边的危机状况相关的区域产生影响。这些区域需要一种干预，超过城墙自身的范围，并影响到那些被定义为"正在关注"的区域：托尔托城墙和波各塞别墅—弗拉米尼奥轴线系统；第布勒蒂纳—马焦雷（Tiburtina-Maggiore）城门和其周边废弃的区域，西斯廷规划系统和圣洛伦佐区内19世纪城市结构之间的渗透性议题；从迪斯达奥（Testaccio）到圣保罗大教堂（St. Paul Basilica）之间的奥斯提安塞区域，这个地区对台伯河沿岸大片工业区的更新与再开发有着重要作用；莱扎纳古埃利（Regina Coeli）和福尔纳奇（Fornaci）路之间的区域需要重新思考绿色空间之间的重新连接。

曼特罗尼亚和圣保罗城门项目

　　这些项目特别关注城市空间在城墙公园交叉点的重组，包含由圣保罗和曼特罗尼亚城门广场形成的具有纪念意义的城市节点和两个地段，分别由曼特罗尼奥

public work, the Integrated Linear Park (Fig.4). In this new entity all the public space will be enhanced in the two ways, culture and tourism, helped by the renovated rejoining of the entire wall circle, with restoration of the broken continuity.
– The second consists of definite urban projects, related to areas that require localized operations for the redevelopment of the walls and can also become driving forces of more extensive urban transformations like Vatican Walls, Portese gate, Sannio road or Castro Pretorio area.
– The third level is the one of complex urban projects that will affect the areas where the walls problems are associated with the critical conditions of surrounding areas. Those ones need a kind of intervention that is beyond the walls territory and affects those areas that are defined as "under attention": the Muro Torto and the Villa Borghese–Flaminio axis system; the Tiburtina–Maggiore gate with its disused areas and the theme of permeability between the Sistine system and the urban structures of nineteenth-century San Lorenzo district; Ostiense area from Testaccio to St. Paul Basilica,

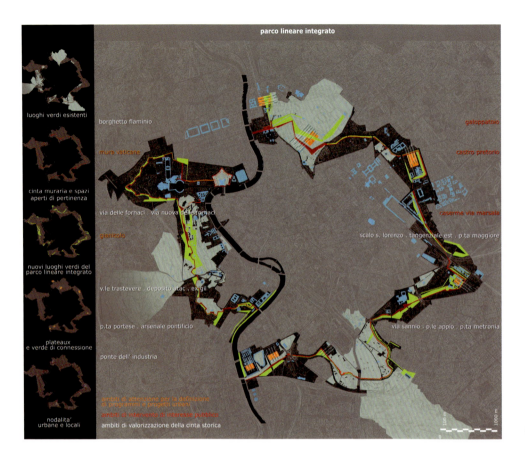

图4 整合的线性公园
Fig.4 The integrated linear park

（Metronio）大道和牛市街为代表。

这两个项目所关注的区域由于现有结构和潜在发展的不同，彼此产生了很大的差异。第一个区域是大罗马纪念系统的一个节点，被强大的基础设施和纪念物包围，传达着"强烈的场所精神"，但其布局混乱、危机日积月累。与此相反的是，第二个地区似乎是一个没有任何"布局"可言、缺少城市发展潜力的地区。不可化解的矛盾在伪三岔路的布局、城墙的环状和不具有纪念样式的城门之间显现出来。城门旁两片相同的区域的作用被降低，仅仅作为不和谐的交叉路口。

高密度的居住片区面向广场前形成的伪三岔路区域，这是一个不同功能的建筑混合体，容纳了高密度住宅和以本地居民兴趣为主导的商店。

城市纪念性的效果，因此与这个街区的空间形态和建筑类型的异质性相矛盾，而缺乏等级性不仅指的是新建筑，而且指的是这些大型街区的布局，这减弱了城门的中心性。

important for the renovation and redevelopment of the Tevere river's large industrial zone; the area from Regina Coeli and Fornaci road that requires a whole rethinking of the reconnection of green spaces.

The projects for Metronia and San Paolo gates

Those projects are focused specifically on the reorganization of the urban spaces at the intersection between the walls park, with its monumental urban nodes of San Paolo and Metronia gates squares, and the two segments represented respectively by Metronio and Campo Boario avenues.

The areas on which the two projects focus are quite different between themselves due to existing structure and potential development. The first one is a node of the great Roman monumental system and is surrounded by strong infrastructures and monuments that, in its chaotic dispersion and

图 5　圣保罗城门项目
Fig.5　The project for San Paolo Gate

关于这两条大街，有两点需要强调：

曼特罗尼奥大道由于几乎沿城墙两侧都分布着大片绿色区域，构成了整合式线性公园的城内部分面积最大的延伸空间之一。否则，屠牛广场（Foro Boario）街现在依然是一条狭窄的小路，限制了重组的可能性，当然除了台伯河和特斯塔（Testsccio）区的连接、屠牛广场的非地与特斯塔丘山考古区的关联之外。牛市的开放区，也是特斯塔丘山的考古区。

在圣保罗地区，规划的主要目的是恢复整个城市体系核心区的优势地位。该区域由切斯提亚金字塔和城门、阿·里伯拉（A.Libera）设计的邮局、前往奥斯提亚利多（Ostia Lido）的火车站以及周边的一些街区组成。这一目的是通过重新铺设步行区域，以及通过将切斯提亚金字塔和城门重新统一起来而实现的，这种统一是通过消除由佩尔西凯蒂（Persichetti）在1950年代造成的城墙中断而实现的（图5）。

accumulation of emergencies, express a "strong genius loci". The second one seems instead as an area without configuration and also lacks of potential urban development. What appears is the irresolvable contradiction between a pseudo-trident configuration, the circularity of the walls and not monumental shape of the gate. The same two areas next to the gate are reduced to mere detuned traffic junctions.
The intensive inhabited district that faces the area, forming this pseudo trident in front of the square, is a mixed ensemble of buildings with different functions: high-density houses and shops of prevailing local interest.
The effect of urban monumentality is then contradicted by the morphological and typological heterogeneity of the blocks, by the low presence of functions and by the lack of hierarchy due not only to the emerging buildings but also to the distribution of these large blocks that contribute to reduce the gate central importance.

在曼特罗尼亚城门地区，由于广场缺少内部的人行空间，因此空间成为一片无组织的空地，不利于交通，实质上也未得到充分利用。该项目重点在于重新布局，与曼特罗尼奥大道的城墙内侧沿线已开发的城市空间连贯起来，改善这条大道和曼特罗尼亚城门之间的空间，最终，使这座城门以及拉丁纳和圣塞瓦斯蒂安城门成为中心考古区遗址的网络关系的首选节点（图6）。

Two points are to underline concerning the two avenues.
Metronio avenue, thanks to the presence of large green areas on both sides of the wall for almost all its length, constitutes one of the greatest extension space of the interior section of the Integrated Linear Park. Otherwise, Foro Boario street is now an almost narrow road with limited reorganization possibilities except for those related to the reconnection with the river Tiber and the Testaccio district, the free areas of Foro Boario and the archaeological space of mount Testaccio.
In San Paolo area, the main aim was to restore strength to the core of the whole urban system, formed by the Cestia Pyramid and the Gate, the Post Office of A. Libera, the Railway Station for Ostia Lido, the surrounding blocks. This result has been reached through the realizing of a new paved area for pedestrian use and through the reunification of the Cestia Pyramid with the gate, realized with the elimination of the break, made in the 1950s by Persichetti (Fig.5).
In Metronia gate area, where the square lacks of an inner pedestrian space and the space is an amorphous void, not good for traffic purpose and substantially underused, the project has focused on a reconfiguration, coherent with the equipped urban space along the interior walls on Metronio avenue with the improvement of the space between the avenue and the Metronia Gate and finally, choosing this gate, Latina and San Sebastiano ones, as preferred node for the network relations with sites of the central archaeological area (Fig.6).

图6　曼特罗尼亚城门项目
Fig.6　The project for Metronia Gate

注释

1. 在编辑中，路易吉·戈佐拉不得不删减了约 2/3 长度的文字，但无法与作者取得联系并向他们致歉，希望不会使内容混乱。同时还使文献资料与附属的插图和照片整合起来。
2. 在 ANCSA 的建议下，城墙地区的设计研究包含在了新 PRG（负责人：M. 马尔切洛尼教授）的编制中，并且由老城办公室（负责人：建筑师 G. 法里纳）带头进行，科研人员：P. 法利尼和 A. 泰拉诺瓦与 E. 卡塔鲁扎，A. 克里科尼亚，C. 斯科佩塔，C. 瓦洛拉尼和 R. 布鲁诺尼，A. 奥塔维亚尼，S. 皮耶雷蒂，D. 塞雷蒂。

Notes

1. Luigi Gazzola had to intervene in the editorial and to reduce the length of the text by about two thirds, but we are unable to contact with the author to whom I make apologizes. Hopefully, it will not upset the contents. It also has integrated documentation with additional illustrations and photos.
2. The design study of the Area of the walls was covered in the formation of the new general plan (Director: prof. M. Marcelloni) with the advice of ANCSA and then in the efforts of the Office for the Old City (Director: Arch . G. Farina), scientific officers: P. Falini and A. Terranova, with E. Cattaruzza, A. Criconia, C. Scoppetta, C. Valorani and R. Brunori, A. Ottaviani, S. Pieretti, D. Serretti.

第五章 城墙与都市项目

5 City Walls and Urban Projects

第一节　南京明城墙风光带规划与实施

5.1 The Landscape Planning and Implementation of the Nanjing Ming City Wall

刘正平　Liu Zhengping

1. 明城墙在今日的地位

明城墙是南京悠久历史的重要象征，是南京历史文化名城的重要组成部分，在南京城市风貌保护区中，明城墙风光带无疑是长度最长、覆盖范围最广泛的一片（图1）。

1. Ming City Wall: today's status

The Ming City Wall makes an important piece of evidence to confirm Nanjing's position as a city with a long history. It is an important part of Nanjing, a historically and culturally famous city. Of the major urban landscapes placed under the Municipal Government's protection, the city wall is the longest landscape that has covered most part of the city(Fig.1).

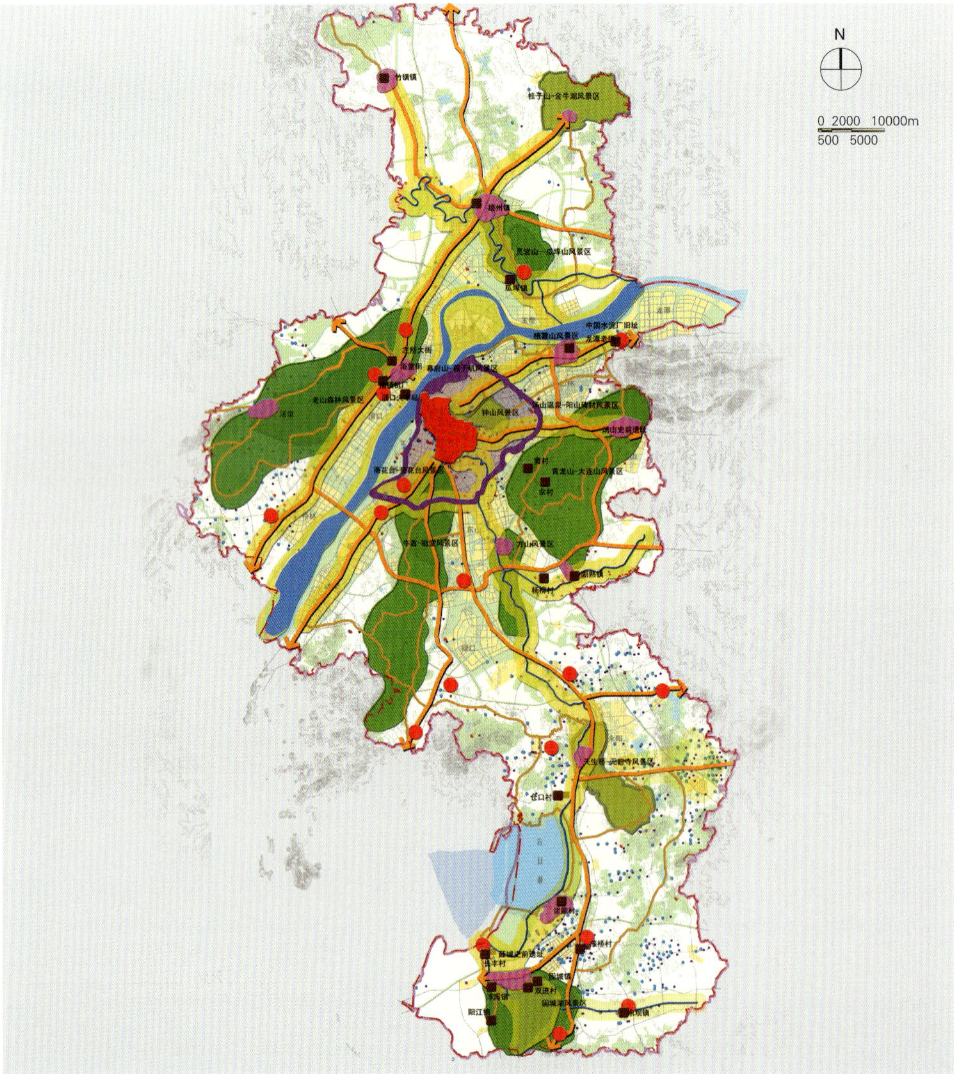

图例

- 老城
- 明外郭
- 环境风貌斑块
- 历史文化斑块
- 古镇古村、历史地段
- 历史文化节点
- 历史文化廊道
- 串联路径
- 绿地
- 水域
- 铁路
- 道路
- 市域界线

图1　南京历史文化名城保护规划图
Fig.1　Conservation plan of historical Nanjing

作为融山、水、城、林为一体，具有古都风貌特色的城市，南京明城墙及其周围山水资源，无疑是最重要的体现（图2）。

南京明城墙是主城绿地系统的主骨架，最为可贵的是，南京明城墙及其周围的绿地分布在最需要绿地的城市中心区，它是一条绿色的项链，将分散的绿地有机组织在一起（图3）。

在当今旅游业迅速发展的情况下，明城墙无疑具有重要的旅游价值，是明文化的重要内容之一，也是南京城墙具备申报世界文化遗产实力的项目之一。

The city wall and ambient mountains/rivers makes Nanjing an ancient capital city intertwined with mountains, waters, urban areas, and forests(Fig.2).
The wall system constitutes the skeleton of greeneries running through the city proper. It is worth mentioning that the walls and ambient greeneries are fortunately located in the center of the city that needs green vegetations most. It works like a green necklace, linking scattered ambient greeneries together(Fig.3).
The Ming City Wall is undoubtedly an important tourist attraction for the booming tourism industry in today' China, an important part of Ming culture, and a heritage qualified to be a World Cultural Heritage.

图2　山、水、城、林的南京古都
Fig.2　Ming Nanjing with the environments of mountains, water system, city and forests

图3　南京城墙绿地系统
Fig.3　The greenery system along the Nanjing City Wall

2. 明城墙风光带规划总体构思

《明城墙风光带规划》的全部构思以保护、利用与保证体系三项为出发点（图4、图5）。

从"人类文化遗产"的高度审视南京明城墙的价值，实行全方位保护；南京明城墙的残缺部分，同样是城墙不可分割的一部分，因此将35.267 km的城墙（包括遗迹和遗址）作为一个整体来规划实行全线保护；作为古代的防御工程和军事设施，应是城

2. Ming City Wall Landscape Belt Planning

The Ming City Wall Landscape Belt Planning is made in line with the principle of protection, utilization, and guarantee (Fig.4, Fig.5).

The planning is supposed to understand the value of the Ming City Wall from the angle of a cultural heritage, advocating an all-round protection. The missing wall sections are deemed an inalienable part of the wall landscape. As a result, efforts have been made to protect the 35.267km long city walls, including both the relics and sites, as a whole. The walls worked with gates and moats as a defense and military facility in ancient times. Therefore, all the three components have to be protected as a whole. The booming development of Nanjing City

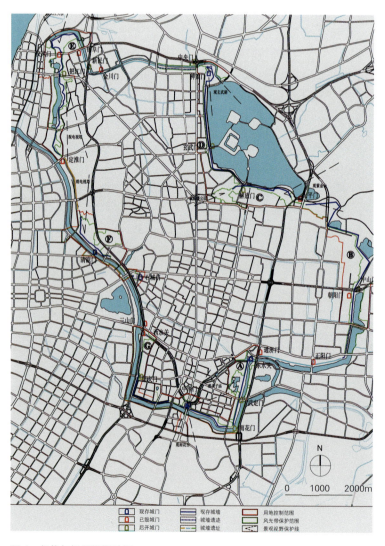

图4　保护与控制规划总图
Fig.4　General plan for protection and control

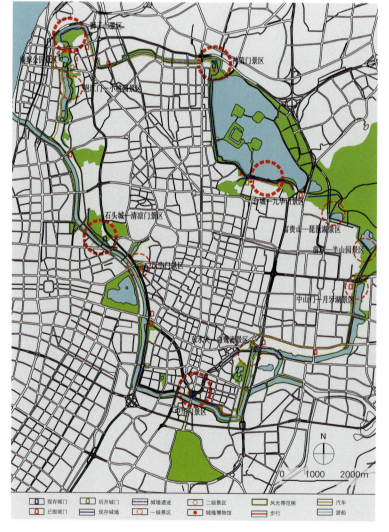

图5　开发与利用总图
Fig.5　General plan for development and utilization

墙、城门、城河三位一体，共同发挥城防作用，因此将三者作为一个整体来考虑，实行全体保护；由于城市的膨胀和违章建设，因此部分城墙周围的环境问题已相当严重，必须将城墙与周围的城市用地实行有效的"剥离"。

以城墙为轴，整理与其相关的山林与水体，在南京主城的中心区，真正形成一道有一定宽度的，连续不断的绿色项链，以展现古代城墙昔日的风采，改善老城的生态环境与城市景观。充分利用以城墙为主体的风景资源，采用多种方式进行开发与利用，发展旅游。

借助法律效力，完善法规体系，保护明城墙及其城墙环境，在《文物保护法》和《南京城墙保护管理办法》的基础上，由市政府颁布《南京明城墙风光带规划管理规定》，成为城墙及其周围环境保护的依据。

3. 保护与控制规划

根据城墙保存情况，可分为三类：现存城墙；城墙遗迹；城墙遗址。其保护与控制规划为：

1）现存城墙

现存城墙是规划的重点。根据现状保存情况，在总体构思的指导下，分为七段：（1）中华门—东水关，全长3.23 km；（2）月牙湖—太平门，全长4.05 km；（3）九华山—台城，全长1.66 km；（4）解放门—神策门，全长4.07 km；（5）狮子山—定淮门，全长3.96 km；（6）石头城—汉西门，全长1.67 km；（7）西水关—中山南路，全长2.11 km。对上述城墙段制定了一套立体的、多层次的保护体系进行有效的保护与控制。

第一层：城墙保护，包括城墙本体保护与城墙安全保护，这是保护规划的基础。城墙本体为绝对保护。如因城市道路建设需要对其有所动作，需报国家文物局审批。保护范围的界定，按照城墙高度的1.5倍并且不少于15 m的原则进行，在该范围之内为禁止建设区。

第二层：环境保护，包括风景资源保护和建设环境控制，这是明城墙风光带保护的重要内容。风景资源保护依据全面保护的原则，根据南京城墙与山林水体的特殊的依附关系而设定。一般情况下，城外至护城河对岸15 m，城内根据山体情况逐段界定，该范围内禁止一切与风景游览无关的建设活动。建设环境控制地带是一种有限使用的城市建设区域，也是城墙风光带的环境风貌协调范围，该范围内的限制要求主要有用地性质、建筑高度、建筑密度三项指标。

第三层：景观视野保护，基于下列两种情况而设立：一是城墙与其依附的山体是观望城市景观的重要景点；二是城墙本身为城市的重要景观。景观视野保护根据视点

and illegal construction activities has worsened the environmental problems surrounding the walls. The walls, therefore, have to be effectively "separated" from the land use in the vicinity.

Protection is made to center on the walls, while taking care of the mountains and waters associated with it. An uninterrupted green "necklace" with the desired width will be built to decorate the center of the city, demonstrating the magnificence of the city walls in old times, and improving the ecological environment and landscape of the old city proper. Additionally, efforts will be made to tap up the wall related landscape resources for tourism development and utilization.

The wall and its ambient environment has to be protected under a legal system. The municipal government is supposed to promulgate a by-law to regulate the management of the city wall landscape belt, in line with the Law of Cultural Heritage Protection and the Methods for Protecting and Managing the Nanjing City Wall, making them the solid legal ground for protecting the wall and its ambient environment.

3. Protection and control planning

The wall is planned to be protected under three categories: surviving walls, wall relics, and wall sites. Their protection and control will be made as follows:

1) Surviving walls

Surviving walls are the focus of the planned protection activities. They can be split into seven sections:(1) Zhonghua Gate–East Water Pass (3.23 km); (2) Yueya Lake–Taiping Gate (4.05km); (3) Mount Jiuhua–Taicheng (1.66km); (4) Jiefang Gate–Shence Gate (4.07km); (5) Mount Shizi–Dinghuai Gate (3.96km); (6) Stone City–Hanxi Gate (1.67km); and(7) West Water Pass–Zhongshan Rd. S. (2.11 km). A three dimensional multi-level protection system will be established to effectively cover the surviving walls.

Level 1: This level of protection makes the physical part of the wall and safety the basic targets of planned conservation. The physical part of the wall shall be placed under absolute protection. Any construction activities that might affect the integrity of the physical part of the wall shall be subject to the approval of State Administration of Cultural Heritages. The wall shall be protected in line with the criteria that no structures shall be built within an area 15m away from the walls, with a control at 1.5 times the wall height.

Level 2: Environmental protection, including landscape resources protection and construction environment control, is a major part of the Ming City Wall landscape protection. Landscape resources

的高度分为高视点保护与低视点保护。

2）城墙遗迹

是指城砖全部驳落，仅剩城芯的残体（土城），现存总长度约 1.8 km，根据全线保护的原则，同样严加保护，具体保护办法分为遗迹本体保护和遗迹环境保护。

3）城墙遗址

是指地面上无遗存的段落，但为了保证明城墙的连贯性，必须明确表示，设置永久性标志和绿带，表明原城墙走向。具体做法有：（1）以河代墙，即城墙已毁而护城河犹存时，在城河边的绿地上设置永久性标志；（2）以路代墙，即城墙城河已不存在，原城墙基上已修道路，可在路边绿地内设置永久标志；（3）以绿代墙，既没有河，也没有路的情况下，在城基上设置绿带，并设置永久标志（图6）。

规划同时对护城河的保护提出要求：分为河床保护与水质保护。明城墙风光带的保护面积为 651 hm²，环境协调面积 465 hm²。

4. 开发与利用规划

明城墙风光带的开发与利用是指城墙及城墙所依附的风景资源的综合开发利用。

图6 绿化作为城墙遗迹的标志
Fig.6 Greenery as the sign to show the city wall site

protection shall be made in an all-round manner, taking into account the special ties between the walls and mountain/forest/water. As a normal practice, an area stretching out from the external part of the wall to the opposite bank of the moat (15m stretching out from the bank) shall be defined to forbid any construction activities that are unrelated to landscape tourism. Inside the walls, the area forbidding any construction activities unrelated to landscape tourism shall be defined in line with the mountains it has encompassed. Construction environment control belt is an area defined for limited urban construction activities, and an area that shall work with the environment and landscape patterns of the wall landscape belt. Such an area shall meet the desired criteria for land use type, structure height, and structure density.

Level 3: Landscape view protection. Protection is needed in the following two circumstances: (1) The wall and associated mountains makes a major scenic spot for landscape viewing; and (2) the wall itself is a major urban landscape. Landscape view protection can be made either as a high viewing site protection, or a lower viewing site protection, in line with the height from which people view the landscape.

2) Wall relics

Wall relics are the earthy core of the walls, uncovered by bricks. The wall relics in the city run about 1.8km long. This part of the wall shall be protected in an all-round manner. It can either be the physical part of the relics protection, or relic environment protection.

3) Wall sites

Wall sites are the wall sections without the physical part of the wall on the ground. To secure the needed continuity of the walls, efforts shall be made to erect permanent signs or grow greeneries to show the course of the original walls. Detailed practice can be: (1) rivers are borrowed to replace the walls. (The practice fits the case when the moat but the wall is still there. A permanent sign shall be erected on the greeneries bordering the moat); (2) roads are employed to connect the walls (The solution is desirable for the case in which both walls and moats are no longer there, and the original wall foundations have been turned into road beds. A permanent sign can be erected on the greeneries on the roadside); and (3) greeneries are employed to connect the walls (Greeneries can be grown on the old wall foundations, when the sites is not occupied by rivers nor by roads. A permanent sign can be erected nearby to show the sites)(Fig.6).

Protection planning also asks to protect the moats. Moats shall be protected in the context of beds and

这种开发与利用对于保护人类文化遗产，改善城市景观，提高老城环境质量，开展专题旅游，无疑都是十分重要的。

南京城墙周边风景资源有：以中华门城堡为城南片景点的核心，城外有雨花台风景区、古长干里，城内有白鹭洲公园、夫子庙、内秦淮河、东水关和传统民居保护区。从城南顺时针向北至下关，明城墙依起伏的丘陵、傍外秦淮河而筑，沿线景点有汉中门文化广场、莫愁公园、鬼脸城、绣球公园、挹江门、小桃园以及新建的狮子山公园。位于南京东北面的明城墙是保存距离最长、完好率最高的一段，自神策门向南，傍玄武湖西岸与南岸蜿蜒向东，经覆舟山，越过钟山余脉折向南，沿琵琶湖、前湖，至月牙湖，此段城墙串联的景点有：神策门瓮城、玄武湖、北极阁古观象台、台城、古鸡鸣寺、明城垣史博物馆、钟山风景区、中山门、月牙湖公园等。

根据城墙保存现状与采用多种方式开发的原则，城墙的开发和利用可以有分段（片）开发与整体开发两种形式，以分段开发方式为主。

根据风景资源情况划分景区，确定景区等级，设置景点。景区等级分为一级景区、二级景区与一般景区三类。一级景区的服务对象主要是外地游客与本地居民；二级景区的服务对象主要是本区居民；一般景区的服务对象为周围的居民。

根据以上原则，整个明城墙风光带共设置一级景区5处，它们是：中华门景区；台城—九华山景区；神策门景区；狮子山景区和石头城景区。另有二级景区7处，它们是：东水关—白鹭洲景区；中山门—月牙湖景区；前湖—半山园景区；琵琶湖—富贵山景区；绣球公园景区；挹江门—小桃园景区和汉西门景区（图7）。

根据城市大交通安排景区出入口，设置登城口与游船码头，并根据景区等级配置旅游服务设施及停车场地。

《南京城墙风光带规划》由南京市规划局组织编制，并召集国内著名专家参与评审。两院院士吴良镛先生在专家评审意见中指出"规划将融山水城林为一体的明城墙、城门、城河三位一体，作为城市绿色的环，将分散的绿地组织在一起，作为发挥城市特色的积极措施是非常正确的……这将成为南京独立于任何其他城市的艺术骨架……"。

1999年南京市人民政府对明城墙风光带规划进行了批复，并且开始风光带的实施。

water quality. The area to be protected across the city wall landscape belt reaches 651hm^2, with a coordinating environment area at 465hm^2.

4. Planned development and utilization

Apparently, the Ming City Wall landscape belt can be further developed and utilized, taking advantage of the landscape resources offered by the wall and its environment. The development and utilization is extremely important to the city, as it protects the cultural heritage, improves urban landscape, raises the environmental quality of old urban areas, and opens up themed tourists routes.

There are numerous landscape resources in the vicinity of the walls: Zhonghua Gate and associated castle makes the core of the southern wall landscape. Outside the walls stands the Yuhuatai landscape and old Changganli. Inside the walls sit Bailuzhou Park, Fuzi Temple, Inner Qinhuai River, East Water Pass, and traditional residential areas. In the southern section of the city, one can travel north to Xiaguan, enjoying the view of the waving mountains and the Qinhuai River along which the walls were built. Along the route, people can also see a range of interesting sites, including Culture Square at Hanzhong Gate, Mochou Park, Guilian Town, Xiuqiu Park, Yijiang Gate, Xiaotaoyuan, and the newly built Mount Shizi Park. The Ming City Wall section sitting in the northeast part of the city is the longest and best preserved one in the city. It starts from Shence Gate in the south, bordering the west and southern banks of Xuanwu Lake, stretching out in a zigzagged manner, crossing Mount Fuzhou and the mountains of Mount Zhong, before turning south, heading for Pipa Lake, Qian Lake, and Yueya Lake. On the way, one can see the fortified outposts at Shence Gate, Xuanwu Lake, an ancient observatory at North Pole Pavilion, Taicheng, Jiming Temple, Ming City Wall museum, Mount Zhong Park, Zhongshan Gate, and Yueyahu Park.

The development and utilization of the walls shall be made in line with the principle of maintaining the current status of the walls, and developing in diverse forms. Specifically, the walls can be developed and utilized either by section, or as a whole, though the former prevails.

Landscape resources shall be rated by class, and categorized by scenic spots. Landscape resource can be rated into three classes: class I, class II, and class mediocre. Class I landscape is designed to mainly serve the tourists from the provinces or cities other than Nanjing and local residents; class II landscape is desirable for the residents living in the area; and class mediocre serves the residents living in the vicinity.

5. 规划实施成果及经验

首先是城墙本体的维护，南京市文物及相关部门几年来投入了相当的资金，抢修了大多数存在隐患的城墙险段，完善了城墙的排水系统。为免于前湖湖水对城墙的侵

The Ming City Wall landscape belt has 5 class I landscapes, including Zhonghua Gate, Taicheng-Mount Jiuhua, Shence Gate, Mount Shizi, and Stone City; and 7 class II landscapes, including East Water Pass-Bailuzhou Park, Zhongshan Gate-Yueya Lake, Qian Lake-Banshanyuan, Pipa Lake-Mount Fugui, Xiuqiu Park, Yijiang Gate-Xiaotaoyuan, and Hanxi Gate (Fig.7).

Municipal authorities has set up entrances and exits to the landscapes, entrances for climbing the walls, ports for tourist boats, and established service facilities and parking lots for the landscapes, in line with the arrangements made by the urban traffic system.

Nanjing City Wall Landscape Belt Planning is prepared by the Nanjing Municipal Planning Bureau, and reviewed by renowned specialists in the country. Mr. Wu Liangyong, an academician of both the Chinese Academy of Sciences and the Chinese Academy of Engineering, pointed out in an expert review: "The planning makes the walls, gates, and moats that built with mountains, waters, urban areas, and forests a green belt, gathering together scattered greeneries in the city. This is correct as it is a positive measure to display the unique features of the city….This will become an artistic skeleton that distinguishes Nanjing from any other cities in the country."

In 1999, Nanjing Municipal Government endorsed the Ming City Wall Landscape Belt Planning, and started to work on its implementation.

5. Implementation, accomplishments and experience to be shared

The implementation of the plan focuses on the maintenance of the physical part of the wall in the first place. In recent years, municipal authorities has invested dearly in repairing the wall sections that had hidden risks, and improving the drainage system. The gap between Qian Lake and the walls have been filled up to be a road, preventing lake water erosion to the walls. A range of walls sections, including Mount Shizi, Qingliang Gate, Shence Gate, and Jiqing Gate, have been reinforced and maintained. A number of old gates, including Yifeng Gate and Wuding Gate, were restored. The removal of industrial gas tanks near Xuanwu Lake, and the withdrawal of military troops from Mount Shizi facilitates the protection, and accelerates the development of landscape belt.

The ambient environment has also been improved, as required by the plan, with laudable accomplishments. (Fig.8 ~ Fig.14) Additionally, it is planned to protect and utilize the defensive walls and forming another green long corridor enriched with historical memories

图 7 明城墙风光带规划图
Fig.7 Ming City Wall landscape belt planning

蚀，已在前湖与城墙间填坝筑路。狮子山段城墙、清凉门、神策门、集庆门等城门及城墙段均得到了加固、维修，并恢复新建了仪凤门、武定门等城门，玄武湖煤气柜的搬迁及狮子山部队的迁移均有利于城墙的保护，也加快了风光带的建设。

城墙周边的环境建设，也完全按规划逐步实施及整治，并已大见成效（图8～图14）。外郭将形成丰富的绿色长廊，成为大南京重要的联系山水的又一条风光带（图15）。

南京明城墙风光带的规划与实施是一项多环节、多层次、浩大的系统工程，不能急于求成，每整治或实施一段都应成为精品。为此，各级政府对明城墙保护工作及环境建设极为重视；其次是制定了较为合理及可操作性的规划，近远期结合，分步实施；第三是坚持社会、经济、环境三方面可持续发展的思路，成熟一段、开放一段，让市民在已整治的城墙段周围近距离地与城墙历史"对话"，感受古都昔日的风采，从中受益；四是加强宣传力度，让全体市民共同关注明城墙的保护与建设，同时使明城墙扩大影响，走向全国、走向世界，为今后申报"世界文化遗产"做好准备。

(Fig. 15).

Nanjing Ming City Wall Landscape Belt Planning and associated implementation is a large multi-link and multi-level project. It takes time to make every phase and every part of the project a fine product. For that, the wall protection and associated environment improvement has to win the firm support of governments at different levels. A reasonable and feasible plan, for both near and long term, shall be prepared, and phased out properly. Protection efforts shall be made in line with the sustainable social, economic, and environmental development. The results of protection can be opened to the public only when they are ready, allowing citizens to "make a dialog" with the history of the repaired walls and improved ambient environment, experiencing the beauty of the old capital city. Efforts shall be made to enhance people's awareness of protection, making the protection a shared cause for all citizens. Meanwhile, efforts shall be made to raise the visibility of the Ming City Wall, letting it be known to the rest of the country and the world, and getting ready for being a World Cultural Heritage.

图8　狮子山段城墙维修后（左）与维修中（右）
Fig.8　The city wall of Mount Shizi section after restoration (left) and under restoration (right)

图 9　修缮后的神策门
Fig.9　Shence Gate after restoration

图 10　修缮后的小桃园段城墙
Fig.10　The city wall of Xiaotaoyuan section after restoration

图 11　台城段城墙景观
Fig.11　The view of Taicheng

第五章 城墙与都市项目 5 – City Walls and Urban Projects

图 12　自城上俯视月牙湖（引自：南京市规划局图片库）
Fig.12　Over looking Yueya Lake from the city wall (from: Photo gallery of Nanjing Planning Bureau)

图 13　修缮后的东水关全景（引自：南京市规划局图片库）
Fig.13　A Panorama of East Water Pass after restoration (from: Photo gallery of Nanjing Planning Bureau)

图 14 东长干巷整修前后（上）；西长干巷整修前后（下）
Fig.14 The City Wall and moat in East Changganxiang section before and after treatment (up); the City Wall and moat in West Changganxiang section before and after treatment (down)

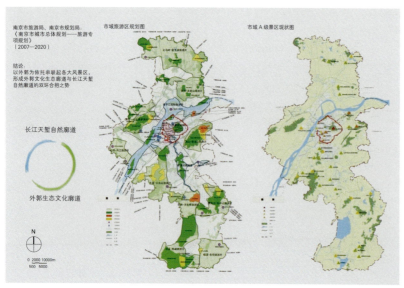

图 15 大南京旅游专项规划图
Fig.15 Tourism specific plan for Modern Nanjing

参考书目

1. 蒋赞初．南京史话：上．南京：南京出版社，1995
2. 刘正平．南京城墙保护规划文本．南京：南京市规划设计研究院，1992
3. 南京市旅游资源开发利用课题组．南京城墙旅游资源潜在价值亟待开发，2000
4. 南京市规划局．南京城市总体规划，1992
5. 南京市规划设计研究院．南京历史文化名城保护规划，1992
6. 南京市人民政府．关于明城墙风光带规划的批复，1999

Reference

1. Jiang Z C. *Nanjing Shihua* (History of Nanjing):1. Nanjing: Nanjing Press, 1995
2. Liu Z P. Nanjing City Wall Conservation Plan. Nanjing: Nanjing Municipal Institute of Planning and Design, 1992
3. Study Team of Tourism Resources Development and Utilization in Nanjing. Nanjing City Wall: a potential tourism attraction to be tapped up, 2000
4. Nanjing Municipal Bureau of Planning. Master Plan of Nanjing, 1992
5. Nanjing Municipal Institute of Planning and Design. Protection planning for Nanjing as a Historically and Culturally Famous city, 1992
6. Nanjing Municipal Government. An endorsement to the Ming City Wall Landscape Belt Planning, 1999

第二节　新罗马城总体规划与战略规划区
5.2　The New Master Plan for Rome and its Strategic Planning Zones

皮耶罗·奥斯蒂利奥·罗西　Piero Ostilio Rossi

新的罗马总体规划（PRG）已编写完成，将在今后的十年内分不同阶段逐步实行（图1）。这份规划法案的起草严格遵照左翼委员会的意见。左翼议会由市长弗朗西斯科·鲁泰利（Francesco Rutelli）和沃尔特·韦尔特罗尼（Walter Veltroni）领导，后者成功地管理了这座城市长达15年（1993—2008年）。

该规划的初稿成于1998年，2003年才正式"颁布实施"（根据意大利法律，市议会的"颁布实施"是总体规划审批的第一个阶段），之后又进行了一系列的修改和重订，直到2008年2月，才获得完全通过。几周之后，市议会就进行了大选，选出了现任市长詹尼·阿莱曼诺（Gianni Alemanno）领导的右翼委员会。新的总体规划是罗马成为意大利首都后的历史上第六次规划，之前的五次分别在1873年、1883

The new Master Plan for Rome (PRG – Piano Regolatore Generale) has been conceived to be implemented in successive stages over a ten year span (Fig.1) and its drafting is strictly linked to the centre–left wing committees headed by the mayors Francesco Rutelli and Walter Veltroni who successively administered the city during fifteen years from 1993 to 2008.

The Plan, first drafted in 1998, was "enacted" in 2003 (according to Italian law, the "enactment" by the City Council is the first stage in approving a Master Plan) and fully approved following a series of changes and re-elaborations, in February 2008, just a few weeks before the council elections which saw the voting in of the centre–right wing committee headed by current mayor Gianni Alemanno. The new Master Plan (PRG) is the sixth in the history of Rome as capital city of Italy, and follows those of 1873, 1883, 1909, 1931 and 1962 (in actual fact formally it is the fifth because the

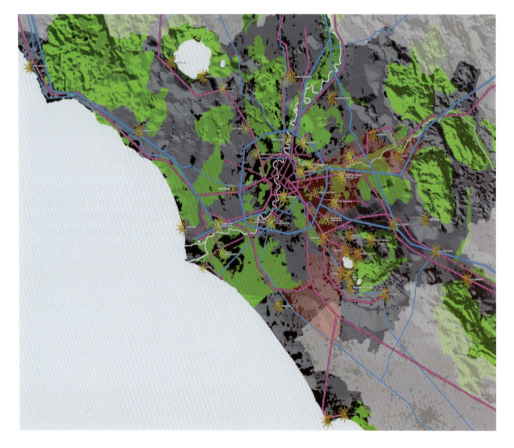

图1　总体规划和大都市战略区的布局：粉红色——地铁线和大都市铁路网络；蓝色——公路网络和主干道；黄色小星形表示城市和大都市中心

Fig.1　Layout of the Master Plan and metropolitan strategic areas: pink – the subway lines and the metropolitan railway network; blue – the highway network and the main roads; the small yellow stars indicate urban and metropolitan centres

年、1909 年、1931 年和 1962 年（实际上这是官方承认的第五次规划，因为 1873 年的规划从未成为国家法律）。

一部新的城市总体规划是一座城市生命中的非凡事件，它标志着这座城市历史中的重要时刻。但是，就罗马而言（特别是涉及最后三次规划），这些规划甚至具有更加特殊的意义，因为它们常常抓住机会对先进的解决方案进行实验，而不用现今正在使用的城市规划方式。这次新提出的规划也有类似的目的。

事实上，新规划最初是通向立法改革的桥梁，它有可能为立法改革分辨目标，但不是立法改革的法律架构。因此，该法案一方面考虑的是城市规划的新工具（"城市肌理"网络）以及大都市核心战略（环境和生态网、铁路交通作为重要的城市化转型的框架、多中心居住模式）；另一方面，作为代替传统的征地方式（在意大利，大部分城市土地归私人所有，为公共使用征地是一种法律手段，允许以低于市场的价格从私人手中购得土地，用于公共项目的建设），新规划引入了诸如城市土地补偿调整这种手段，或更有甚者，作为将土地用于公共事业用地的回报（即使对于单一土地所有权，新开发土地位于别处），准许共享新的开发的利益。这样做是因为考虑到，尽管过去的想法有可能是错误的，但是，目前可用的资源，仅仅利用公共基金，再也无法支付公共服务设施建设的成本，私营领域的参与不仅是必需的途径，而且是现行规划实施中最重要的一种方式。

在确保"提议的计划"转变成"有效的"总体规划的大量技术和政策调节措施当中，有一些创新举措已经失去了一点优势，尽管最近一次的国务院法令（2010 年 7 月）已经裁定了诸如特别税和有补偿转让（compensated handovers）这样的重要而创新的措施具有法律效力。例如特别税，它有可能带来通过扩大建筑体量或改变土地使用类型来提升一个地段的价值的可能性（所获利益并不完全归私人土地所有者所有：大约三分之二要归重新投资开发公共事业的市议会所有）。有补偿的转让政策允许市议会征用私人所有土地，将其分配用于公共事业发展，给土地所有者最少量、但今后具有发展潜质的份额。

我深信，只有当一座城市的新理念建构起来后，一个新的总体规划才真正成型，新的理念明确了所要达到的目标，因此创造出启动所必须的条件：实际上，总体规划的角色在于为这座城市提供理念——既具有战略分量又具有技术深度。1995 年到 2000 年间，在鲁泰利政府"实干规划"（planning by doing）政策的倡导下，实施了一系列可操作的创新举措，罗马的城市新理念已经诞生。

罗马已经被构想为一个多中心的城市，由新建成的大都市区组成，既包括市中心，也包括片区中心。这些可以通过经验证的关联的铁路交通走廊和由受到保护的公园和农业用地网络组成的环绕的"绿带"得以实现。

这是一个有限增长的城市，在这种发展中，不仅要利用其历史中心的城市品质，

1873 Plan was never formed into State Law).
A new Master Plan is an extraordinary event in the life of a city and marks an important moment in the city's urban history, but in the case of Rome (especially for what concerns the last three ones) they are even more exceptional because they have often been the occasion to experiment more advanced solutions than those currently utilised in the urban planning of the country. The new proposed Plan has an analogous aim.
Originally in fact it was intended as a bridge towards legislative reform, for which it was possible to discern the objectives, but not the legal structure. Therefore if on one hand it considered new tools for city planning (the network for the "urban fabric") and metropolitan focus strategies (the environment and ecological networks, rail transportation as the framework for important urbanistic transformations, the polycentric settlement model) on the other, it introduced, as alternative to the traditional method of expropriation (in Italy the bulk of urban areas are private property and the expropriation for public use is the legal tool that allows acquisitions at lower than market prices in order to realise public projects) tools such as the urban compensatory adjustment, or rather, the granting of new development shares (even if located elsewhere with respect to the single landed properties) in exchange for the use of areas destined to public use. This is due to the consideration that despite what was wrongly thought possible in the past, the available resources can no longer cover the costs of realising facilities and services on public funding alone, and the involvement of the private sector is not only an obligatory passage, but one of the foremost tools for the implementation of the current Plan.
In the myriad of technical and political mediation necessary to ensure that a "proposed Plan" turns into an "effective" Master Plan, some of these innovations have lost a little of their edge, even if a recent court ruling from the State Council (July 2010) has decreed the validity of important and innovative tools such as extraordinary levies and compensated handovers. With extraordinary levies, it is possible to introduce the possibility of increasing the value of an area by increasing the cubage or changing the land use category (the increase in value does not go entirely to the private landowner: two thirds are appropriated by the Council who re-invests in public works). Compensated handovers allow the Council to acquire private property areas and assign them to public use leaving a minimal but subsequently developable share to the landholder.
I am convinced that a new Master Plan comes alive only when a new idea of city is constructed,

图2 新总体规划：红色——历史城区；橙色——转型城区；深绿色——公园；浅绿色——乡村地区
Fig.2 The proposals for the new Master Plan: red – the historic city; orange – the city of transformation; dark green– parks; light green – rural areas

而且也要利用分布广泛的在世纪之交就逐渐成型的城市肌理的潜力。通过这样的方式可以重新定义郊区，对其实施一系列的改造转型计划（图2）。

这次规划大体上建立在五个策略选择之上。

大都市区的面积范围，紧扣住一个由数个自治区组成的远景规模，这些自治区与拉齐奥区1997年法案所确定的公园体系整合在一起，促进了大都市区规模的流动性，将部分城市中心设置在市议会的领土之外。

经整合的交通系统，已经做出了多种努力来改进公共交通系统，特别要提及三条地面城市轨道线和四条地铁线（A线和B线已投入使用但仍需改进，C线和D线为新建），连接了更多的重要的城市发展区域。

环境作为可持续发展的城市的支持与根基，也是基于历史与自然价值的城市规划

which defines the objectives to be reached and thus creates the conditions necessary to begin: the role of the Master Plan is in fact to give this idea of city, a strategic weight and technical depth. Thanks to a practical series of initiatives undertaken by the Rutelli Administration between 1995 and 2000, under the "planning by doing" policy, a new idea of city has taken shape in Rome.

Rome has been conceived as a polycentric city made up of newly built-up metropolitan areas, both urban and local (centres), accessible through empirically relevant transport corridors on rail and surrounded by a "green belt" built up of a protected network of parks and agricultural areas.

A city with a restrained growth in which to exploit not only the urban qualities of its historic centre, but also the potential of the widely distributed urban fabric that stems from the turn of the century onwards, and through which redefine the suburbs with a series of improvement and transformation schemes (Fig.2).

The Plan, in essence, is built upon five strategic choices.

The size of the metropolitan area, anchored to a vision of scale built up of several municipalities integrating in a system of parks defined by a 1997 Act of the Lazio Region, promoting the fluidity of the metropolitan scale and locating some urban centres outside of the council's territory.

The integrated transport system, that has joint efforts to improve the public transport system, in particular with reference to the three over-ground city rail links and the four subway lines (A and B already in use but requiring improvement, C and D new) in conjunction with the more significant urban developments.

The environment as support and basis for a sustainable city and as expression of an urban planning based on the values of history and nature, considering them as frames of reference with which to evaluate and enact transformations to the contemporary city space.

The qualification of the existing urban fabric defines a plan declaredly driven to re-claiming the existing city as well as descriptive of the methods of construction and implementation of the Plan itself. This is the purpose of the "guidelines" (which supply information on the criteria and strategies for implementing the directives of the Master Plan – PRG) inserted in the administrative processes to instruct the work of urban planners, and of the "supplemental programs" strategically included for the implementation of works that transform or renovate the city.

The re-organisation of urban peripheries, according to the polycentrism model. The concept of new

的表达，可将之视作评估与实施当代城市空间转型的参考框架。

现有城市肌理的限制条件，决定一个可公开启动修复现有城市的规划基础，并使得建设和实施的方法可以描述。这就是"导则"的目的所在（为实施总体规划的目标提供标准和战略方面的信息），且已纳入行政程序用来指导城市规划者的工作，这也是"补充方案"的目的所在，在这里，战略性地包含"补充方案"是为了实施城市转型或更新方面的措施所在。

城市边缘区的重组，依据多中心的城市模型来操作。不同层次——大都市区、市区、郊区的新中心区的理念（例如，具有管理和第三产业性质的城市活动、商业、居住和娱乐中心），以及引入优于传统的城市规划做法的程序方法，以运用适应当代城市的标准，形成了在未来几年里衡量该规划成效的准则。

新总体规划（PRG）放弃了传统的功能区划方法，转而采用互为交织的城市网络的结构体系方法，既包含现有的城市网络，也包含未来的城市网络。现有的城市网络被划分为三类：历史城区、整治过的城区和待更新的城区。同时未来的城市网络是城市转型的一部分，这既包括目前愿想的转型项目（不仅是新建建筑，还包括新城市中心的战略发展），也包括那些从1962年总体规划继承下来的部分。

按照新规划提出的布局，市域范围内历史城区占大约6%、整治过的城区占13%、待更新的城区占6%、城市转型区占大约9%，同时被保护的环境网络遍布全市范围的65%以上。同样重要的是，应注意到新总体规划引入"质量地图"作为其管理工具的一部分，这是令人赞叹的、覆盖全市的数字化信息网络，在运行中经常得到更新，目前包括将近25 000栋人造构筑物（图3）。该数据库收集了不同研究小组的研究数据，用来分析市区的整个领土，以便发现城市环境中可以赋予以"质量的要素"（bestowing quality）（此文献由此得名）。数据库内包含城市广场、花园、林荫大道、考古遗址、塔楼、建筑物、古代构筑物、教堂及在社区中有重要地位的建筑物、节点和地方名胜，尤其是精心实施的城市肌理中的要素，在建筑学上具有重要意义的建筑物和地区，无论它们是在城市中还是在环境区、住宅、学校和任何在所建造

centralities (i.e. centres of urban activity of an executive and tertiary nature, commercial, residential and entertainment) of various levels, metropolitan, urban, local; and the introduction of a procedural approach that surpasses traditional methods of urban planning in order to apply criteria for a contemporary city, form the testing bench on which the efficiency of the Plan will be tested in the coming years.

The new Master Plan (PRG) moves on from a traditional functional zoning to favour a structure of interwoven urban networks that includes those present and future. Existing urban networks are structured in three categories: The historic city, the consolidated city and the city to renovate, whilst the future urban networks are part of the city of transformation, which includes both the desired current projects of transformation (not only new buildings but also the strategic development of new centres) as well as those inherited from the 1962 Master Plan.

In the arrangement proposed by the new Plan, the historic city comprises about 6% of the council's territory, the consolidated city 13%, the city to renovate 6%, the city of transformation about 9%, whilst the protected environmental network is spread over more than 65% of the territory. It is also important to note that the new Master Plan has introduced as part of its management tools, the "Quality Map", an impressive computerised network of information on the territory, running and constantly updated, that currently includes nearly 25,000 man made structures (Fig.3) and which collects the research of various groups that have analysed the council's territory in order to uncover any elements capable of "bestowing quality" (hence the document's title) to the urban context in which they belong. Town squares, gardens, boulevards, archeological sites, towers, buildings, ancient structures, churches, buildings that play an important role in the community, nodal points and local attractions, particularly well executed elements of the urban fabric, architecturally significant buildings and areas, be they urban or environmental, housing, schools and any estates that create identity in the areas in which they are constructed. Amongst the various sector studies, there is one of particular relevance, not least because it represents a completely new approach to the urban planning process of this country: "Surveys on the contemporary city"[1] identifies buildings, man made structures, real estate developments and suburbs realised from the turn of the century till now, in which are recognised significant architectural, urban or functional qualities.

Albeit with differing approaches and procedures, it is planned to use a direct (meaning it avoids the precautionary drafting of implemental tools) approach in the urban fabric of the historic and the consolidated city, which on one hand needs to take into account the high degree of consolidation and identity of these areas (and therefore of the laws that manage them) whilst on the other it can take advantage of more flexible tools such as the guidelines, which can suggest the criteria and an abacus of solutions and procedural directives. In the other typology of urban networks the indirect approach refers (as in the case of renovations) to procedures that are centred on targets and functions compatible with the particular weave of an urban area. In the case of those areas in need of transformation, the mechanism proposed is the "urban project", a tool that is capable of identifying a theory of organisation for a specific part of the city, ensuring functional integration, supplies of the necessary equipment and shared objectives. In both cases it is necessary that the procedures be self-funded, and realised with the greater share of contributions sourced from within the private sector.

的地方能够产生特色的建筑。在不同领域的研究中，有一点显得特别具有针对性，尤其是因为它代表了这个国家城市规划过程中的全新方法："对当代城市的调查"[1]确定从本世纪初开始直到现在建成的建筑物、人造构筑物、房地产开发和郊区的发展情况，从中辨别重要的建筑、城市或功能品质。

虽然有很多不同的方式和程序，在历史城区和格局已经稳固的城区中仍然允许直接干预形式（即先前规划预料之外的干预计划）的存在"。这类直接干预，一方面，必须高度重视城市肌理的巩固和肌理特征的识别性（即需依照用于整理该地块有机组成的相关规划法规），另一方面，可以借助于一些更加灵活的手段，例如一些能够在标准，系列解决方案以及操作程序等方面提供建议和启示的一些不同性质的导则。在另外一类城市网络中，非直接的干预方式指的是（正如在城市更新区的情形中），关注于基于目标和功能的程序，这些目标和功能与一个城区的特定肌理是相融的。在需要进行城市转型的区块中，所提出的机制是"城市项目"（urban projects），这是一种能够为城市中的一个特定部分确定一种组织理论的方法，确保功能上的整合、提供必要的设备并共享目标。在这两种情形中，必须可以自筹资金，其实现必须有来自私营领域的更大的贡献。

通过对城市肌理群的解读，新的规划因此提出一个"璀璨群星"式的规划策略。该策略建立在优先选择以及植根于历史城区和城市自然结构中一系列的"雄辩的标志"的基础上。它们由五个战略性的区域组成，这些区域不仅积聚了大量的复杂问题，同时也具备那些能够构建大型的，城市尺度下的"意义单元"的要素。其实，它们是城市空间和形态的精巧关节系统，是城市自然环境和历史发展中留存于城市物质结构中的沉淀物；也正是它们给予城市以形式，特征和内涵。

这些区域整合了一些重要的地块，包括已建地和空地，他们分布在：

— 台伯河和安妮河 (Aniene) 两岸；
— 奥勒良城墙；
— 阿皮亚古道考古公园及其中心考古区；

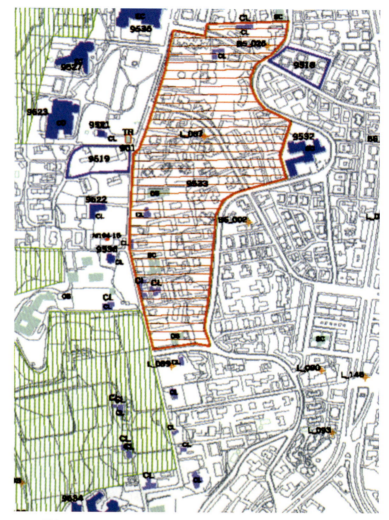

图3　城市西段详图
Fig.3　Detail from the quality map for the western sector of the city

The new plan accompanies a reading of the city according to its urban fabric, with a constellation of strategies built on the basis of priority choices and rooted on a series of "eloquent symbols" from the city's urban history and from its natural configuration: they are the five aims of strategic planning, which are simultaneously areas of accumulation of complex problems as well as elements capable of generating significant "units of meaning" in the urban scale. They are in fact articulated systems of spatial morphology that history and nature have deposited within the physical structure of the city giving it form, identity and meaning. The targets unify significant areas – whether built up or not – distributed along:
– the banks of the rivers Tiber and Aniene;
– the Aurelian Walls;
– the Appia Antica Park and its Central Archeological area;
– the north to south principle motorways between the Italic Forum and

— 由北向南，自意大利广场（Italic Forum）至博览会新城（EUR）管理中心区一线，即1930年代建成的沿弗拉米尼亚路—科尔索路（Via del Corso）—克里斯托弗·哥伦布路的南北向主干道一线。

— 由铁路环线和公路环线沿线的环形区域，正如在1909年的总体规划中的构想，本区域已成为老城区和新城区的边界。

不难发现，这五个区域可以分为三个线性系统：台伯河和安妮河水道、由北到南的城市轴线以及阿皮亚古道考古遗址公园；和两个环形系统：古城墙和环形铁路系统（图4）。

它们按照形态的相似性把这座城市的一些城市节点主题拼合起来，是构成市民"城市心理地图"的重要元素。沿着这五个区域的交界处，及边界周边的部分，集中了一些充满机遇的地段和高质量的资源，尤其是历史和艺术遗产方面的。它们以深厚的历

the executive centre of EUR built in the thirties along the Via Flaminia – Via del Corso – Via Cristoforo Colombo main roads system;
– the layout built up of the ring rail and the ring road, as drafted in the Master Plan of 1909, that currently acts as a boundary between the historic and the consolidate cities.

It is simple to note that these five strategic aims, target three linear systems – the course of the rivers Tiber and Aniene, the north–south axis and the Appia Antica archeological park area; and two beltway systems: the ancient walls and the ring rail (Fig.4).

They piece together in morphologically homogenous terms some of the nodal themes of the forma urbis of the city and constitute important elements in the mental map of the city for its inhabitants. Along and around its demarcations are significant concentrations of opportunities and resources, especially in terms of a historical and artistic heritage. They are characterised by deep cultural–historical foundations and by a prevalent relational nature with a strong morphological and functional integration to the urban scale. They form in other words, additional systems and can therefore be read as structural elements of the urban network, capable of re–qualifying and enhancing the value of some of the important symbols of nature and history.

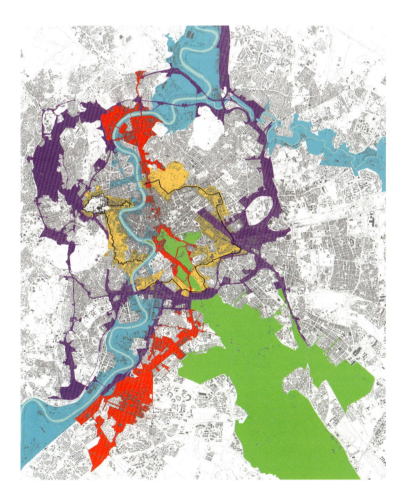

图4　总体规划的五个战略规划区：蓝色——台伯河与安妮河；黄色——奥勒良城墙；绿色——阿皮亚古道考古公园和中心考古区；红色——意大利论坛和博览会新城管理中心；紫色——铁路环线系统

Fig.4　The five strategic planning zones of the Master Plan: blue – thc Tiber and Aniene rivers; yellow –the Aurelian Walls; green – the Appia Antica Park and Central Archeological area; red –the Italic Forum – EUR corridor; purple – the Ring Rail system

史文化为特征，也拥有显著的"关联"属性：它们的存在既是对城市整体形态，也是对城市整体功能的补全。也就是说，它们可以被解读为构成城市网络的结构元素系统，具有使得大型城市历史和自然标志物得以复兴和再利用的能力。

卡罗·噶斯帕瑞尼（Carlo Gasparrini）曾写过："看待一个城市，不是将城市的各部分简单地累加，而是将之视作各部分之间的关联体系，这一点非常重要。在城市中，各部分之间的关系比各部分自身更为重要。这是因为城市现象产生于满足沟通与合作的需要，或换句话说，是来自互相关联的需要。"2

对于这五个规划策略区域的资源和目标的初步研究，在总体规划设计之初便开始了——在本书之前提到的奥勒良城墙项目研究中所呈现的——其中部分研究后来发展成规划导则，分别在规划和实施等层面上作出了限定。例如，在台伯河和安妮河的河流体系项目中，卡罗·噶斯帕瑞尼和马里奥·马涅里·埃利亚（Mario Manieri Elia）（他们是罗马城市总体规划的历史城区方面的顾问）设计的方案是与台伯河的城市水道相关的干预，将水道线诠释为一个拥有横向骨架穿插其间的南北向线性体系，其横向骨架由位于切多萨输水道（Acqua Cetosa）区域和嘎勒巴代拉（Garbatella）地区之间的九个横向节点组成。其中一个节点设计，位于阿文提诺山和雅尼库伦山之间（它们被河床分成两部分），该方案目前已顺利进展到实施项目阶段（图5）。

Carlo Gasparrini has written – "It's important to consider the city not so much as the sum of its parts, but as a system of networks between its parts; in a city, the relation between the parts is more important than the part itself, and this is due to the fact that the urban phenomenon is born out of the need for communication and collaboration, in other words out of the need to relate."2

Preliminary studies on the resources and objective aims of the Master Plan began during the development of the plan itself – as is illustrated by the case of the project for the Aurelian walls, mentioned in the earlier pages of this book – and some of them have subsequently been defined as project guidelines, thus defining their scheduled and implemental aspects.

With regard to the project for the Tiber and the Aniene fluvial system for instance, Carlo Gasparrini and Mario Manieri Elia, (who were consultants for the historic city aspects of the Master Plan), have put together a project of intervention relating to the urban course of the Tiber that interprets the flow of the river as a linear framework for a north–south system of nine transversal nodes between the areas of Acqua Cetosa and Garbatella. The project in one of these transversal nodes, the one between the Aventine hills and the Gianicolo, (which is in turn divided in two by the riverbed), has been successfully developed to an executive project level (Fig.5).

图5 卡罗·噶斯帕瑞尼，马里奥·马涅里·埃利亚. 台伯河战略规划项目指南. 2008. 阿文提诺山与特拉斯特韦拉（Trastevere）广场之间的人行天桥

Fig.5 Carlo Gasparrini, Mario Manieri Elia. Project Guide for the strategic Tiber area, 2008. The footbridge between the Aventin hill and the Trastevere quarter

该项目预见了一系列后续的工作,旨在重新构建成形河流和城市之间的关系。这个关系曾由于1890年河堤改造而被彻底改变,而在这个项目中则构想了一个新的交通体系以实现河与两山的沟通。³

The project foresees a series of works that aim at re-constituting and re-configuring the city's relation to the river, (which was completely altered by the construction of the Muraglioni (city walls) in the 1890's) and at creating new systems of access and connection from the level of the river bed to that of the two hills[3].

注释

1. 罗西 P O. 当代城市与"质量地图".〔意〕城市规划,2001,116(1-6):121-124。当代城市的质量地图由拉萨皮恩扎大学建筑规划系在1999到2006年间开发,由皮耶罗·奥斯蒂利奥·罗西(学科带头人)、弗兰切斯卡·罗曼娜·卡斯泰利、安德烈亚·布鲁斯基和劳拉·耶尔马诺(1999—2004年),亚历山德罗·弗兰凯蒂·帕尔多和卢卡·斯卡尔韦迪(1999—2001年)以及亚历桑德拉·卡潘纳(2002—2006年)创建,由多梅尼科·佛朗哥进行数据和图形处理。
2. 加斯帕里尼 C. 罗马城墙内外的历史. 从历史中心到历史城市 // 戈佐拉 L. 意大利修复. 意大利和中国的古迹修复和城市恢复. 罗马:拉萨皮恩扎大学出版社,2007:112-115
3. 斯卡哥里奥 P. 感性景观设计. Monograph.IT,2010,2(5):222-231

Notes

1. Cfr.Rossi P O, La città contemporanea e la. Carta per la Qualità. Urbanistica, 2001(1-6): 121-124. The Quality Map of the contemporary city was developed between 1999 and 2006 by the Architecture and Projects Department of the Universita' della Sapienza, formed by Piero Ostilio Rossi (head of sciences), Francesca Romana Castelli, Andrea Bruschi and Laura Iermano (from 1999 to 2004), Alessandro Franchetti Pardo and Luca Scalvedi (from 1999 to 2001) and Alessandra Capanna (from 2002 to 2006) Processing of data and graphics by Domenico Franco.
2. Gasparrini C. La storia dentro e fuori le Mura di Roma. Dal centro storico alla città storica // Gazzola L.(a cura), L'Italia restaura. Restauro dei Monumenti e Recupero urbano in Italia e in Cina. Roma: Published by Università La Sapienza, 2007: 112-115
3. Scaglione P. Landscape Sensitive Design. Monograph. IT. 2010(5): 222-231

结语

陈薇

Conclusions

Chen Wei

当城墙界定了城市范围时，也界定了一种文化；当城墙投射出城市变化时，也投射出历史进程。

南京城墙作为明代都城的见证，罗马城墙作为大帝国的表征，都极富文化特色和历史厚度。

在进行南京和罗马城墙在历史演变，城墙、景观与城市肌理，城墙修复，城墙规划，城墙与都市项目方面的平行比较后，我们不难发现它们的同质异构。有如其下：

同质一，城墙作为城市的一个界面，形成相对稳定的范围：南京明城墙串联历史遗留城墙并扩展成总长 35.267 km，围合城市面积 41.07 km²，外郭总长 60 km，形成 230 km² 的都城；罗马全盛时期奥勒良城墙总长 18.837km，围合面积约 13.7 km²，作为罗马帝国时期的城市，已十分庞大。

异构一，城墙作为城市的一部分，建立起的秩序是不一样的：上述城墙围合的面积差异，也在一个方面表现出同为城市，但是体系不一样。明南京墙体除城墙外，内建有皇城和宫城，外筑有郭城，这样的四套城制实质为严密加强防御，最中心的部分是皇权所在。在南京的历史上，从孙吴建城到六朝建康，从南唐加强南部城墙，到明代扩展东部、西部和北部城墙，都是为皇帝及子民建立一个坚实的堡垒，并保证足够的用地备战储粮。而罗马古城其实是整个罗马帝国的权力象征，其野心和扩张，表征在以此为发动机，由条条渡槽、栈道和铺路，将帝国的痕迹通往欧洲的各个地方建立不同的城镇实体，而心脏本身（圣城）范围并不广袤，以保证合理和可控的管辖。这样的不同秩序从根本上来自于文明建立的核心理念：中国传统"筑城以卫君，造郭以守民"，其防御心理本质上出于山川环抱的地理环境适于农耕和稳定；而罗马沿用古希腊"卫城—城邦"体系，每个城市面积不十分大以保证民主自治，卫城是圣城。明城墙围合起的南京，代表了中国

When defining the boundary of a city, the city wall also defines a culture. When mirroring the change that a city has undergone through, the city wall also mirrors a historical process.

The Nanjing Wall, as a physical evidence of the capital city in the Ming Dynasty, and the Roman Wall, as a witness to the Roman Empire, are unique in culture, and affluent in historical anecdotes.

When making a parallel comparison between the Nanjing Wall and the Roman Wall of the evolution history, physical walls, landscape and urban fabrics, wall restoration, wall planning, walls and urban development, one would automatically be led to the following similarities as well as differences:

Similarity One: City wall, as an interface of the city, defines a relatively stable boundary. For example, the Nanjing Wall in the Ming Dynasty was physically erected on the relic walls stemmed from the previous dynasties, stretching as long as 35.267km, and enclosing an urban area of 41.07 km². The external rims of the wall, 60km long, encompassed a capital city of 230 km². The Aurelian Wall was 18.837km long in the heyday of the Roman Empire, covering an area of approximately 13.7 km², a large city judged by the then standard.

Difference One: The two city walls, as part of the city, were established under different orders. The difference between the two cities in physical size shows the fact that both of them were created as a city, but under different systems. For example, in the Ming Dynasty, the Nanjing Wall was built to be a fortified defensive structure made up of not only the wall but also an imperial compound and a palace compound, defended by an external wall. The central part of the wall is the place where the imperial power stays. In the history of Nanjing as a city, all the efforts made by the rulers to build the city, from the city built by Sun Wu to the Jiankang City built by the Six Dynasties, from the enhancement of the southern section of the wall in the South Tang Dynasty to the expansions in the eastern, western, and northern sections in the Ming Dynasty, are meant to build a stronghold for the emperors and their people with sufficient food reserves. The ancient city of Rome is literally a symbol of the Roman Empire, and a powerhouse for expansion ambitions. It was connected to other places in Europe through the roads radiating from Rome, allowing the Empire to build an array of townships there. The heart of Rome, or the holy city, was purposefully not made into a large entity for the convenience and controllability of jurisdiction. Apparently, the order was derived from the fundamental core idea of civilization. For example, Chinese tradition advocates "build the city to defend the Emperor, and build the wall to defend his people". The defensive mentality was grown out from the

古代城市内向的、对外设防的城市基本性质和思路；奥勒良城墙围合起的罗马，则体现了自希腊传统延续的、以圣城为主体向外扩展的组织架构和层级秩序。

同质二，城墙建造沿用旧有遗构，变化扩展因地制宜：南京和罗马城墙都是巧用历史上历代城址进行联系，或加筑加宽，同时根据当时需要，善用地形进行建造的。整个城市城墙呈现不规则状态，顺水、架山或联系历代城址，都是善用自然和人工的智慧体现。

异构二，城墙的建造内容和功能不尽相同：南京城墙毫无疑问是为了防御，即使是占地面积很大的瓮城，里面有足够的可居面积；也是为了屯兵，曰"藏兵洞"，城楼和箭楼除了彰显城市外，更主要是为登高望远、观察敌情和组织御敌。而罗马城墙除御敌外，在建造时常考虑将已有的塔楼、营房、金字塔甚至是墓地整合进去，形成可以日常使用的具有混杂性质的城墙。因此，在废弃城墙原有军事功能进行转换时，我们可以看到，南京城墙的使用显得比较单一，主要用于登高观览；而罗马城墙的使用则丰富多彩，也和现代城市生活（如转换为博物馆、花园）有更密切的关联。

同质三，城墙建造的尺寸和材料基本相似：南京城墙除架山墙、包山墙，使得墙体和山体融为一体外，在平地上建造的城墙高度为 10～20m，宽度为 10～20m；罗马城墙记载高有 6m、9m、10m、15m 等几种。反映了出于军事目的，城墙的基本高度是和人体尺度、御敌方式有关，差异不大。在材料上，罗马城墙和南京城墙均用砖石进行建造，墙体坚实牢固。

异构三，修缮的观念和技术路线存有差异：尤其是南京城墙的"修旧如旧"和"原材料原工艺"原则，与罗马城墙修复注重"易识别性"（如用区别古砖的红砖或黄砖）和采用"新材料新工艺"（如涂料和微型绑定技术），有迥异差别。从技术路线看，这样的不同有着传统做法的根源；而从本质上看，是对待文物或遗产的观念不同。20 世纪上半叶，从事文物建筑保护的意大利派吸取总结了历史上的合理理论和做法，于 1931 年制定的《雅典宪章》和 1964 年制定的《威尼斯宪章》，均强调反映文物建

philosophy that a geographical environment surrounded by the mountains is desirable for farming and stability. Rome was built following the So-called Acropolis and city-state system prevailed in ancient Greece. Each city was not large in size to ensure a proper self-government, and the Acropolis was the holy city. The Nanjing City that was enclosed by the wall in the Ming Dynasty demonstrates a defensive philosophy of governing the city. In comparison, ancient Rome that was surrounded by the Aurelian Wall shows a structure and level of order designed to expand from its core, bearing the signature of the Acropolis and city-state system.

Similarity Two: The two walls were built on the old structures, and the expanded part was built tailored to the local conditions. The city walls in Nanjing and Rome were skillfully rebuilt, reinforced, or widened on the old sites, allowing a connection to the past, with expansions being made taking advantage of the natural curves of local terrains. Borrowing the natural lines of waters and mountains, or connecting the sites of past dynasties, the city walls are presented in an irregular pattern to show the wise combination of nature and human wisdom.

Difference Two: The two walls are not quite the same in contents and functionalities. For example, the wall in Nanjing was undoubtedly built to defend, as it was designed with sufficient space for dwelling and stationing troops, even with the fortified outposts that occupied a sizable area. The gate tower and watch tower aligned with the wall was purposefully built to observe the movement of enemy and organize the defense from a raised point, though they had also been deemed as skyline structures highlighting the grandness of the city. The Roman Wall was built to be a mixture of diverse functions, as a living place, a tower, a barrack, a pyramid, and even as a cemetery. Consequentially, one can see that the Nanjing Wall has become rather monotonous in functionality, mainly as a sightseeing site for people taking a bird's-eye view of the city, after it ceased to be a defensive stronghold. On the contrary, the Roman Wall is much colorful for its non-defensive utilities, and became part of the modern urban life, as a museum, as a garden, or others.

Similarity Three: The two walls are similar in dimension and materials used. For example, the Nanjing Wall measured 10-20m high above a flat ground, and 10-20m wide, except the sections built on or enclosing the mountains. The Roman Wall was built at different heights, mostly at 6 m, 9 m, 10 m or 15 m. The wall height, betraying the military purpose it desired, is associated with human's physical height and with the way the defense was organized. The two walls both were built with bricks and rocks.

Difference Three: The two walls saw noticeable differences in maintenance and associated techniques. Particularly, the Nanjing Wall is required to be restored as it was using original materials and original techniques. On the contrary, the Roman Wall was repaired to show its identity, for example, using red or yellow bricks to distinguish from ancient bricks, and using new materials and new techniques, such as coating and micro-bonding. Technically speaking, these differences reflect the traditional practices prevailed in the two countries. To the essence, however, they are the difference of philosophy in treating a heritage. In the first half of

筑的历史真实性，强调着眼于保留文物建筑所携带的全部历史信息，并且"必须利用……一切科学技术来保护和修复文物建筑"（《威尼斯宪章》）。这两部宪章代表了西方文物建筑保护的基本准则和意义，也是欧洲工业革命社会条件下的必然结果。我国在 1961 年制定《文物保护管理暂行条例》，其中第 11 项指出：文物建筑"在进行修缮、保养的时候，必须严格遵守恢复原状或者保存现状的原则"。这在相当长时期内对我国的文物建筑修缮起到指导性的作用。从审美角度而言，西方注重的求真实和中国的重美善，也从不同的文化心理加速不同的修复观念和技术的分野。尽管当今这两大派别有交流、有渗透，但在具体实践中，长期形成的传统做法和价值取向还是在操作与对策中产生不同的应对，如南京城墙的保护十分注重收集旧砖，而罗马城墙的保护对于不断更新的技术的使用始终走在前列。

同质四，城墙系统在应对城市发展时，均是动态变化的：如开墙修路，如开放城墙两侧的绿地和水系，如结合当代都市发展如何进行应有的城墙系统价值实现等，南京和罗马城墙均有不俗的追求和实践探索。

异构四，新旧城市形态带来的冲突是不同的：由于历史原因，南京城墙围合的范围是比较封闭的，城墙围合的城市相对平坦，适于生活甚至是种植，当时的水路是沟通内外交通的重要方式，而陆路则比较注重在四套城内部的道路关系和连接。相比较而言，罗马城墙从开始就是一处圣地，其文化基石是古伊特鲁里亚文化，建在高岗上，由它向外延伸到"殖民"城镇或"纳贡"城镇，道路注重对外联系。这使得两个城市形态很不一样。当今天面临都市发展时，从某种程度上而言，罗马古城和外围的新城更容易建立文脉上的联系，四通八达的发散道路体系是最好的衔接。比较而言，南京城墙面临的城墙的"围"和道路的"穿"的矛盾则格外突出，近年不断引发的破墙开洞问题层出不穷。但是，当我们从历史的角度冷静而审慎地关照城市发展时，欣慰地发现，地铁正以它独特的方式修正和弥补发展带来的遗憾。无疑，南京主导的线性地铁线和罗马主打的地铁环道，是科学合理的。如此，传统交通线和当代交通线相互补充、共同形成网络系统，满足新旧

the 20th century, the Italian school that advocated heritage protection enacted the *Athens Charter for the Restoration of Historic Monuments* in 1931, and later the *Venice Charter* in 1964, based on the rational theories and practices proved in the past. The two Charters stressed the reflection of the historical originality of old buildings, preserving all the historical information embedded in them, and "protecting and repairing the buildings...using all scientific and technological means available" (the *Venice Charter*). The two Charters are the embodiment of the basic principles applied by Westerners in protecting old buildings, and an inevitable result of the Industrial Revolution prevailed in Europe. China enacted an interim by-law to protect cultural heritages in 1961. It pointed out in provision 11 that old buildings, as a heritage, "shall be repaired and maintained strictly in line with the principle of restoring to its original form, or maintaining its status quo". The policy has long been a benchmark for repairing and maintaining the heritage buildings in the country. From the perspective of aesthetics, Westerns pay more attention to the originality, while Chinese to the beauty and goodness, which mirrors the differences in culture as well as in mentality, and is strengthened in the philosophy and techniques that were applied to repair or restore a heritage structure. The long lasting traditional practice and sense of value would automatically lead to a different practice and strategy in dealing with the protection of heritage buildings, though the two schools have shared their views and experience, and found mutual influence. As a result, the Nanjing Wall protector attaches great importance to collecting old bricks, while the Roman Wall protector is a forerunner applicator of constantly updated technologies.

Similarity Four: The city wall system has been changed in a dynamic manner to respond to the urban development. Both the Nanjing Wall and the Roman Wall have made laudable pursuits and exploration in coping with the changing world, including running a "hole" through the wall to facilitate traffics, opening up the greeneries and water systems on both sides of the wall, and making the wall useful to the contemporary urban development.

Difference Four: The two cities act differently in dealing with the conflicts between their old and new urban forms. For example, the area enclosed by the Nanjing Wall was technically closed, desirable for dwelling and planting, thanks to the relatively flat terrains. Waterway was at the time an important way of communication for both internal and external traffics, with land roads mainly serving as a connection in the city. In comparison, the Roman Wall emerged as a holy land right from the beginning, with the ancient Etruscan culture as the cornerstone. Built on the hill, the wall reached out to the "colonized" or "vassal" towns. Roads were built to facilitate the reaching-out. The roads culture stemmed from the two cities is quite different from one another in urban forms. In the context of modern urban development, the ancient part of Rome is, to some extent, more relevant to the new town built on its rims, thanks to the radiating road system that reaches all the directions. In comparison, the Nanjing Wall has been fighting with the attempt for running a "hole" through the

城市联系的发展需求。

　　无论是同质还是异构，我们在进行南京和罗马城墙比较后，更加自信：城墙作为一种遗产，不仅是独特文化的重要表征和传承，还是城市发展建立步骤和策略的重要基准，以及不断探索科学保护的重要载体。有了先进的科学手段，城墙可以永久保存，城墙内外的人们也将生活得更加美好。

2012年4月4日清明节定稿于金陵

wall to facilitate the traffics between the two sides of the wall. Fortunately, we are pleased to see that subways are remedying the regrets brought up by the urban development in a unique manner, after we have been calmly and carefully dealing with the urban development from the perspective of history. Undoubtedly, the linear subway system in Nanjing and the Metro ring in Rome have been built with a rational design, allowing" the traditional and modern road systems to work together, accommodating the development needs of both old and new urban areas' communication. The comparison of the two city walls makes people enlightened about the wall as a heritage, regardless of the similarities as well as the differences. They are not only representing and carrying forward a unique culture, but also create an important benchmark for developing a city and for preparing urban development strategies. Additionally, they are a major carrier that attracts increasingly enhanced scientific protection. Thanks to the scientific and technological advancement, the wall can be preserved in a permanent manner, and the people inside and outside of the wall will live a better life.

Finalized on April 4, 2012, Qing Ming Festival, in Jinling

作者及简介（按出现次序排列）
Authors and Introductions (appear in sequence)

陈 薇
Chen Wei
东南大学
Southeast University

路易吉·戈佐拉
Luigi Gazzola
罗马萨皮恩扎大学
Sapienza University of Rome

诸葛净
Zhuge Jing
东南大学
Southeast University

张剑葳
Zhang Jianwei
东南大学
Southeast University

是霏
Shi Fei
东南大学
Southeast University

杨 俊
Yang Jun
东南大学
Southeast University

绘理奈·平田
Erina Hirata
罗马萨皮恩扎大学
Sapienza University of Rome

费德里科·斯卡洛尼
Federico Scaroni
罗马萨皮恩扎大学
Sapienza University of Rome

钟行明
Zhong Xingming
东南大学
Southeast University

薛 垲
Xue Kai
东南大学
Southeast University

亚历桑德拉·德·塞萨里斯
Alessandra De Cesaris
罗马萨皮恩扎大学
Sapienza University of Rome

杨新华
Yang Xinghua
南京市文物局
Nanjing Administration of Cultural Heritage

罗萨纳·曼齐尼
Rosanna Mancini
罗马萨皮恩扎大学
Sapienza University of Rome

贾亭立
Jia Tingli
东南大学
Southeast University

保拉·法利尼
Paola Falini
罗马萨皮恩扎大学
Sapienza University of Rome

刘正平
Liu Zhengping
南京市城市规划编制研究中心
Nanjing Urban Planning & Research Center

皮耶罗·奥斯蒂利奥·罗西
Piero Ostilio Rossi
罗马萨皮恩扎大学
Sapienza University of Rome

译者 Translators

中译英 (Chinese to English)：邹春申 Zou Chunshen
英译中 (English to Chinese)：邢晓春 Xing Xiaochun　高文娟 Gao Wenjuan
意译中 (Italian to Chinese)：杨 慧 Yang Hui　贾亭立 Jia Tingli

说明 Notes

1. 陈薇、诸葛净、是霏、贾亭立系东南大学建筑学院教师和东南大学城市与建筑遗产保护教育部重点实验室成员
   Chen Wei, Zhuge Jing, Shi Fei, Jia Tingli, Teachers of School of Architecture, Southeast University, also members of Key Laboratory of Urban and Architectural Heritages Conservation (Southeast University), Ministry of Education, China

2. 该著作得到国家自然科学基金重点课题"中国城镇建筑遗产适应性保护和应用的理论和方法"（51138002）基金资助
   This book is supported by NSFC "On the Theories and Methods of Adaptive Preservation and Reuse of Urban Architecture Heritage" (51138002)

图书在版编目（CIP）数据

南京城墙与罗马城墙比较：汉英对照/陈薇，〔意〕戈佐拉著.
--南京：东南大学出版社，2013.5
ISBN 978-7-5641-3854-7

Ⅰ. ①南… Ⅱ. ①陈… ②戈… Ⅲ. ①城墙—比较研究—南京、罗马 Ⅳ. ①K928.77②954.67

中国版本图书馆CIP数据核字（2012）第267699号

南京城墙与罗马城墙比较
Comparative Study on the City Walls of Nanjing and Rome

著　者	陈　薇　　〔意〕路易吉　戈佐拉 Chen Wei　　〔Italy〕Luigi Gazzola	
出版发行	东南大学出版社	
地　址	南京四牌楼2号　（邮编 210096）	
出版人	江建中	
网　址	http://www.seupress.com	
经　销	全国各地新华书店	
印　刷	利丰雅高印刷（深圳）有限公司	

开　本	889mm × 1194 mm　1/12	
印　张	17 2/3	
字　数	439千	
版　次	2013年5月第1版	
印　次	2013年5月第1次印刷	
书　号	ISBN 978-7-5641-3854-7	
定　价	198.00元	

本社图书若有印装质量问题，请与营销部联系，电话：025-83791830